Feminist Visual Culture

Edited by

Fiona Carson and Claire Pajaczkowska

EDINBURGH UNIVERSITY PRESS

Edinburgh University Press Ltd
22 George Square, Edinburgh

Typeset in 10pt Sabon by
Hewer Text Ltd, Edinburgh, and
printed and bound in Great Britain by
The Cromwell Press, Trowbridge

A CIP Record for this book is available from the British Library

ISBN 0 7486 1046 4 (paperback)

Contents

List of illustrations

Dedication

During the four-year gestation of this book, eight babies were born to the contributors; the book is dedicated to these babies, with love:

Theodore Jerzy Raoul Curtis
Holly McIntosh
Sam Knight
Jake Knight
Eloise May Cadman
Jules Orion Francis de Souza Glaves-Smith
Louis Robert Harding

And Jessica and Paul's baby whose gender and name are still a mystery . . .

THIS BOOK DRAWS ON nearly thirty years of feminist scholarship and visual practice, and the dawn of the new millennium seems an appropriate moment at which to celebrate this achievement. By juxtaposing essays on fine art, design and popular culture in one volume, rather than keeping them separate as is usually the case, it is possible to see the range and depth of that juxtaposition, the cross-fertilisations, common concerns and theoretical heritage of feminist visual culture. While attempting to be comprehensive, we must in the end be selective. Nevertheless, we hope the book gives a sense of a shared history of feminist ideas and interactions, applied in and altered by very specific contexts.

The contributors to this book are all engaged at different levels in the teaching and learning process in higher education, mainly in 'new university' contexts, and they have been chosen because of their specialisation and their investment in feminist ideas and research. This book has come together slowly and with some difficulties. Its contributors often pursue complicated and demanding domestic careers as well as academic ones. These perspectives also influence the writing and research agenda.

The paradox of feminist scholarship and practice is that although it constitutes a separate sphere of work, this sphere cannot be separated from the practice of everyday life. Unlike the old universities, which based themselves on the structures of the church and of monastic devotion to the celestial life of the soul and the mind, feminism, which was born of modernity and modern life, depends on the experience of quotidian living for its meaning and direction. Therefore, devotion to our loved ones informs and directs devotion to our work.

This book has been some four years in gestation and during

those years the authors have lived through many of the more extreme experiences of 'life's rich tapestry': parents have died, babies have been born, illness and disability have been encountered, and through those experiences endures the privilege of reflecting, thinking, learning and theorising. Feminist scholarship is not practised somewhere apart but is the product of the thought we give to the problems, and pleasures, of life. In this thinking, we are helped by the culture that we inherit from our predecessors, which is the product of their thinking about their lives.

We have dedicated the book to the babies that were born to us over the last four years because they represent the future, to which the work is humbly offered in the hope that others may find in it something of value and significance. Feminism – by default as much as by revolutionary intent – has mapped hitherto uncharted territories: the 'dark continent' that was femininity in the eyes of masculine scholarship, and the voyages of discovery that are the courage to 'leave home' and take up the power and responsibility of representation.

Living at a time which is sometimes called post-feminist, the contributors demonstrate that although several battles have been won, the war is far from over. The approach of each author is unique and original, and each brings her own understanding of feminism and sexual difference to her case-study. The result is a collection that is 'rich and strange' as well as being scholarly and accessible. You are invited to join this celebration.

RSVP to c.pajaczkowska@mdx.ac.uk or f.d.carson@uel.ac.uk

Fiona Carson and Claire Pajaczkowska

Acknowledgements

The editors would like to thank all the contributors for their hard work and patience, and all the artists and photographers whose work is reproduced. Thanks also to Sadie Coles HQ and The White Cube, the Jo Spence Memorial Trust, Mary Shemza, Graham and Nancy Wood, MUF Design Group, Women's Design Research Unit, the Potteries Museum and Art Gallery, and Birmingham City Art Gallery. Thanks also to Bruce Carson for support and proof reading, to Shiona Burris, Helen Robertson, Sarah Burnett, James Dale and Hazel Bell for bringing the project to completion.

Fiona Carson would also like to thank Cathy Blackford for holding the fort, the University of East London for research time, and also Maggie Humm and Jackie Jones at Edinburgh University Press for initiating the project.

Claire Pajaczkowska, Sally Stafford and Sarah Chaplin would like to thank the Research Team of the School of Art, Design and Performing Arts at Middlesex University for funding and research time.

Jessica Evans would like to thank Terry Dennett at the Jo Spence Memorial Archive for giving kind permission to reproduce the photographs in Chapter 5.

Teal Triggs wishes to thank those who generously read and commented on Chapter 7, Siân Cook, Rick Poynor, and Roger Sabin. Her essay is dedicated to her father Edward E. Triggs (1930–99).

Janis Jefferies wishes to dedicate her chapter to Shireen Akbar with whom she worked on the tapeslide *Field of the Embroidered Quilt* for the exhibition 'Woven Air: Textiles from Bangladesh' held at the Whitechapel Gallery in 1998. She would also like to thank Alexia Defert, Lisbeth Tolstrup and Melissa E. Feldman.

Issues in feminist visual culture

Claire Pajaczkowska

ALL CULTURES HAVE A visual aspect. For many people, the visual aspect of culture – its imagery, signs, styles and pictorial symbols – is the most powerful component of the complex and sophisticated systems of communication that are a constitutive part of culture. The seen may be the surface of an underlying and unseen system of meaning, such as the pictorial aspects of writing; it may be a component part of scriptovisual signification; or it may comprise both signifier and signified, as in iconic forms of signification.

The seen has a complex relation to the unseen. The seen is considered evidence, truth and factual, as sight establishes a particular subject relation to reality in which the visual aspect of an object is considered to be a property of the object itself. This differentiates vision from other sense data, such as tactile and acoustic, which are associated more with the subjective relation between subject and object. Acoustic information is received through the resonance that soundwaves create within the body, and this seems to materialise the space between receiving subject and the source of sound. This quality of offering an apparent autonomy of distance and 'separateness' to the spectator is an important feature of vision and, by extension, of visual culture, and it has contributed to the evolution of a structure of subjectivity with specific consequences for the cultural representation of sexual difference.

Although much is understood about the structure of language, its biological bases and social effects, the history and politics of literacy, education and social privilege, much less is known about the communicative nature and the internal structure of imagery. Visual culture has an impact that is immediate, and often compelling, from its overdetermined origins in the documentary genre of cartography and the mapping of private property, alongside the visual symbols depicting the mysteries of the unseen and invisible. The power of the image has long been recognised and has been ascribed magical qualities, such as the cave paintings of Lascaux, the Buddhist mandala, Byzantine icons, Semitic scriptures, and Islamic geometries through to contemporary and secular equivalents in cinema and television, art, design, advertising, fashion, architecture, and cyberculture. These are some of the component objects of study of the new and burgeoning field of visual culture.

Whereas these different systems of representation were originally the objects of such disparate and specialised disciplines as archaeology, theology, art history, media, cultural and film studies, the new interdisciplinary study of visual culture allows the concepts and methods of these original fields of research to be pooled. Conceptual frameworks derived from anthropology and psychoanalysis are now available to inform the questions and methodologies that were once limited by the boundaries of thought considered 'proper' to the discipline; and although the troubling problem of material and intellectual 'property' is neither dissolved nor resolved through this pooling process, it does become part of a new problematic for the study of questions of property, authorship, ownership and power in visual culture. The new practical, intellectual, professional, academic field becoming known as visual culture is growing in significance precisely because the juxtaposition of questions from a range of academic disciplines has multiplied the avenues of enquiry into the meaning of imagery in our culture and in everyday life.

Integration and difference

The cultures discussed here are modern, or postmodern, and are mostly European and Judaeo-Christian in origin, being the components of what many contemporary theorists call 'Western civilisation' or the 'Western episteme' characteristic of modernity. The extent to which this culture might be considered global, through the technological determinist views of the ubiquity of such structures as cinema, television and cyberculture; or through the economic determinist views of the economic domination of multinational capitalism are issues discussed in the following chapters. Postcolonial politics, a vital part of postmodern visual culture, are an integral part of the questioning of modernity advanced by feminism over the last four decades. The historical axis of postcolonial theory allows European historical chronology of the twentieth century to be related to the 'other' histories of non-European cultures. We can then wonder why Hegel was able to declare that 'Africa has no History', and why Picasso, in *Les Demoiselles d'Avignon* was able to incorporate allusions to African masks, unconsciously, unknowingly, in his cubism. The structure underlying Hegel's thinking, and Picasso's painting is not limited to European reflection on Africa, but is characteristic of a more ubiquitous 'logic' of misunderstanding cultural difference that is visibly manifested in most representations of 'racial' and sexual difference. It is the patterns which govern the refraction and distortion of difference in the visual culture of European modernity that enable observers to perceive structural similarities between feminist and postcolonial research questions and methodologies.

Contemporary theories of the construction of difference in culture offer a framework for understanding these structural similarities. Psychoanalytic theory, especially, extends the analytic concepts of postmodernism, anthropology, politics and common sense into thinking about the origins of discursive structures, and about the patterns determining the aetiology of cultural misunderstanding. Through a synthesis and juxtaposition of historical, theoretical and psychoanalytic methods of research, we can recognise the field of visual culture as a heterogeneous but integrated field of enquiry which generates questions previously obscured by the divisions and boundaries between academic specialisms. The new field of visual culture, then, includes questions from visual anthropology such as the social production and exchange of signs, and their function in offering a vehicle for social cohesion or rebellion, to questions from art history about style, the significance of form. the nature of the sublime, together with questions from other fields like design history and cultural studies. These are approached using methodology from history, such as in the work of Foucault, or the British tradition of social history, the study of material technologies as different as pottery is from cyberculture, or methods of interpreting unconscious fantasy such as through psychoanalytic theory. Within visual culture, feminist methodology is indispensable for opening and disinterring the repressed and troubling questions of sexual difference that inflect the visual. Feminist exploration of visual culture aims to loosen the ties that bind gender and sexuality to visual representation in such limited, repetitive and stereotypic ways, and to understand the relation of representation to the psychic economy of thought, fantasy and emotion. Just as all cultures have a visual aspect, every culture has complex ways of encoding and decoding the biological differences that exist between the two sexes of all animal species. The enigma of sexual difference and the fact of sexual reproduction that makes us akin to, and different from, other animals is probably the greatest enigma that faces human thought, and evidence of the symbolic attempts to resolve this enigma is visible in all cultures. Although anthropologists have identified the structure of the mind's attempts to explain and fathom this enigma as universally inherent in myths, narratives, rituals and religious ceremonies, we are particularly interested in the part played by visibility and visual culture in representing solutions to this invisible mystery.

Invisibility and enigma

The invisibility of this enigma of our similarity to, and difference from, other species exerts a kind of gravitational pull on the visualisations of difference that circulate in culture. Surprisingly perhaps, the representations of the enigma of sexual difference that we find in contemporary postmodern culture are no more sophisticated than those found by anthropologists in premodern and even primitive cultures. It seems that just as gravity is a geographical constant so the human mind's need to decipher the enigma of origin is a historical constant. Both forces require specific sciences that enable them to be understood, accepted and overcome. Part of feminist practice is comparable to the rational and cerebral enquiries that are the basis of all scientific development and progress in modern culture, and part of what is denoted by the term feminist visual culture is this rational, scholarly and academic enquiry into the complex codes that govern the allocation of meaning to sexual difference as represented in our society's visual culture. There are a number of well established research questions and methods that have emerged and have been developed over the last forty years in academic feminism. It is the coherence of these questions and the methodological practices they entail that has enabled feminism to become one of the most exciting and productive problematics to have evolved in the twentieth century. Beyond the subjective perspectives which define whether feminism is experienced as revolutionary or metonymically as a mere 'nuisance' there is the objective fact that the result of work produced by feminist research over the last century has been a paradigm shift whose effects have been felt in all academic disciplines and institutions. This shift has also affected the research methods themselves, so that, for example, postfeminist anthropology is more self-reflexive than was the 'science of man' before it; women anthropologists began to use the evidence of women 'informants' in assembling data on societies they studied which changed the definition of the process of collecting data, of the nature of 'data' itself and of the gender balance of society. Similarly, psychoanalysis has changed its view of the part played by maternal influence on the development of subjectivity, and therefore on the influence of pre-Oedipal fantasy on culture, which changes the Freudian view of society as a product of a patrilineal Oedipal dynamic. Similar changes in the methods of semiotics, historical analysis and the textual analysis of imagery are also explained in the following chapters.

One way to loosen the ties that bind gender and sexuality to visual representation is by investigating the topography of knots, and this is a metaphor much used by the post-Freudian psychoanalyst Lacan and his feminist interpreters. The controversial concepts that issue from the discourses of structuralism, poststructuralism and postmodernism have been found, in their focus on process and intersubjectivity, to be compatible with forms of feminist research. The benefits and disadvantages of the structuralist and Lacanian influences on feminism are further explored here. These theoretical discourses are used by many of the authors in this book, each of whom outlines the theoretical issues specific to her field of research, its methodological procedures and intellectual traditions, before going on to apply these to the study of her selected examples of contemporary feminist visual culture. However, the historiographical issues raised by feminism's engagement with poststructuralism require a more general comment.

From structuralism, feminism received the conceptualisation of culture and society as 'language-like' structures of exchange and circulation. The structuralist method of analysing cultural discourses as constituted through systems of binary oppositions proved a helpful and incisive form of thinking about and analysing the social refraction and misrepresentation of biological sex differences. If, as structuralists claim, no thought can carry meaning except through reference to its definition in relation to its opposite, then the implicit pattern or 'structuring absence' of the unspoken non-concepts can be intuited beneath the surface cohesion of the logic of language. If the humanist concept of 'man' or mankind, widely used in the prestructuralist discourses of philosophy, anthropology, politics and the humanities, carried denotative meaning only by implicit reference to its negative, then feminist research had to be into the negativity of the unspoken communications concealed within explicit discourse. This negativity was sometimes gendered otherness, 'racial' otherness, class otherness, or the otherness of an imaginary animalesque alterity, and the structure of 'otherness' could also be the content of the category of 'other'. The fact that binary opposition is a feature of language means that it invariably has a structuring presence in culture, when the latter is defined as a 'language-like structure', so that its meanings are understood as created through metaphoric and metonymic patterns of difference between signifiers. The enigma for structuralism was to ascertain the extent to which binarism was an inherent structure of the brain, and therefore inherent in the biological bases of language. If the brain is a neural network that functions through the digital coding of electrical impulses firing across synapses between nerve cells, as some structuralists understand it to be, then it may be that the structure of binarism is 'printed' into the circuitry of the 'hard disk' of our brains. All other subjective and psychological processes would then be understood as a by-product of this neural pattern. The question of the relation between neurological descriptions of the brain and central nervous system and the psychoanalytic descriptions of the mind and body remains to be fully explored, and the results of such exploration will extend feminist understanding of sexual difference.

Alongside the question of the body's relation to the structure of signification, structuralists also explored the cultural existence of a concept of the mediating category produced by the fact that the analogical reality of life cannot easily be digitalised into the neat binaries required by the cybernetic coding of language, and possibly the brain. For example, our culture uses a concept of 'life' that has meaning only in contrast to the antinomy of 'death', and because the science of physics tells us that matter is neither created nor destroyed but is transformed, there is a contradiction between the analogical reality described by science and the reality of the digital coding of human experience into language. This contradiction, which issues from the monological belief that language denotes reality, is symbolised in representational form by what structuralism calls 'mediating categories', concepts that contain the contradictory ideas that are mutually exclusive to the antonymic categories. In our example, the mediating categories include concepts such as the religious concept of an 'afterlife', or the superstitious concepts of the 'undead' or ghosts. As mediating categories embody the evidence of the arbitrariness of the logic of binarism, they are particularly anxiogenic and the concepts they contain tend to be either idealised or denigrated, for example the afterlife is traditionally considered divine and ghosts absurd.

To take an example that leads us back to our questioning of sexual difference, the primary contradiction between concepts of 'nature' and 'culture' creates a mediating category in which the concept of sexuality is found. Most art is interpreted by structuralist thinkers as representations of the transformation of 'nature' into 'culture', and as a form of 'play' with the conventions of representation. The antinomy between nature and culture rests partly on the paradoxical status of language itself which is natural, instinctive and biologically based, but is simultaneously cultural, differentiating humans from other species. However, language is rarely the object of language and therefore the concept that mediates between nature and culture is the idea of sex. If sex is what we share with the dumbest of sexually-reproducing species and all other animals, it is also the libidinal basis of culture and symbolisation. The etymological roots of the concept of sex demonstrate its relation to segmentation, such as in the insect's segmented body, and to division. Thus, difference is at the core of the fission and fusion generated by our concept of sex, and it is this fact of difference that troubles the narcissism that equally defines human agency. According to the logic of binarism, sex may 'stand for' language and vice versa, such as we find in the concept of 'intercourse'. Each denotes the segmentation, division and articulation that are metaphors for the enigma of human society. As a concept, sex is particularly anxiogenic in our culture and tends, therefore to be idealised in romantic, divine and sublime love or to be debased as carnal, instinctive or perverse, as dirt. This is where structuralist explanation ends and psychoanalytic theory is needed, if feminism wants to understand the origins of the particular contradictions around sexuality and representation.

However, the structuralist method provided feminism with the conceptual tools for separating from the liberal humanism which seemed to accommodate all claims to 'individual' humanity. The prestructuralist answers to the question of what it is to be human were phrased in terms of philosophical concepts such as 'self-knowledge', 'consciousness', and 'thought', which emphasise the significance of self rather than the significance of division. Early feminists such as Virginia Woolf can be understood as creating a modern textual practice in which the limitations of liberal humanism are contested in order to find a cultural practice in which the 'divided self' can be described, explored and reconstructed. Her most feminist books are also those in which she actively deconstructs the patrilineal tradition of authorship in which she found herself. It was, in Freudian terms, the triumph of the ego instincts over the sexual instincts that appeared to be the only route to humanity. This paradigm remains active in a broad range of contemporary social and cultural institutions, which consider the ascension of the human over the animal as the triumph of repression over sexuality. But feminists know better, and Virginia Woolf intuited that the problem is more complex than this because it has to do with aggression and death instincts rather than with sex.

The feminist challenge to both liberal humanist and structuralist thinking is based on the observation that the two terms of the antinomy – man and woman – are concepts that are unstable, neither complementary nor opposites, and that their relation is profoundly asymmetrical. The feminine is ubiquitously used to connote secondary status, and is often used to signify the cause of

the anxiety that the cultural representation of the fact of difference creates.

Symbolic assymetry

The reasons for this symbolic asymmetry are the terrain of
feminist research, and the poststructuralist theory of 'deconstruction' used by Derridean thinkers which identifies the radical
instability of language as the basis of the inequality that lies
hidden beneath the apparent antinomy of binarism. Deconstructionists refer to the imbalance between the two terms as the 'logic
of the supplement', as there is one term which is used as supplementary to the other. This discursive fact is, according to Derri-
deans, the cause of power differences in culture. What might be
called a discursive determinism has been widely employed in
feminist research as it conveys the political importance of textual
analysis. 'To deconstruct is to reconstruct' is a dictum that
dissolves or contests the traditional distinction between artist
and critic and enables art to be conceived as a critical practice of
playing with, and thus destroying, convention, and enables criticism to be appreciated as a creative act of giving representational
form to new thoughts as exegetic to existing discourses. The logic
of the supplement extends the analysis of gender difference to
challenge other binaristic incongruities such as those of white and
black, centre and margin, rational and irrational, and infantile
and adult.

Taking exception to this method of textual analysis are feminist
historians. To the historian, a text is a document which refers to
some empirically-defined external or extra-textual reality, rather
than a monument to be deconstructed. The historian 'finds' texts,
often by assigning new meanings to existing texts or by reposi-
tioning texts within the classificatory order in the archive. For
example, paintings by Pop artist Pauline Boty were found in
1992, forgotten in a shower room outbuilding of an uncle's
house, and were exhibited alongside the work of her peers,
thereby being rescued from oblivion and restored to the canon
of British Pop artists. For research in visual culture, this includes
the research that 'discovered' the work of artists, designers and
filmmakers whose work had been considered anonymous, or

misattributed to (often male) colleagues, or consigned to the obscurity of historical oblivion. Historians find texts and reconstruct a missing piece of the historical record. This research was the earliest and the most extensive form of feminist scholarship in visual culture. The work of restoring women practitioners to the historical record also raises the question of accounting for the dynamics that actively consigned them to oblivion.

The controversy between deconstructionists and historians is not quite as clearly adversarial as this slightly dramatised account would have it. Every historical excavation of a forgotten woman designer or artist changes not just the historical record, but the definition of history. The historical record is not an additive or cumulative quantity of knowledge but a dynamic process of remembering and forgetting, of knowledge illuminated by illusion or obscured by fear. History is a discursive practice as well as an archival ordering, classifying and interpreting of documents. Many feminist historians have read the work of Foucault with sympathy and interest. Foucauldian historians extend the concept of archive to include all signifying systems, but analyse these in relation to the systems of power that connect juridico-discursive institutions to the structures of subjectivity. Feminist Foucauldians have made use of two aspects of his work. The first is the concept of history as discourse, as an active dynamic, and the second is his history of sexuality with its emphasis on gender difference as inherently embodied in performance or performativity, thus contesting the structuralist concept of gender as a product of a static structure. Developed by some as 'post-feminism', and as 'queer theory', this critical practice rests on an appreciation of those discursive manifestations of gendered performativity, that travesty, negate or hyperbolise the cultural assigning of gender difference.

One of the first Foucauldian paradigms used in feminist research in visual culture was the interest that many photographers had in Foucault's investigation into the 'eye of power', originally an interpretation of how rationalist philosophy and eighteenth-century prison architecture of the panopticon cohered in manifesting the intrasubjective equivalence between vision and control. By extension, this analysis of the interrelation between vision and control was of interest to those who were curious about the visual representation of sexual difference in contemporary culture.

This was extended into an exploration of the 'apparatus', an enquiry into how the technology of perception and photographic reproduction in still and moving images, of photography and cinema, and was a development of a subjectivity first described through the mathematical perspective systems of Renaissance painting, the *camera obscura* devices used by painters to reproduce pictorial realism, and through a succession of conventions that defined the 'classic realist text' that reached its apex in late nineteenth-century European art. The apparatus is not merely the technology of optical devices that are used to extend human eyesight in various ways, but is a metaphor for how regimes of representation construct a subject spectator for whom the coding of visual representation offers a transcendence, the illusion of omniscience or centrality which belies the contradictory and heterogeneous experience of reality. This coding of the illusion offered by classic realism, with its apparent transparency of meaning, is thought to be analogous to the work of ideology. Ideology, such as the ideology of liberal humanism, creates the illusion of the centrality of an undivided 'individual' self, whose relation to external reality is rational and instrumental. For feminists, this analysis of the apparatus enabled the deconstruction of classic realism and the practice of various kinds of modernism to be contemplated as feminist practice. This informed the study and practice of visual culture in ways that differentiates it from feminist research in other disciplines.

Technologies of vision

In visual culture, the methods of textual deconstruction and historical reconstruction are subject to particular techniques of analysis which are responsive to the different forms taken by visual representation. Materially, the technologies of the image have significance for feminist research. The difference between technologies considered 'hard' and 'soft' has been used to adjudicate the boundaries of those arts to which women were allowed access and those from which they were debarred or discouraged access. The troubled history of feminism and architecture within modernism bears witness to some exemplary case studies of active exclusion. This is in sharp contrast to other cultures within South Africa in which women are expected to be the designers, builders and decorators of domestic buildings, but where this work is, in the traditions of vernacular building, anonymous or 'unauthored'. The newer information technologies produce a virtual public space which both replicates traditional, conservative, demarcations of gender and allows a new cyberfeminism to be developed.

The technologies of visual representation offer a rich source of textual analysis; the meaning of the New York 'hard-edge' school of abstract painting of the 1950s, or the gendering of intellectual work in 'conceptual art' have elicited feminist analysis of the troubled instability of masculinity's self-definition in art. The difference between carving in marble and modelling in clay, between painting in oils on canvas and watercolour on paper, between woodcut and etching, between designing furniture in tubular steel or designing decoration for fabric, are all differences which connote chains of meaning associated with a range of social and gender differences.

The most crucial structuring of sexual difference through vision and visible differences in visual culture is through the 'gaze'. The methodological issues raised here are developed from the structuralist and poststructuralist methods just described and are an extension of the concept of the 'apparatus', relating it to feminism's encounter with psychoanalysis. Developed by Christian Metz and Laura Mulvey, the theory of the gaze demonstrates how scopic structures developed by technologies of cinema and textual codes of realism combine with the organisation of the psyche into different processes of unconscious, preconscious and conscious representation to characterise the relation of spectator to spectacle in an intricately gendered system. If classic realism is organised into narratives composed of different points of view, these differences are structured into a hierarchy of discourses, with the most subjective ranked as least authoritative and the 'voice' of the author, or the point of view of the omniscient eye of cinematic realism, being the most authoritative, or the 'truth'. In cinema, this relates to the juxtaposition of visual and acoustic tracks in such a way that they either synthesise to produce the illusion of homogeneity of representation, or vie with each other for authority. With the coding of classic realism and its illusion of transparency, a hierarchy of discourses and the depiction of reality as uncontradictory and homogeneous, the psychic structure of the dominance of the ego is reinforced. This facilitates the process of repression through which the ego can remain unaware of unconscious impulses of sadism and masochism, voyeurism and exhibitionism associated with looking. The cinema spectator, in the comfort of the dark and lulled into regression by the luminosity, size and pleasure of the screen images, relives a 'mirror moment' described by Lacan: in this moment, the psyche becomes alienated from itself through a perverse act of dividing ego ideal from the ego, projecting it onto the screen persona and seeking reunion of the divided ego through reintrojection and identification of ego with image. The division is further exacerbated through the projection of idealised exhibitionism and narcissistic unity onto the screen persona and the intensification of the envious aggression of the voyeuristic drive which incorporates its image/object in a way that satisfies both the aggressive and libidinal drives, through 'sex' and 'death'.

Laura Mulvey further advances the analysis by pointing out that the visual codes of classic realism tend to associate female with passive, exhibitionistic objects and male with active, voyeuristic subjects. This pre-Oedipal, perverse dynamic is then further bound into an Oedipal structure in which the image of the woman comes to symbolise both sexual desire and the threat of castration. As castrated other, female characters are then either sadistically punished for representing this 'lack' or else fetishised and endowed with phallic attributes to make good their lack. The oscillation between sadistic voyeurism and fetishistic stasis is manifested in the narrative tempo, and changes of narrative to celebration of 'pure looking' or primary identification. In cinema, the hierarchy is established between three gazes, so that the spectator's gaze at the screen is paralleled by the camera's look at the pro-filmic event and these are both subjected to apparent domination and substitution by the characters' looks at one another within the diegesis. This 'hierarchy of discourses' simultaneously subjugates the feminine, passive spectacle to the masculine active voyeur, and subjugates the primary identification of the unconscious to the secondary identification of more conscious ego processes. In this way, Mulvey shows us, a form of visual culture exactly replicates the structure of the patriarchal unconscious.

Mulvey's revolutionary juxtapositioning of feminist research questions with structuralist and psychoanalytic methods generated a new field of enquiry into the female gaze, the spectatrix and into other feminist uses of Freud, Lacan and other psychoanalysts such as Luce Irigaray, Julia Kristeva, Janine Chasseguet-Smirgel and Juliet Mitchell.

Difference as separation

There are a number of questions that psychoanalysis generates in its encounter with visual culture, but the most central issue is the way it can explain the misrepresentation of sexual difference as a product of unconscious fantasy, that is as a misplacing of generational difference.

As Freudians explored the mechanism of the scopophilic instinct and identification, the enigma of the anxiogenic nature of sexual difference became clearer. The sphinx's riddle to Oedipus needs a tripartite answer. The first is self-knowledge, the second refers to the temporal axis of human maturation, and the third, as invisible to Oedipus as his own gender, is the different relation that male and female have to the process of reproduction. It is this invisibility, male narcissism, that casts Oedipus' interlocutor as monstrous. The seductive and destructive sphinx is the repressed knowledge of the fact of maternity within a patrilineal culture. Woman is not simply the complement or obverse of Man, but is also a part of the infant-adult relationship on which evolution, play, language and therefore culture turn. Psychoanalysis refers to this repression of the significance of the maternal, and its recoding into the symbolic binarism of sexual difference as the 'castration complex', an unconscious predicament entailing the symbolic loss of an imaginary object. Feminist research into visual culture has found psychoanalytic theories of the part played by such unconscious fantasies an indispensable part of interpretation. Whether Freudian, Lacanian, Kleinian or using the thinking of other psychoanalysts, this area of theory enables another dimension of the extra-textual to be understood. The psyche, as distinct from the soma, and from the socially determined definitions of gender performance, is a powerful determinant of meaning, and is especially so in visual culture.

Feminist psychoanalysts such as Kristeva have argued that the balance of meaning in language is a question of ratio between meaning that is transmitted through symbolic forms such as syntax and logic, and meaning that is transmitted through what she calls the 'semiotic'. The semiotic, in this respect, refers to the pre-symbolic forms of communication such as rhyming, prosody, allusion, music and imagery. Visual representation with its lines, colour, texture, luminosities, physical space in sculpture, architecture and design, temporal rhythms and narratives in film and television, constitutes a language with a high ratio of semiotic to symbolic meaning. It is, for linguists and theorists of discourse, enigmatically closer to the non-rational side of the ratio of meaning. As a science of the irrational, psychoanalysis unravels the ties that bind the meaning of sexual difference so closely to visible difference in our culture. Based on an evolutionary theory of biological development, psychoanalysis locates the body at the centre of representation; because the ego is 'first and foremost a body ego', the echoes of bodily imagery extend into discourse, culture and society. It places the psychic representation of bodily instincts, the drives, as a fundamental part of the metapsychology, the general theory of mind which it applies to understanding society and culture as much as to intersubjectivity. Lacanian theory accords greater meaning to the topography, or spatial representations of the psyche, especially as this is mapped onto discursive structures, than does Freudian. For Freudians, it is the drives as energies cathected to impulses, objects, signifiers, affects, defences and other vicissitudes that constitute the economic field of the metapsychology, and which motivate the complexities of its dynamic axis.

According to Kristeva, the 'semiotic' aspect of meaning refers more closely to the body and to the unconscious than does the symbolic which demands a greater transformation of energy into the sublimated and symbolically mediated form of language. Visual representation communicates through signifiers with meanings of proximity, with signifiers whose relation to their signifieds is not completely arbitrary or conventional. There is an interesting field of research into the relation between verbal and visual representation, some of which explores the idea that imagery is more intimately connected to the pre-Oedipal world of the primary processes, infant-mother communication, and the unconscious.

Unconscious, or primary process, representation is concrete

rather than abstract, visual rather than verbal, affective rather than conceptual, and is organised into 'scenes' or compositions known as unconscious fantasy. These can be communicated indirectly to other parts of the psyche or intersubjectively. One of the most urgent functions of primary process representations is in the pre-verbal intuitive communication that exists between a mother and an infant. The infant communicates its moods, needs, fantasies and thoughts quite dramatically with a range of gestures, noises, bodily states and expressions which the mother internalises and interprets and to which she (or he, as this function may be fulfilled by a man) responds. This process of internalising inchoate communication and transforming it into meaning, through the mechanism of emotional receptivity, is known in psychoanalytic theory as maternal 'containment'. It is the process through which sensation becomes significance, and is the intersubjective basis for what will become the infant subject's capacity for intrapsychic communication, thought and language. That this first relation is communication of matters of life and death or survival, between infant and a life-support system who will eventually become recognised as a person or mother is deeply relevant in two ways. First, it becomes repressed as the infant separates from the mother, and develops in autonomy, thus forming the bedrock of the unconscious. This is the content of the 'semiotic' ratio of language which subtends the symbolic. It represents the relationship which is renounced in order to achieve independence and that is recreated, differently, in order to become social, a human destiny.

The second aspect of its relevance is through the social fact that most of the people who do this work of emotional receptivity are women. Thus the first relationship, which is one of absolute dependence on a woman, is already gendered. This process of pre-verbal communication which is repressed at the Oedipal stage and which persists in adult subjectivity as an unconscious process, can often be observed in irrational forms of communication in adults. There is a form of relationship, sometimes thought of as psychotic, which is used to a greater or lesser degree by all subjects and is called 'projective identification'. When projecting communication about an experience for which the subject is lost for words but which he has an urgent need to share, he elicits the emotional receptivity of an interlocutor who is placed in the position of the maternal container, and who is 'given' the experience which the subjects are unable to represent, symbolise or metabolise for themselves. In this way, unconscious messages, usually about unbearable pain, are transmitted more or less directly into the mind of another. This process of projective identification has been observed in a range of ideological institutions and in culture as well as in intersubjective relationships of love. The asymmetry of the relation is based on the emotional need that the 'projector' has for the containing function of the receptive thinker, who can help him understand his experience as his own, and help him find words or symbolic forms in which the experience may be more socially communicated, expressed or considered. This need is concealed, often from the projector himself, as the communication takes place in a relationship of apparent equality and reciprocity. To a spectator, the exchange looks no different from any other inter-course or communication. An apparently binary structure is used to conceal the imbalance of need, in a way that is mirrored by the inequality of the binary opposition described by the textual struc-ture of the logic of the supplement. This textual logic of power is the discursive manifestation of the psychological process of pro-jective identification, through which a concept is given clear boundaries through the projection of the contradictory meanings which it cannot contain into another supplementary concept: 'man' and 'woman', 'sense' and 'nonsense', 'white' and 'black', 'familiar' and stranger' and so on.

Mothers and other lost things

The structure of discourse determines the form given to a parti-cular affective, or emotional labour, which is generally unac-knowledged in our patrilineal culture because it is based on a form of apprenticeship which infants undergo for many years before becoming human subjects. Psychoanalysts suggest that this first relationship lies at the origin of love and hate, and therefore at the 'transitional space' between subjectivity and intersubjec-tivity that is the cradle of culture. The psychic mechanism of projective identification has been used to understand behaviour as different as child abuse, serial murder, anti-semitism and racism, identification in cinema and visual spectatorship, roman-

tic love and psychoanalytic transference. It has much to contribute to the analysis of sexual difference in visual culture, and
can do so through a combination of theoretical research and the
development of subjective intuition and intelligence. Because the
mechanism lies at the borders between thought and emotional
experience, it cannot be observed through intellectual skill alone
but requires a synthesis of knowledge and sensitivity. Until
neurologists can more accurately describe the biochemical effects
of emotional experience on brain activity (neurons and synapses
making 'pathways of interconnections'), psychoanalytic theory
remains the most useful map of the topographies of conceptual
and affective borderlines in the mind. It is the 'emotional intelligence' of women and reputed 'oversensitivity' that makes them
particularly suited to this work. However, as it recapitulates the
highly idealised, and denigrated, work of maternal labour it is in
permanent danger of being repressed, forgotten, denied and
unacknowledged in the same way that infants cannot recognise
their 'life support system', or need-satisfying object, as a person.

What are the effects of this on visual culture? The traditional
overestimation of independence which can be seen in the fetishisation of authorial innovation in modern art is more easily legible
as a defence against the ambivalence of a return to primary
dependence on maternal origination. That this is particularly
active in architecture is not unrelated to architecture being what
Stokes calls 'the mother of the arts'. The defensive use of narcissism is legible as an indication of an inadequately completed
separation from primary dependence, or a fear of the fantasy of
being returned to dependency; of being 'contained' rather than
'container', passive rather than active, the recipient rather than
the originator. If current forms of authorship in art tend to
fetishise the 'name of the father', this defence raises a number
of cultural issues for feminist research: how might fatherhood be
more adequately recognised and developed in visual culture,
rather than relegated to the distant idealised power of nomination? Can paternal labour be acknowledged as the work of
'containment' that is usually ascribed to the maternal? Can
authorship be understood, and recognised as a relationship rather
than fetishised as a conceptual production of an independent
individual? Can masculinity be described and mapped rather than
remaining the 'dark continent' of an unknown interiority?

Although projective identification is a mechanism of communication used by both sexes, the cultural representation of masculinity makes it more difficult for men to understand themselves as recipients rather than as penetrators. Once the emptiness of masculine narcissism is uncovered as a complex structure of reactions, defences and unconscious fantasy, the visual culture which bears the imprints of this gendered ignorance will be freer for women to work in.

The other axis of questions raised for feminist research relates to the forms of identification for women artists and designers in a culture where there are few examples of precursors or indications of trajectories of working in visual culture. If creativity in the cultural sphere has unconscious Oedipal connotations as well as historical determinants, there are specific fantasies attached to the identity and work of practising in visual culture; if the maternal position is not defined as a potentially productive place from which to work, do women become rebel daughters, pioneering and inventing the territory they stand on? Is a girl's identification with an Oedipal father a helpful ideal for conceiving a sense of destiny, as it may be for her brother? What are the difficulties, ambivalences and anxieties that a patrilineal cultural history produces in identification with maternal or feminine work? If conceptual fertility depends, at least in part, on the subjective capacity for integrating an unconscious idea of a dynamic coupling, and of containing the affective intensity of fantasies associated with procreation, is there a distinctive difference in a man's and a woman's identifications within this subjectivity? The masculine tradition of authorship in visual culture demonstrates an ambivalence between the desire to identify as the 'name of the father' and the conflicting desire to be the rebel son that transgresses the rules and conventions governing meaning. If there is an equivalent feminine ambivalence of desires for similarity to and difference from the Oedipal mother it entails the subject's questioning of being 'whose daughter' and 'whose mother'?

In psychoanalytic theory, the discussion of the psychic consequences of extended infant-maternal dependency that pre-dates language and subjectivity and the relationship enabling the capacity for the 'transitional space' of culture to be developed, centres on the resolution of Oedipal infantile sexuality, and on its dissolution and subsequent repression. The relationship to the primary object, or mother, is transformed and 'resolved', by the Oedipal triangulation which structures the psychological birth of the subject-in-culture. The 'kernel' of the unconscious in the castration complex is the condition for entry into subjectivity, culture and society. Lacanian analysts suggest that this process can be metaphorically represented by an equation in which the 'desire for the mother' becomes subsumed by a relation of identification with the 'name of the father'. This casts fatherhood in the role of agent of separation of infant from mother, and casts 'woman' as a negative unconscious concept. Feminist Lacanians find truth in the congruence between Lacan's theory and the structure of the unconscious within patriarchal society. Other, less Lacanian, feminists have offered theories of the transition from pre to post-Oedipal subjectivity which do not depend on the replacement of the maternal by paternal prohibition, and which suggest that there is a different female Oedipal complex. These involve a recognition of the effects of the primary identification, of children of both sexes with the mother, and an acknowledgement of the traces of this pre-verbal apprenticeship to subjectivity in the cultural forms which may be the documents of, and monuments to, its original significance. The pre-Oedipal mother may be an emotionally charged object, and subject to a range of perverse sexual fantasies, but she is also the object to which some of the strongest physical, sensual and bodily experiences of ego are cathected. The adult ability to paint or draw synthesises the libidinal cathexis to the memory of the unconscious object of the mother with the mastery of hand and eye coordination. Other signifying systems of visual culture give a different form to similar fantasies and energies.

Visual representation shares many registers of meaning with other aspects of the unconscious 'primary process'. An image can coexist in unconscious and conscious parts of the mind, and imagery is close to 'mood' and affect, as is music, and is readily transformed into the synaesthesia of 'inspirational' experience. The concept of synaesthesia refers to the process by which the barriers that usually differentiate representational registers of auditory, visual, kinetic, olfactory, and tactile signification, can, under certain circumstances, become permeable, thereby connecting the experience of the sound of a noise, for example, with the feel of a texture. Synaesthesia is a common experience before the separate organs of sensation are 'organised' by the developing ego and through different forms of language or different registers of representation. Specific forms of coordination between visual, acoustic, kinetic and symbolic registers make reading and writing verbal language possible, but generally in adults synaesthesia, as a merging of sensory experiences and representations, is limited to certain cultural forms, notably visual culture, and is often described as its principal pleasure, most compelling attraction and source of meaning. Thus visual culture becomes a privileged site for the production and deciphering of the unconscious in culture. The specific techniques of analysis that enable spectators to deconstruct and understand the unconscious are an indispensable component of feminist visual culture. Whereas other disciplines such as cultural studies, art and design histories, and media studies have made tangential use of theories of sexual difference and of psychoanalysis, the new emerging field of feminist analysis of visual culture maintains a central focus on how issues of gender, sexuality and power are inextricably intertwined in all aspects of our society's visual culture.

The fifteen chapters that follow are written specifically for this collection by authors who are known and recognised in their specialist fields as practitioners, theorists or both. Each author reviews the most relevant theoretical literature in her field, explaining the main issues and most significant debates, before presenting a case study or current example of feminist practice in contemporary visual culture.

The result is a selection of fifteen different perspectives on the production and the analysis of feminist visual culture. They give some sense of the range of research methods currently in use in feminist scholarship, and a sense of the scope and range of research questions and debates being generated by this opening-up of the mysterious universe of sexual difference and visual representation.

Part I

Fine art

New-type glass for RCA television picture tubes filters unwanted light, to give sharper, clearer images.

Wayward light is <u>*disciplined*</u> *— for better television!*

Now television pictures gain still greater contrast and definition—through research originally initiated by scientists at RCA Laboratories.

Their discovery: That wandering light waves inside a picture tube—and inside the glass itself—may cause halation and blur an image's edges. By introducing light-absorbing materials into the glass, the wayward flashes are absorbed so that only the light waves which actually make pictures can reach your eyes!

Glass companies, following this research, developed a new type of glass for RCA . . . *Filterglass.* Minute amounts of chemicals give it, when the picture tube is inactive, a neutral tone. In action, images are sharper—with more brilliant contrast between light and dark areas. Reflected room light is also reduced.

* * *

See the latest in radio, television, and electronics at RCA Exhibition Hall, 36 West 49th Street, N. Y. Admission is free. Radio Corporation of America, RCA Building, Radio City, N. Y.

The new Filterglass faceplate gives you more brilliant pictures on today's RCA Victor television receivers.

 RADIO CORPORATION *of* **AMERICA**
World Leader in Radio — First in Television

Feminist debate and fine art practices

Fiona Carson

The model and the muse

In the seamless trajectory of Western art history, one might be forgiven for assuming that art is the province of men and that the place of woman is in the picture, as model or muse. The stock-in-trade of art history is the monograph, or specialist study of an individual artist, and most of these are about men. However, the fact that an increasing number are being published about women, and that whole sections of specialist bookshops now address issues of gender and representation, is attributable to the past thirty years of feminist art theory and practice, to which this book is a further contribution.

In 1972, John Berger initiated the debate about the politics of representation and the gaze with his observations on the different ways in which men and women were represented: 'Men act and women appear. Men look at women. Women watch themselves being looked at.'[1] In his discussion of the tradition of the Renaissance reclining nude, Berger described the female nude as the objectified possession of the male spectator-owner. However, he saw Manet's famous nude of 1865, *Olympia*, as a turning-point: 'If one compares his *look Olympia* Olympia with Titian's original, one sees a woman, cast in the traditional role, beginning to question that role, somewhat defiantly. The ideal was broken.' Olympia gazes back at us. For the female art historian Eunice Lipton, writing in 1970, this returned gaze was a defining moment: 'I saw that the model surveyed the viewer.' This simple shift of perspective opens up a whole new set of questions that have revolutionised the concept of art history.

It is now rather difficult to imagine art without politics, ideology or social context. However, Lipton reminisces on art history in the 1960s: 'reading historical events into the style of works of art was forbidden in art history . . . Abstraction was sacred.'[2] As a Courtauld Institute student in the mid-1960s, my experience was similar. The list of books *not* to be read included those by John Berger, along with Hauser's *Social History of Art*. Lipton also describes an encounter in 1970 with Linda Nochlin, a female art historian who dared to ask questions about political and social meaning in art history, and one very famous question in particular: 'Why have there been no great women artists?'

ISSUES.

These two issues – the objectification of the female body in art, and the marginalisation of women as artists – have been the most important concerns for feminist theory and practice over the past thirty years.

Marginalisation

Linda Nochlin's explanation for the lack of female genius in art was two-sided. First, she examined the concept of genius, what she terms the 'golden nugget' theory lying at the heart of art historical structures. The idea of artistic genius as a god-given essence, 'subject of a hundred monographs', was a myth with its origins in Pliny, reiterated by Vasari about Giotto and Michelangelo, and embodied in modern times by Picasso. It was a male myth, a myth about masculinity, a myth that could be subject to deconstruction. In fact, most male 'geniuses' were precocious in their access to intensive training from an early age – Michelangelo and Picasso being good examples. By contrast, until the end of the nineteenth century, women artists were denied access to the training necessary to become professional artists, especially the study of the nude body upon which high-status narrative painting was based. Those few exceptional women – like Artemisia Gentileschi, Rosa Bonheur and Berthe Morisot – who achieved careers as professional artists, tended to be members of artistic families.[3]

Rozsika Parker and Griselda Pollock's book *Old Mistresses* (1981) went much further in its analysis of why women artists were excluded from the canon of art history. In the book's devastating conclusion, they propose that women artists 'are mentioned in order to be categorized, set apart and marginalized' within the 'masculine discourses of art history'. This marginalisation functioned to support the centrality and 'hegemony of men in cultural practice, in art'. Not only were women artists marginalised, they were *supposed* to be marginalised.

Parker and Pollock also concluded that women artists would be bound up with and discussed in terms of contemporary definitions of femininity and the perpetuation of the feminine stereotype. Individual female artists in turn would negotiate in different ways with these ideologies. Thus, the female Surrealist Leonor Fini engaged wholeheartedly in the role of Surrealist muse, dressing up and being photographed in mythic guises but painting from the perspective of a female consciousness and sexuality. As predatory black sphinx watching over the slight body of her reclining lover, she is 'the power of woman, the watcher'.[4]

The art/craft dichotomy

Rozsika Parker's analysis of the art/craft dichotomy underscored another way in which the feminine stereotype was linked to art production.[5] She traced the privatisation of female embroidery skills and their role in the inculcation of an ideology of femininity as devout, chaste and obedient, which culminated in the Victorian cult of medieval embroidery. During the Renaissance period, fine art was established as a public activity of high status associated with male professionals, while embroidery became a low-status craft associated predominantly with women and domestic spaces. Where it was professionalised, women were excluded.

The implications of this social stratification are still in place. Sculptural fibre art, for example, is exhibited as craft. Therefore, Magdalena Abakanowicz, a sculptor working in fibre, was never discussed in art magazines until she began to sculpt in bronze or wood. Eva Hesse, who pushed sculpture to its limits in tenuous fibrous forms like *Ennead* (1966) and *Right After* (1969), came from a fine art background and was discussed as a Minimalist sculptor, making 'vulnerable'and 'feminine' forms in contrast to Sol Le Witt's mathematical grids. Context was everything in terms of how these two artists' work was exhibited and reviewed, and consequently, Abakanowicz's powerful work remains relatively unknown.

The personal as political

The early 1970s saw the political explosion known as the Women's Liberation Movement. Fine art, like other cultural forms, was used as a medium for the expression of feminist politics. One of its most enduring slogans was 'the personal as political', described by Laura Mulvey in her catalogue entry for the Whitechapel Gallery's 1982 exhibition of Frida Kahlo and Tina Modotti as 'the political nature of women's private individualised oppression'.[6] The Mexican artist Frida Kahlo became an early heroine of the Women's Movement because of her ability to express powerful emotional experiences graphically, and to exorcise traumatic events in paint. It was in Kahlo's work that we first see the inner and tabooed aspects of the female body revealed in order to express such events. Her paintings, which show graphic depictions of physical injury to the body, imagery of birth, abortion and wounding, and the breaking-open of the body surface to reveal a dripping heart or a fractured spine, portray physical and emotional pain intertwined.

Goddess culture

Feminist art of the 1970s is characterised with hindsight as monocultural and essentialist, dominated by a preoccupation with goddess culture and vaginal iconography, which came to be viewed as anathema from the 1980s perspective of deconstruction and multiculturalism. By the 1990s, this polarisation had begun to acquire a historical perspective.

The idea of a 'utopian vision of lost maternal power regained'[7] perhaps explains part of the appeal of 1970s goddess culture and its fascination with myths of ancient matriarchy, which even led artists like Mary Beth Edelson to perform goddess rituals at ancient sites and declare that patriarchy's 5,000 years were over.[8] The Cuban artist Ana Mendieta, explaining the reasons for making the *Silhueta* series in 1981, stated, 'My art . . . is a return to the maternal source. Through my earth/body sculptures I become one with the earth.'[9]

The Dinner Party

The most famous and controversial icon of 1970s feminist art, Judy Chicago's *The Dinner Party*, brought together a number of contemporary concerns. This large triangular table, set with embroidered runners and vaginal plates, aimed to rescue female achievement in history from invisibility and to celebrate it – it was a dinner party for those 'consumed by history'. Chicago's use of craft skills associated with domestic femininity in a high art context challenged the traditional hierarchy of art and craft and drew attention to its gender politics. The overtly 'high church' atmosphere of the display with its female Last Supper connotations and goddess numerology imbued it with a religious atmosphere. But it was the use of vaginal imagery for the place settings of women as diverse as Virginia Woolf and Sacajawea that gave *The Dinner Party* its lasting place in controversy. Condemned in the United States Congress as 'pornography on plates' and criticised by 1980s feminists as essentialist, *The Dinner Party* remains homeless twenty years after its creation. Amelia Jones, attempting a critical rehabilitation of the piece, discusses Chicago's intentions in her use of vaginal imagery to portray an active and creative sexual energy: 'the vagina as temple, tomb, cave, flower, [or] the Butterfly Vagina which gets to be an active vaginal form'.

Jones notes how, when a 'paradigm shift' to a poststructuralist feminist art theory occurred in the 1980s, an opposition was set up against the 'body-oriented, utopian, transformative art of the 70s'. The range and challenge of this art tended, she claimed, to be 'collapsed into *The Dinner Party*, which was then cited as exemplary of its problems'. Mira Schor, meanwhile, observed that the label of 'essentialism' conferred on the work was a term created by its opposition.[10]

Deconstruction

An influential article by Judith Barry and Sandy Flitterman categorised women's art practices, only to condemn those that did not promote social analysis.[11] The 'celebratory' strategies of 1970s feminist aesthetics were compared unfavourably with 'deconstructive' strategies that used Marxism, structuralism, and psychoanalytic theories of the gaze to unpick dominant representations of women and reveal the workings of ideology. Such strategies saw the dominance of theory over making processes, and of photography over fine art media, and the development of a hegemonic 'scriptovisual' style in which text was often as important as image. The psychoanalytic theories of Freud and Lacan elaborated by Laura Mulvey in relation to the gaze had a strong influence on this type of work, which dominated the early 1980s in a series of exhibitions such as 'Issues' (Institute of Contemporary Arts, 1980), 'Sense and Sensibility' (Nottingham, 1982), and 'Beyond the Purloined Image' (Riverside, 1983).

In 1987, Griselda Pollock lent weight to this paradigm in her introduction to *Framing Feminism*, a compilation documenting the course of feminist art in Britain over the period 1970–85, by discussing Mary Kelly's Lacanian analysis of motherhood, *Post-Partum Document* (1975–8), as an illustration of Barry and Flitterman's thesis. She cites their view that artistic activity is a 'textual practice which exploits the existing social contra-dictions [in patriarchy] towards productive ends'. Kelly's work documented the mother-child relationship as a gendered ideo-logical process ending with the child's entry into language. The absent body of the mother was reconstituted as the narrative text: 'What I have evacuated at the level of the look (or representational image) has returned in the form of my diary narrative.'[12] Pollock argues elsewhere that *Post-Partum Docu-ment* uses Brechtian techniques of defamiliarisation, such as multiple registers of representation, to distance the audience from autobiographical identification or voyeuristic exploitation of the maternal image.[13]

Kristeva

The high level of theoretical understanding required by scripto-visual work, its rejection of traditional fine art media, and ultimately its orthodoxy eventually generated challenges. The pro-painting lobby criticised the emphasis on photographic media and the rejection of painting. Angela Partington[14] and Sarah Kent[15] defended the accessibility of less intellectualised and celebratory strategies for their accessibility and engagement with the audience. Katy Deepwell argued in favour of painting and a plurality of strategies including 'woman-centred, and sometimes essentialist views'.[16]

The dominance of the Lacanian model of woman as a sign of absence and lack presented something of a visual *impasse*, which could only be sidestepped by recourse to post-Lacanian psycho-analytical theories and a return to populism and a preoccupation with the body. The influence of Julia Kristeva, Hélène Cixous and Luce Irigaray's ideas about *l'écriture féminine*, the possibility of feminine languages outside the Freudian/Lacanian notion of the 'law of the father' that was inscribed in language and even the structures of the unconscious, seemed a way out of the *impasse* of lack and had particular relevance to the practice of abstract painting. Even more influential were Kristeva's description of the mother as 'custodian of the clean and proper body' in the prelinguistic phase of childhood development, and of the importance of purity and pollution rules in the organisation of the female body under patriarchy. The relevance of these ideas to the nude and to feminist critiques of it was explored by Lynda Nead in *The Female Nude* (1992) and I discuss them here in Chapter 2.[17] Jo Spence's photographic series about cancer, *Narratives of Dis-ease* (discussed in Chapter 5) sets out to challenge normative assumptions about the body and disability. Spence's invention of 'phototherapy' resituates 1980s class and gender analysis and psychoanalytical theory within a consciousness-raising framework by drawing on co-counselling and psychodrama skills to revisit her personal history. From my own experience of teaching feminist theory/practice, there is much mileage to be drawn from this conjunction of art practice and feminist theory applied to experience.

Identity politics

As Heidi Safia Mirza wrote in *Black British Feminism* in 1997, whereas 1970s and 1980s feminism centred on the 'right to be equal', the postmodern feminism of the 1990s turned to the celebration of the 'right to be different'.[18] The late 1980s were characterised by the growing importance of identity politics and an increasing mistrust of grand narratives, of which feminism was perceived to be one. Poststructuralist ideas about the primacy of text over authorship and the fracturing of the unified subject made political cohesion more difficult. This situation was desirable from several perspectives. Black feminists condemned earlier phases of the women's movement as middle-class and racist, and the 1980s saw the emergence of a Black Arts Movement, and within it the distinctive voice of a black feminist avant-garde was apparent in a number of exhibitions and writings. Eleven black women artists, including Lubaina Himid, Sutapa Biswas, Sonia Boyce and Chila Burman, exhibited in 1985 in the seminal exhibition 'The Thin Black Line'. These issues are discussed further by Pauline de Souza in Chapter 4.

As Sunil Gupta describes, the 1990s also saw a 'coming out of the closet for lesbian and gay artists dealing with issues of their own identity'.[19] The lesbian photographic compilation *Stolen Glances* (1991) sought a greater visibility for lesbian representation in the wake of discrimination created by the Section 28 legislation of 1988 which prohibited British local government authorities from 'intentionally promoting homosexuality' in schools.[20] The compilation *Outlooks* (1996) reflects the 1990s concept of a 'queer sensibility' and cultural activism. Emmanuel Cooper defines queer art as 'part of a continuing search for a visual language which expresses the hopes, anxieties, desires of queers/gays/lesbians/dykes/bisexuals'.[21]

The 1990s saw a diversification of feminism and some would argue a process of fracturing. In terms of the mainstream, a generation of young women artists has emerged for whom feminism is a backdrop rather than an identity, something taken for granted rather than admitted to. But feminism's importance remains as an evolving critique of representation and of the dominant structures of the art world, which remain basically unchanged. Griselda Pollock described feminism in 1996 as 'standing for a commitment to the full appreciation of what women inscribe, articulate and image in cultural forms; interventions in the field of meaning and identity from the place called "woman" or the "feminine"'.[22] The metaphor is both geographical and spatial. As a black feminist, Razia Aziz argues for recognition of the fluidity and fragmented nature of racialised and gendered identities, but she also argues for the importance of cohesion and activism – escape from the '*cul de sac* of identity politics' by means of 'a powerful, conscious form of political agency'.[23] It is these tensions between cohesion and difference that continue to generate an exciting body of theory and practice in the field of feminist visual culture.

Notes

1. Berger, *Ways of Seeing*, ch. 3.
2. Eunice Lipton, *Alias Olympia* (London: Thames & Hudson, 1993), pp. 5–11.
3. Nochlin, *Women, Art and Power*, ch. 7.
4. Parker and Pollock, *Old Mistresses*, pp. 139–41 and pp. 169–70.
5. Parker, *The Subversive Stitch*.
6. Laura Mulvey and Peter Wollen, *Frida Kahlo and Tina Modotti* (London: Whitechapel Gallery, 1982), p. 13.
7. Adrienne Rich, *Of Woman Born* (New York: Norton, 1976), pp. 238–40.
8. Lucy Lippard, *From the Center* (New York: Dutton, 1976), p. 21.
9. M. Kwon, 'Bloody Valentines, Afterimages by Ana Mendieta' in C. De Zegher (ed.), *Inside the Visible* (Cambridge, MA and London: MIT Press, 1996).
10. Jones, *Sexual Politics*, pp. 85–100.
11. J. Barry and S. Flitterman, 'Textual Strategies: the Politics of Art Making', *Screen*, (1980) vol. 21, no. 4.
12. Mary Kelly, quoted in Parker and Pollock, *Framing Feminism*, p. 49 and pp. 96–7.
13. Pollock, *Vision and Difference*, pp. 171–2.

14. Angela Partington, 'Feminism and Avant-gardism' in H. Robinson (ed.), *Visibly Female, Feminism and Art Today* (London: Camden Press, 1987).
15. J. Morreau, and S. Kent, *Women's Images of Men* (London: Pandora, 1985).
16. Janet Wolff, *Feminine Sentences* (Cambridge: Polity Press, 1990), ch. 6.
17. Lynda Nead, *The Female Nude: Art, Obesity and Sexuality* (London and New York: Routledge, 1992).
18. Mirza, *Black British Feminism*, pp. 12–13.
19. S. Gupta, 'Culture Wars', in Horne and Lewis, *Outlooks*, p. 171.
20. Anna Marie Smith, 'Which One's the Pretender?' in Boffin and Fraser, *Stolen Glances*.
21. Cooper, E., 'Queer Spectacles' in Horne and Lewis, *Outlooks*, p. 13.
22. Griselda Pollock (ed.), *Generations and Geographies in the Visual Arts* (London: Routledge, 1996), p. 8.
23. R. Aziz, 'Feminism and the Challenge of Racism' in Mirza, *Black British Feminism*, pp. 70–7.

Bibliography

Berger, John, *Ways of Seeing* (Harmondsworth: Penguin, 1972).
Boffin, T. and Fraser, J., *Stolen Glances, Lesbians Take Photographs* (London: Pandora Press, 1991).
Horne, Peter and Reina Lewis, *Outlooks* (London: Routledge, 1996).
Jones, Amelia (ed.), *Sexual Politics, Judy Chicago's Dinner Party in Feminist Art History* (Berkeley and London: University of California Press, 1996).
Kelly, Mary, *Post-Partum Document* (London and Boston: Routledge, 1983).
Lippard, L., *Eva Hesse* (New York: New York University Press, 1976).
Mirza, H. S., *Black British Feminism* (London: Routledge, 1997).
Nochlin, Linda, *Women, Art and Power* (London: Thames & Hudson, 1989).
Parker, Rozsika, *The Subversive Stitch* (London: The Women's Press, 1984).
Parker, Rozsika, and Griselda Pollock (eds), *Framing Feminism: Art and the Women's Movement 1970–1985* (London: Pandora, 1987).

Parker, Rozsika, and Griselda Pollock, *Old Mistresses: Women, Art and Ideology* (London: Routledge, 1981).

Pollock, Griselda, *Vision and Difference: Femininity, Feminism and Histories of Art* (London: Routledge, 1988).

Rose, B., *Magdalena Abakanowicz* (New York: Harry N. Adams, 1994).

Spence, Jo, *Cultural Sniping* (London: Routledge, 1995).

Chapter 1

Painting

Fran Lloyd

PAINTING BEARS WITNESS TO some of the most dramatic
shifts in the past thirty years within feminist artistic practice in
Britain. Rejected by many earlier feminists, painting is now visibly
established as an important and vital area of feminist activity.
This chapter explores how and why such a major shift has
occurred, by mapping out the complex and often contradictory
issues that have surrounded painting as a feminist practice since
the 1970s, and showing how these, together with more recent
theory, have helped to shape the richness and diversity of feminist
painting at the turn of the century. Such a description is necessarily brief, selective, and dependent on previous explorations.
However, my central concern is to revisit painting as one of
the most undervalued sites of feminist practice in Britain and to
provide a sense of its continuities and potential. A fuller history of
the complex lineage of feminist painting in Britain has yet to be
written or curated.

Painting, feminism and feminist paintings

Like other forms of cultural activity, painting does not exist
independently. It is part of the complex web of political, social
and economic practices and their accompanying ideological
values that constitute society at any given time. Painting is
'simultaneously a medium, a critical category, a form of economic
investment, a curatorial term and a symbolic system'.[1] Because it
is always defined in relation to other cultural practices, its meaning changes in relation to these 'extratextual' conditions.[2]
In the same way, feminism is not one fixed thing. There are

many feminisms and there are also 'different generations and geographies'.[3] Here, I am taking feminist art practice to be any intervention in the dominant system of artistic production and reception which has historically excluded or marginalised women. This viewpoint may focus on women as active producers – as artists – and/or it may critique the naturalised assumptions of masculinist culture. The specific forms of such social intervention, in this case within the confines of painting in Britain, will be different at different times and for different audiences.

The mapping of feminist painting is therefore complex. It is multifarious and multi-sited and it is constantly working against and through other, often dominant, positions: painting by men, alternative practices such as installation or performance, the art market, curatorial policies and so on. As this chapter sets out to demonstrate, there is no single model of feminist painting; its forms cannot be predetermined nor its readings narrowly prescribed. It is an interactive process where meaning is always in production.[4]

Looking back: easel answers and the politics of representation

Feminist art practice in Britain grew out of the contemporary women's movement in the late 1960s and early 1970s.[5] Through the ground-breaking work of feminist writers, it became evident that women artists, particularly painters, had always existed but they had been marginalised by the dominant practices that controlled the dissemination and mediation of art and the criteria used for defining 'greatness'.[6] In particular, modernism, the dominant cultural practice from the mid-nineteenth century, was shown to privilege art (that is, painting and sculpture) as self-expression and the male artist as the universalising voice, free of the constraints of gender.

It is this intersection of the various critiques of modernism, at the level of both individual practice and institutions, that has made painting a difficulty for some feminists. In the 1970s, painting was associated with a male-dominated tradition, and was seen as a private as opposed to a collective activity, with a modernist emphasis on the medium and the autonomy of painting. It was also associated with the 'virility and domination' of the phallus and implicated in maintaining the very categories of art history – the artist, genius and individual expression – that feminist writers had shown to have excluded women.[7]

Many artists associated with feminism in the 1970s had been trained as painters within an art school system that perpetuated modernist values. Not surprisingly, several rejected painting in favour of photography, performance or conceptual art , forms of expression which were widely associated with an adversarial, avant-garde practice and were less burdened by historical pre-cedent. Those women who continued to engage in painting employed various strategies to disrupt the dominant modernist values, including a conscious exploration of women's experience and the undermining of the dominant forms of abstraction that inscribed art as 'purely an optical experience' (gender-free and universal) and perceived the 'representational', and the 'literary' or narrative as pollutants of this pure art.

In Britain, the issue of painting and feminism initially centred on the use of figuration which had emerged within the Women's Liberation movement in the early 1970s and is exemplified by Monica Sjoo's infamous painting, *God Giving Birth* (1968). Shown in 1973 as part of a figurative group show called 'Woman-power', Sjoo's painting depicted a centralised image of a non-white female giving birth. It effectively used figuration to reclaim the female nude (usually the object of male desire), to celebrate female creativity, and to focus on female experience through the depiction of childbirth. It also contested the naturalised myths of male power in Western culture and challenged the modernist view of painting as pure, aesthetic experience.

As the exhibition titles suggest, the paintings by figurative artists shown at 'Womanpower' and later exhibitions, such as 'Women's Images of Women' (1977) and 'Womanmagic' (1978), were women-centred images. They attempted to challenge the predominantly negative representations of women circulating in culture by offering alternative, positive images exploring specific areas of female experience that had previously been ignored. Like much American work at that time, the paintings focused on fertility, childbirth, the goddess, mythology or the artist's body. While the popularity among women of these images was evident, many feminists, particularly in Britain, were wary of them.[8] How could positive images of women be effective in a culture where female experience was denigrated and the female body was always open to recuperation by the male gaze, especially in painting?

This wariness was rooted in the specificities of British feminism, as Amelia Jones has shown. British feminists at that time focused on socialist politics and a growing body of feminist practice that, drawing upon psychoanalysis (especially Lacanian) and recent theories of representation, questioned even the possibility of representing woman in a system that saw woman as absent, as the 'other' and as objects of the male gaze.[9] Laura Mulvey's 1975 essay on 'Visual Pleasure and Narrative Cinema', together with Mary Kelly's 'paradigm-shifting' *Post-Partum Document* (1974–9), 'moved the terms of feminist art practice' by focusing on the systems that constructed the female rather than on direct imaging.[10] Kelly later described her work as a 'rupture' which divided 'feminist debate within the movement' and 'questioned the explanatory power of experience that gave the emerging movement ideological as well as organisational cohesion'.[11]

Feminist art practice in Britain became dominated by such poststructuralist models of signification, while painting became increasingly positioned against the supposedly more radical 'document' work of Kelly and others.[12] Celebratory images were seen as 'biological essentialism' against 'those who insist that femininity is socially and historically constructed' and, significantly, artists were urged to 'resist visual pleasure' since it was seen as central to painting and the male gaze.[13] For a period during the 1970s, 'this produced a "negative aesthetics" among certain feminists, a radical distanciation from any aspect of the spectacle and visual pleasure, a distrust of the visual image, of the iconicity especially of women.'[14]

However, painting continued to effectively confront issues of women's history and experience in the public realm of the gallery as the 1976–7 canvases of Margaret Harrison and Rose Garrard demonstrate.[15] Similarly, it is clear from the writings of Sjoo, Jacqueline Morreau and others that their move to celebratory figuration was a strategic intervention, no less deconstructive, informed by specific historical, social and political conditions, and equally important to the feminist project.[16]

Changing conditions: postmodernism and the return of painting

By the late 1970s, it was evident on several fronts that major cultural shifts were taking place, and this was encapsulated by the widespread acknowledgement of the postmodern. Postmodernism seemed to mark a general dismantling of the modernist project and its concomitant grand narratives, which feminists (alongside others excluded from modernism through race or sexuality) had helped to achieve.[17] Central to this shift was the recognition of multiplicity and difference at all levels of society including that of the individual subject. Thus, 'woman', once a secure category for feminists, was now theorised as one among a number of intersections (including class, race, sexuality and geography) in a 're-centred' postmodern culture of partial and provisional meanings and fluid subjects. This recognition of difference (in both producers of art and their audiences), together with the dismantling of modernism and the related return of figurative painting in the international art market, provided further impetus for feminists to rethink the place of painting within feminism.

The exhibition 'Women's Images of Men', held at the Institute of Contemporary Art (ICA) in London in 1980, was 'perfectly timed' given these changing conditions.[18] Organised in direct protest against an Allen Jones exhibition and encouraged by the 1978 'Hayward Annual' (selected by women) in London, 'Women's Images of Men' aimed to reach a wide audience and to present feminist, issue-based, figurative art in a major public arena. Continuing the self-help strategies of earlier collective exhibitions, it included thirty-five artists, ten of whom were painters representing various generations from Morreau (one of the organisers and an established feminist activist) to the recent graduate Eileen Cooper.

This exhibition, alongside other feminist events of 1980, helped to focus the fierce debate around feminist painting on issues of the 'efficiency and function of art within a political movement' and the question of the effects on audiences.[19] While the dominant discourse was for a negative aesthetic, the exhibition clearly demonstrated a need to consider female pleasures for both the producers and the audiences. Thus, despite the dominance of 'scriptovisual' work, feminist painting emerged once again in the 1980s as an effective form of practice.[20]

Building upon previous feminist practice and encouraged by the recent visibility of women's painting, feminist painters continued to explore critically a wide range of female experience that undermined both past and current attitudes to painting. Conceptual artists such as Alexis Hunter returned to painting to employ psychoanalytical theory to parody male myths and question female desires,[21] while younger artists such as Eileen Cooper and Amanda Faulkner concentrated on rethinking the complex pleasures and pains of the gendered female body, notably the experiences of motherhood and childbirth.

Mythology, meanwhile, continued to serve as a potent device for both actively reclaiming and rewriting women's histories and for imaging the present and the future. Morreau's large mythological triptychs explored women's presence as active subjects in culture and the forgotten continuities of mother and daughter.[22] The large themed collective exhibition 'Pandora's Box' (1984) enabled many painters to use myth to comment on political issues of class, sexuality and gender.[23]

Equally important in the early 1980s were exhibitions that focused attention on black women's experience.[24] Like earlier feminist exhibitions, these were the result of women's collective action and most took place in alternative spaces rather than in mainstream galleries. Lubaina Himid, Sutapa Biswas and Sonia Boyce used painting as a critical and radical form for imaging their presence and difference in a predominantly white, male British art world.

Thus, while painting's much lauded return to favour in the international art world in the early 1980s did not in itself embrace women, the changing climate of postmodernism, combined with the increasing championing of nationalistic art, did provide some mainstream visibility for feminists through the British art shows, and through exhibitions of Scottish art, Irish art, and even the London school.[25] There was also some recognition at this time for artists such as Paula Rego and Evelyn Williams who had pursued issues of women's experience in seeming isolation during the 1970s and early 1980s.[26] However, in most cases, feminism was written out of the account.

Painting difference in the 1980s and 1990s

The younger generation of women painters who emerged in the 1980s had a different relationship to feminism, painting and the art market. A postconceptual generation, trained in the late 1970s and early 1980s, their approach to painting, and its traditions and procedures was informed by a substantial body of feminist practice which, together with other deconstructive theories, encouraged a critical attitude to any naturalised order within the seemingly more open art market. It was also informed by new approaches to 'writing the body'.

L'écriture féminine emerged within French feminism as an attempt to reconsider Lacan's psychoanalytical theories of the female as absent 'other' or as the passive recipient of the male gaze.[27] Although the ideas of Julia Kristeva, Luce Irigaray and Hélène Cixous are radically different from each other in many respects, they all focus on the 'feminine' in culture. For Kristeva, this resides in the 'semiotic', a pre-linguistic realm of bodily drives and pulsations which is repressed on entry into language but may emerge from the unconscious at a later stage as a 'feminine' language that disrupts patriarchal language and carries traces of the repressed maternal body. This exploration of the material of language itself as a site of disruption offered the potential for disrupting and reformulating the very language of painting.

By contrast, Irigaray and Cixous propose a form of writing the body that is ultimately based in the specificities of the experience of living in a female body where sexuality is multiple, fluid and decentred. This embodied experience (neither available to nor mediated by men) acknowledges alternative ways of knowing and negotiating the world which do not privilege the mind/body duality or sight (the mastery of the gaze). Lisa Tickner's key article on 1970s feminist body art recognised that 'living in a female body is different from looking at it, as a man',[28] while, more recently, Rosemary Betterton describes it as a shift 'from questions about representation – how the female body should be represented – to the question of subjectivity – what it means to inhabit that body: from the problem of *looking* (distance) to the problem of *embodiment* (touch)'.[29]

These theories, however problematic, have been enormously

important for artists.[30] 'The emphasis on materiality, touch and embodiment offer ways of discussing what is specific to the procedures, and the effects of making objects, images, for people to look at . . . use and be affected by'.[31] In particular, they have provided a renewed confidence that painting, long associated with the disembodied eye of pure vision, can operate as a radical and critical practice on a number of levels.

The effects on feminist painting practice have been dramatic and far reaching. The most obvious is the increasing number of women painters who see their experience of difference as central to their work, and not as a separate, uneasy fact. This experience informs their painting in a number of different and interconnected ways: at the level of mark-making, where traces of the gendered body reside; through the use of materials (the materiality of paint having long been associated with the skin of the body); through the subject matter; and finally in the effect of these on the body of the viewer.[32]

In the mid-1980s, women painters explored all of those levels. Maria Chevska and Therese Oulton focused on landscape painting (a male tradition associated with mastering nature) exploring the literal and metaphoric use of layering and weaving to directly reference a lost history of women's labour as active producers and to simultaneously embody the feminine presence through an emphasis on the materiality of the paint, the decentring of the controlling gaze and the division of subject/object.[33] Others, such as the Irish artists Alice Mahler and Mary McGowan, continued to expand the forgotten histories of oral traditions, fables and myths to include women's memories of place and an 'archaeology of the self'.[34] These complex and often contradictory issues of cultural identity in terms of race, class and religion are central to much recent painting.[35]

Not surprisingly, the imaging of the female body has once again become a major site for intervention, both to reclaim the repressed and to deconstruct embedded masculinist values. Alison Watt, for example, deconstructs dominant ideas of beauty and containment while Jenny Saville and Gwen Hardie emphasise the materiality of the female body as a critique of the male objectifying gaze and related systems of institutionalised control.[36] Nicky Hodge and Julie Roberts confront such systems within medical science, while Glenys Johnson focuses on media control.[37] Recent group exhibitions have portrayed the under-valued areas of women's experience including issues surrounding motherhood and the repressed maternal body.[38] Self-portraiture, working across many of these sites, has become particularly prevalent, as recent publications show.[39]

Similarly, the repressed lesbian body has become an important site within feminist art practice for acknowledging difference. Aware of the current curatorial strategy of the 'homogenisation of contemporary art by lesbians under a rubric of "bad girls" or dysfunctional sexual alienation', Cherry Smyth's recent book presents a broad range of work involving all areas of lived lesbian experience.[40] Several of the painters it features, clearly informed by earlier feminist strategies, use figuration to disrupt notions of the female lesbian body. Rachael Field and Sadie Lee, for example, contest accepted ideals of feminine, heterosexual beauty and desirability, while Patricia Hurl's 'frank vulvic portraits' subvert a long tradition in Ireland of both revered romantic landscape painting and the land as 'asexual mother'.[41]

However, the most striking change in contemporary practice is the rethinking of non-representational painting as a site for feminist intervention. Given the perceived links between abstraction and modernist (male) practice in the 1970s, it was difficult to see how such work could be shown to engage with feminist issues, despite the presence of established women painters such as Bridget Riley and Sandra Blow. Recently, however, feminist writers and artists have begun to question and explore this forbidden territory and, as Betterton states, 'the idea of the body of the artist, female embodiment and female subjectivity' are central to this exploration.[42] Using Irigaray's theories, Betterton identifies several strategies in women's contemporary abstract painting that reclaim femininity and disrupt the 'binary oppositions which enshrine sexual difference'.[43]

The rethinking of the process of painting and its material existence has opened up other possibilities. As the recent exhibition 'Inside the Visible' showed,[44] the idea of 'feminine inscriptions' allows both a way of looking back to previously marginalised art in order to uncover feminine traces and a way of understanding the process of making as an act of discovery or becoming. Thus, painting is not necessarily a representation of the already known but can be a process of uncovering or articulating that is able to create new identities and new conditions for the future. This is important for feminists: while recognising social and historical positioning such an approach offers the possibility of imaging change. It also renegotiates the once fiercely defended boundary between feminist painting and women's painting, which has worked to exclude and divide.[46]

In order to explore the diversity of feminist painting in the 1990s, I will concentrate on two different contemporary artists whose work is informed by feminism: Jenny Saville, a figurative painter, and Monair Hyman, a non-representational one. Both trained as painters in the late 1980s, both graduated in 1992 and both have begun to enter the more diverse art market system of recent years.

Saville studied at Glasgow School of Art, famous for its continuous tradition of drawing, its 1980s 'new image' painting and its output of high-profile male painters. Within this masculinist climate, Saville focused on the painted nude female – well aware that she was 'making an issue of the institution of "the Nude" – a territory traditionally occupied by male artists and female models: the assessor and the assessed'.[46]

As Lynda Nead has shown, the female nude is 'a particularly significant motif within western art and aesthetics'.[47] It both 'symbolizes the transformation of the base matter of nature into the elevated forms of culture and the spirit' and acts to controls 'this unruly body . . . [by] containing femininity and female sexuality'.[48]

Figure 1.1 Jenny Saville, Untitled, 1994, oil on canvas 210 × 150cm/ 7ft × 5ft. Collection of Graham and Nancy Wood. Photograph by Ray Main, courtesy of Mainstream.

Saville's huge oil paintings directly confront these naturalised conventions; her figures are physically large, they display an excess of flesh heightened by the tactile materiality of the painted surface, and they continuously resist containment through their ambiguous placement and through distorted perspectives that threaten to exceed the limits of the canvas. For example, in the 1994 work *Untitled* (Figure 1.1), the nude, with Saville's self-portrait as the face, overspills the stool (a sign of the model as object?) and pushes towards the spectator, forcing an awareness of the body as living and moving flesh. Simultaneously, the blood-red marks on the knee and the grey and yellow skin tones suggest wounds, decay and the hidden, visceral interior. Distinctions between interior and exterior become blurred. In Kristevan terms, this represents one

aspect of the 'abject', the recognition that the body, and therefore identity, is unstable, impermanent and continuously changing, a state that Western culture has tended to repress.

Saville's representations of the female nude are strategic interventions. They disturb dominant ideals of femininity and expose the diverse systems of science, medicine and the binaries of nature/culture that map the female body. Simultaneously, they raise issues about the fears and desires associated with different bodies (the maternal, the obscene, the ageing), including the body of the spectator.[49]

Monair Hyman, by contrast, studied painting as a mature student at Leeds Metropolitan University. Her recent large oil canvases resist immediate recognition. There is no centralising focal point, no brilliant splashes of diverse colour and, most crucially, no overt object. Instead, in works such as *Fugitive* (Figure 1.2), one is presented with a flowing pattern of grey marks on a shining white ground, which have been dragged or disrupted by intermediary white strokes. The effect is of something out of focus or partially covered, and it is unclear whether these markings were once more visible (disappearing) or are just becoming visible (emerging). They simultaneously imply depth and surface, absence and presence, inside and outside, and work to unfix the body of the spectator: is one looking into, through, out of or from behind a screen?

Hyman's works show a preoccupation with the 'processes of reclaiming memory and examining experience'.[50] They are consciously multilayered, referencing the stereotypical attributes of female artists (decorative marks and so on), the repetition of wallpaper or fabric, or the memories of elaborate ironwork. Such structuring devices are undone through the dragging and blurring effects that disrupt the binary oppositions, and through the patterns that never repeat.[51]

The recognition of the presence of, and the need for, multiple perspectives and meanings is central to Hyman's work and her interest in other cultures. The paintings literally and metaphorically explore the way in which patterns shape our lives and how memory, experience and the constructions of femininity are embodied. They also emphasise the instability of these conditions: they can be changed, and even undone, through the process of active intervention.

*Figure 1.2
Monair Hyman,
Fugitive, 1996,
oil on canvas
183 × 152cm.
Courtesy of
Monair Hyman.*

Equal difference in the marketplace?

Irigaray's image of an unhierarchical, equal difference (not same-ness) is clearly not yet in view. The conditions of production, distribution and consumption are still far from equal in Britain, as many writers have shown.[52] Women artists are still under-re-presented, especially in full-time positions within art colleges and universities and in the mediated spaces of art magazines and exhibitions. The increasing success of women painters in the marketplace is attributable partly to the fact that they have such urgent issues to explore and partly to the fact that the market-place has expanded and diversified. The recent interest in con-temporary art, the emergence of agents rather than dealers, and changing patterns of sponsorship have provided women painters with some crucial support. Similarly, while the cooperative fra-meworks essential to feminists in the 1970s and early 1980s have radically altered, they still remain an indispensable element of the politics of visibility.[53]

However, the increasing number of successful women paint-ers is important – they provide a lineage and a diversity of approach which builds multiple bodies of work that visibly intervene to change dominant masculinist values and are pre-sent for successive generations. This may be 'seeking women's equal rights to the body of the artist', but it is not the same body. These bodies have been inscribed differently and the recognition of difference is vital in a culture that excludes or marginalises on any grounds.

Notes

1. Pollock, 'Painting, Feminism, History', in Barrett and Phil-lips, *Destabilizing Theory*, p. 174.
2. Wolff, *Feminine Sentences*, p. 96.
3. Pollock, *Generations and Geographies*, p. 19.
4. Marsha Meskimmon 'In Mind and Body', *make*, no. 79, March–May 1998, p. 5.
5. Parker and Pollock, *Framing Feminism*, pp. 4–26.
6. Linda Nochlin, 'Why Have There Been No Great Women Artists?' in T. Hess and E. Baker (eds), *Art and Sexual Politics* (London and New York: Collier Macmillan, 1971).

7. Carol Duncan, 'Virility and Domination in Early Twentieth-Century Vanguard Painting', *Artforum*, December 1973, pp. 30–9; Parker and Pollock, *Old Mistresses*.
8. Parker and Pollock, *Framing Feminism*.
9. Jones, *Sexual Politics*, pp. 155–6.
10. Ibid. p. 27.
11. Kelly, *Imaging Desire*, pp. xvii–xviii.
12. Jones, *Sexual Politics*, p. 38.
13. Parker and Pollock, *Framing Feminism*, p. 29 and pp. 232–48.
14. Pollock, 'Inscriptions in the Feminine' in de Zegher (ed.) *Inside the Visible*, p. 79. See also Pollock, *Vision and Difference* (London: Routledge, 1988), pp. 155–99.
15. See 'The Issue of Painting', Rochdale Art Gallery, 1986, and 'With Your Own Face On', Plymouth and Nottingham, 1994–5.
16. See Sjoo's text 'Towards a Revolutionary Feminist Art' in Parker and Pollock, *Framing Feminism*, p. 5.
17. See Wolff, *Feminine Sentences* and Weedon, *Feminist Practice*.
18. Kent and Morreau, *Women's Images of Men*, p. 3.
19. Parker and Pollock, *Framing Feminism*, pp. 245–6.
20. See Angela Partington's 1984 paper, 'Feminist Art and Avant-gardism', reprinted in Robinson, *Visibly Female*, pp. 228–49, and Katy Deepwell, 'In Defence of the Indefensible: Feminism, Painting and Postmodernism', *Feminist Art News*, vol. 2, no. 4, pp. 9–12.
21. Caroline Osbourne interview in Robinson, *Visibly Female*.
22. *Jacqueline Morreau: Myth and Metaphor* (London: Artemis Press, 1989).
23. *Pandora's Box, Women's Images* (London: Trefoil Books, 1984).
24. 'Five Black Women Artists', African Centre, Covent Garden, and 'Black Woman Time Now', Battersea Art Centre, both 1983; 'The Thin Black Line', ICA, 1985.
25. See 'A New Tradition: Irish Art of the Eighties', Douglas Hyde Gallery, Dublin, 1990.
26. For Rego, see Melanie Roberts, 'Eight British Artists – Cross Generational "Talk"' in Lloyd, *From the Interior*; Evelyn Williams, 'Encounters 1992–96', Manchester City Art Gallery, 1997.
27. See de Courtivron and Marks, *New French Feminisms*.
28. Lisa Tickner 'The Body Politic: Female Sexuality and Women Artists Since 1970', *Art History*, June 1978, vol. 1 no. 2.
29. Betterton, *An Intimate Distance*, p. 7.

30. See Wolff, *Feminine Sentences*, and Jane Kelly, 'The Point is to Change it', *Oxford Art Journal*, vol. 21, no. 2, 1998, pp. 185–93.
31. Pollock 'Trouble in the Archive', *Women's Art Magazine*, no. 54, Sept/Oct 1993, p. 11.
32. This formulation is indebted to Hilary Robinson, 'Border Crossings' in Pollock, *Generations and Geographies*, pp. 138–46.
33. See Anna Bonshek, 'Feminist Romantic Painting – a Re-Constellation' in Robinson, *Visibly Female*.
34. See 'Myth, Dream & Fable', Angel Row, Nottingham 1992.
35. See Betterton, *An Intimate Distance*, pp. 161–93, and Bohm-Duchen and Grodzinski, *Rubies and Rebels*.
36. See Lloyd, *From the Interior*; Duncan MacMillan, *Scottish Art in the Twentieth Century* (Mainstream Publishing, 1994); Alison Watt, 'Fold', Leeds Metropolitan University Gallery, 1998.
37. Roberts concentrates on the distancing gaze of medicine in obstetrics and gynaecology, while Hodge's recent work explores the confinement of birth. For Johnson see 'The Issue of Painting', Rochdale Art Gallery, 1986.
38. 'Mothers', Ikon, Birmingham, 1990 and 'Reclaiming the Madonna', Lincolnshire County Council, 1993.
39. See Meskimmon, *The Art of Reflection*, and Borzello, *Seeing Ourselves*.
40. Smyth, *Damn Fine Art*, p. 2.
41. Ibid. pp. 24–5.
42. Betterton, *An Intimate Distance*, p. 94. See also S. Kaneda, 'Painting and its Other', *Arts Magazine*, Summer 1991, pp. 58–64; Rosa Lee 'Resisting Amnesia: Feminism, Painting and Postmodernism', *Feminist Review*, no. 26, July 1987, pp. 5–29; Rebecca Fortnum and Gill Houghton 'Women and Contemporary Painting', *WASL*, no. 28, pp. 4–18; Joan Key, 'Models of Painting Practice' in Deepwell, *New Feminist Art Criticism*, pp. 153–61.
43. Betterton, *An Intimate Distance*, pp. 94–9.
44. See Zegher, *Inside the Visible*.
45. Deepwell, *New Feminist Art Criticism*, p. 1.
46. Lloyd, *From the Interior*, p. 86.
47. Nead, *The Female Nude*, p. 2.
48. Ibid. p. 2.
49. See Alison Rowley, 'On Viewing Three Paintings by Jenny Saville' in Pollock, *Generations and Geographies*; Marsha Meskimmon, 'The Monstrous and the Grotesque', *make*, no. 72, October/November 1996, pp. 6–11; 'Sensation', Royal

Academy, 1997, and C. Townsend, *Vile Bodies: Photography and the Crisis of Looking* (Munich, Prestel in association with Channel Four Television, 1998).

50. Kevin O'Brien in *Monair Hyman* (Leeds: University Gallery, 1997), p. 7, and Nancy Procter, 'Like a Squeegee on Glass', *make*, no. 75, April–May 1997, p. 26.
51. *Monair Hyman*, p. 15.
52. See Deepwell, *New Feminist Art Criticism*, p. 58.
53. Group exhibitions remain one of the most effective strategies for women. Collections such as the Women's Art Collection in New Hall, Cambridge, the MAG Collection, Ferens Art Gallery, Hull and the activities of the Foundation for Women's Art, London are important in maintaining visibility.

Bibliography

Barrett, Michele, and Anne Phillips (eds), *Destabilising Theory: Contemporary Feminist Debates* (Cambridge: Polity Press, 1992).

Betterton, Rosemary, *An Intimate Distance, Women, Artists and the Body* (London: Routledge, 1996).

Bohm-Duchen, Monica, and Vera Grodzinski (eds), *Rubies and Rebels: Jewish Identity in Contemporary British Art* (London: Lund Humphries, 1996).

Borzello, Frances, *Seeing Ourselves: Women's Self-portraits* (London: Thames & Hudson, 1998).

de Courtivron, Isabelle, and Elaine Marks (eds), *New French Feminisms* (Brighton: Harvester Press, 1981).

Deepwell, Katy (ed.), *New Feminist Art Criticism* (Manchester: Manchester University Press, 1995).

Jones, Amelia (ed.), *Sexual Politics: Judy Chicago's Dinner Party in Feminist Art History* (Berkeley and London: University of California Press, 1996).

Kelly, Mary, *Imaging Desire* (London: The MIT Press, 1996).

Kent, Sarah, and Jacqueline Morreau (eds), *Women's Images of Men* (London: Pandora, 1990).

Lloyd, Fran (ed.), *From the Interior: Female Perspectives on Figuration* (London: Kingston University Press, 1997).

Meskimmon, Marsha, *The Art of Reflection: Women Artists' Self-Portraiture in the Twentieth Century* (London: Scarlet Press, 1996).

Nead, Lynda, *The Female Nude: Art, Obscenity and Sexuality* (London: Routledge, 1992).

Parker, Rozsika, and Griselda Pollock, *Old Mistresses: Women, Art and Ideology* (London: Routledge, 1981).

Parker, Rozsika and Griselda Pollock (eds), *Framing Feminism: Art and the Women's Movement 1970–1985* (London: Pandora, 1987).

Pollock, Griselda (ed.), *Generations and Geographies in the Visual Arts: Feminist Readings* (London: Routledge, 1996).

Robinson, Hilary (ed.), *Visibly Female: Feminism and Art Today* (London: Camden Press, 1987).

Smyth, Cherry, *Damn Fine Art by New Lesbian Artists* (London: Cassell, 1996).

Weedon, Christine, *Feminist Practice and Post Structuralist Theory* (London: Basil Blackwell, 1987).

Wolff, Janet, *Feminine Sentences: Essays on Women and Culture* (Cambridge: Polity Press, 1990).

Zegher, Catherine de (ed.), *Inside The Visible, an Elliptical Traverse of 20th Century Art* (London: MIT Press, 1996).

Chapter 2

Sculpture and installation

Fiona Carson

SCULPTURE'S TRADITIONAL PREOCCUPATION with the relationship of the body to space makes the 'gendering' of sculpture a fruitful topic for feminist investigation. In this chapter, I look at the historical relationship of the female body to the gendered division of public and private spaces, through reference to sculpture and installation by women artists from the mid-nineteenth century onwards.

At first glance, the 'Sensation' exhibition held at London's Royal Academy in 1997 seems an unlikely starting-point for my discussion, since it involved scarcely any work that one would describe as traditional sculpture, and had little overt identification with feminism.[1] This exhibition was a major public showcase for the 1990s generation of young British artists spearheaded by Damien Hirst, and the most discussed female 'bodies' in the exhibition (apart from the heavily guarded portrait of the murderess Myra Hindley by Marcus Harvey) were the antics of two 'bad girls', Tracey Emin and Sarah Lucas, self-mocking laddesses with an ambivalent attitude to feminism's legacy.[2]

On closer examination, another theme emerged from the three-dimensional work of women artists in the show: the incorporation of the female body into pieces of furniture and its association with food and domestic interiors. Sarah Lucas's table piece, *Two Fried Eggs and a Kebab* (1992), was juxtaposed with Mona Hatoum's white-clothed table *Deep Throat* (1996), while Jane Simpson's refrigerated chest, *Sacred* (1993), was housed in an adjacent room. All three artworks made references to food, sexuality and the female body. Elsewhere, Rachel Whiteread's reverse casts of chairs, baths, a sink and a whole room made reference to inert domestic spaces. By contrast, Tracey Emin's tent was a temporary structure with strong connotations of home and womb. In terms of discourses about the female body, this group of works provides food for thought. While not explicitly situated within a feminist theoretical framework, each exhibit used the postmodern shock tactics of a provocative subject matter and a powerful sense of irony to explore contemporary issues pertaining to the female body. It thus becomes relevant to locate this contemporary work within continuing debates about female representation, and in particular to situate it within a historical framework that reveals the developing dialogue in sculpture between the female body and gendered spaces from the mid-nineteenth century onwards.

Separate spheres

The gendered division of space into the public world of work and the private sphere of the home in nineteenth-century industrialised society is widely discussed in sociological literature as an ideology of separate spheres in which the geography and architecture of the city reinforced the gendered division of labour. The suburbs and interior domestic spaces were the domain of women, the boulevards and open spaces of the city the territory of men. In Griselda Pollock's influential study of the Impressionists Berthe Morisot and Mary Cassatt, she analyses the way in which a gendered experience of space was inscribed in their work.[3] Their paintings describe an interior territory of dining and drawing rooms, bedrooms, balconies and private gardens, and Pollock argues for a correlation between the compressed spaces of their paintings and the social confinement of respectable bourgeois women at this time, seeing the interior not just as a place but as an idea to be expressed. Whereas male Impressionists such as Manet and Degas roamed the public world of bars, boulevards and street women in search of inspiration, Morisot negotiated the contradictions of her conflicting roles as hostess, mother and artist by both working and entertaining in the living-room where her painting materials were kept in a cleverly concealed closet.[4] To break out of this domestic stereotype and pursue the bohemian artistic lifestyle was a project fraught with difficulty, as the haunting stories of Camille Claudel, Suzanne Valadon and Gwen

John attest. Moreover, whereas it was possible to write or paint in a domestic environment in the nineteenth century, the activity of sculpture required a more public and professionalised environment, making it an extremely rare pursuit for women.

Public sculpture

Elsen describes sculpture in 1900 as 'the celebration of the nation's heroes, institutions and middle-class values. To educate, elevate and delight, and in that order, were the purpose that guided the making and judging of sculpture since the middle ages.'[5] The place of women in this tradition was most likely to be as sculptural object, as the personification of beauty or virtue, rather than as practitioner. Thus, to be a female sculptor was a contradiction in terms. Art history constructs the great sculptors of the Western tradition, such as Michelangelo, Bernini, Rodin and David Smith, as flawed but heroic men engaged in a physically demanding struggle with durable materials and gargantuan tasks. The practice of sculpture has until very recently been intimately interwoven with machismo. Pre-1900 female sculptors faced problems of access to professional training, to the study of the nude (which was essential to success), and to the means and status to establish a workshop set-up. There were, however, exceptions, for example the 'white Marmorean flock' described by Henry James, a privileged group of independent American women sculptors working in Rome in a neoclassical style. Among them was Harriet Hosmer, who felt it necessary to choose celibacy over marriage, fearing to be 'neither a good wife nor a good artist'.

> I honour every woman who has strength enough to step out of the beaten path when she feels that her walk lies in another, strength enough to stand up and be laughed at if necessary . . . But in a few years it will not be thought strange that women should be sculptors and everyone who comes after us will have to bear fewer blows.[6]

Despite running a large studio employing between twenty and thirty workmen and making large-scale monumental sculpture,

Hosmer still found her work disparaged by gender stereotyping. She was also criticised on the grounds that she did not do her own carving, a practice that was widespread among male sculptors of the day. Another member of the group, Edmonia Lewis, was the first artist of colour to achieve recognition.[7] A gifted carver limited by contemporary neoclassical taste to working in white marble, Lewis often used subject matter that referred to oppressed peoples: 'I have a strong sympathy for all women who have struggled and suffered.'

Modernist sculpture

In the early twentieth century, sculpture began to abandon the plinth and its high moral tone, becoming object-like and increasingly abstract under the influence of cubism and African sculpture. Definitions of what sculpture could be were radically changed by the Dadaists and the Surrealists. Born out of the stagnation and waste of the World War One, Dada challenged the sculptural tradition of the monument and the figure, proposing instead that ordinary objects like a bicycle wheel or a coat-rack could be a work of art.

In the interwar years, the Surrealist movement opened up the field of art to the irrational and the unconscious, promoting the female body as the supreme object of desire.[8] The female body appeared everywhere as exotic muse and in the feminising of domestic objects from crockery to furniture, such as in Meret Oppenheim's *Fur Breakfast,* an erotic fur-lined breakfast cup and saucer. Ironically, Oppenheim's artwork continued to have a life as a non-utilitarian surreal object, but its maker slipped out of the textbooks – a classic example of the disappearing woman artist.[9] However, the artist and the artwork, reunited by feminist scholarship, now adorn the front cover of Rozsika Parker and Griselda Pollock's book about women's art practice, *Old Mistresses: Women, Art and Ideology.*

In the 1930s, the young English sculptors Henry Moore and Barbara Hepworth, working alongside each other in London, began to develop a reputation for the direct carving of increasingly abstract forms. Unlike Hosmer, Hepworth was able, despite great poverty and struggle, to combine carving with motherhood, and to make private domestic experience the subject of her work. The critic Adrian Stokes recognised that 'life, birth and infancy' were 'the underlying subject' of Hepworth's work at this time.[10]

The vulnerable body

The idea of sculpture as a totemic monument to the survival of a cataclysmic event is another important aspect of modernist sculpture. The German sculptor Kathe Kollwitz evoked the protective power of the mother in the face of external threat and struggled to memorialise her grief at the loss of her son in World War One. Postwar reconstruction after World War Two and an expanding artistic sector sponsored by public funding offered women sculptors such as Barbara Hepworth, Elizabeth Frink and Germaine Richier undreamt-of opportunities in public sculpture. Hepworth's exceptional status as a woman in a male-dominated profession was recognised with the award of a CBE in 1958.

During the 1950s an 'aftermath' aesthetic developed, revealing the sculpted body in a new light – vulnerable, imperfect and temporary. The aesthetic was typified by the wounded, scarred bodies of Germaine Richier's spectres from the unconscious, and the fragile partial bodies in cast fibre of Polish textile sculptor, Magdalena Abakanowicz. During the 1960s, there were still echoes of the Holocaust in the work of the minimalist Eva Hesse, in whose hands sculpture became soft, tactile, and fragile, developing into a formal 'language' with which to express subjective experiences inflected by a female psyche and bodily experience.[11] The materials used were no longer permanent or heroic, and the female body was being projected into space in new subjective ways, which the critic Lucy Lippard interpreted as protofeminist.

The female body-house

Lippard's 1966 exhibition of 'sensuous geometric work', called 'Eccentric Abstraction', brought together the work of Louise Bourgeois and Eva Hesse.[12] Bourgeois, in much of her work, makes connections between her own emotional life and a sculptural iconography based on the body, fused with the domestic interior. The metaphors of the domestic interior and the interior of the female body often become interchangeable, as environments in which psychodramas of the nuclear family are re-enacted. Her roots lie in Surrealism, but she now insists that her work is existentialist, dealing in real, not imaginary feelings. Her work draws cathartically on her own traumatic emotional experiences. The female body as house was one of her first and most central visual images and it is one to which she has constantly returned. In a series of early prints and paintings, Bourgeois explored the imagery of the *femmes-maisons* (Women-houses) in which the female body and the house merged. The works were based on autobiographical memories of the houses she had lived in, particularly her family home at Choisy-le-roi in France.[13] Lippard described them in 1976 as 'uneasy spaces' and saw in them a sense of containment, anxiety, and the desire for escape. Throughout her long career, Bourgeois has used the imagery of the domestic interior and the female body as interior space in which to articulate personal feelings about the power politics of the family. Most famously she took revenge on her father by making him the object of a cannibalistic meal in *The Destruction of the Father* (1974), while some twenty years later she turned her mother into a space-engulfing monster in *Spider* (1997).

Womanhouse

Writing about the emergence of feminist art in the early 1970s, Lippard noted the importance for women of domestic imagery as a starting-point 'because it's there, because it's what they know best, because they can't escape it.'[14] The cathartic exploration of strong emotions within a domestic framework is also to be found in the Womanhouse project, run by Judy Chicago and Miriam Schapiro at the California Institute of the Arts in 1971. The students involved in creating this environment pictured themselves as struggling to escape from the confines of a domestic straitjacket in which they perceived themselves as trapped: the bride by the cobwebbed stair, the dummy in the linen closet and the nude in the bath, petrified by the appearance of a phallic snake coursing towards her across the floor. This was the world described in Betty Friedan's *Feminine Mystique*: 'fulfilment as a woman had only one definition for American women after 1949 – the housewife mother.' Equally, there was a desire to escape from the confines of the idealised, sanitised, female body.' as expressed in Judy Chicago's *Menstruation Bathroom* in which menstrual debris was viewed through a blue net screen.[15]

Vaginal iconography and its critics

During the 1970s, feminist art historians also began to theorise about a feminist politics of the body. Lisa Tickner, writing in 1978, described the female body in geographical terms as 'occupied territory' and articulated the need for women artists to reclaim their bodies from appropriation by male fantasies and desires.[16] She called upon women artists to create a revolution in erotic representation and to articulate the difference between living in a female body and looking at it. Of necessity, this meant giving visual form to hidden and tabooed aspects of female bodily processes and sexuality. Tickner discussed performance artists working with the body, such as Hannah Wilke and Eleanor Antin, and more controversially, she also examined the use of vaginal imagery as an aesthetic form in the work of Suzanne Santoro, Judy Chicago and others.

   In the feminist art of the 1970s, vaginal iconography was intended as a power symbol of female sexual difference, a defiant challenge to phallic authority. From the perspective of the 1990s, Chicago's use of vaginal symbolism seemed utopian and floral,[17] but still is etched with the stain of essentialism, subsuming all womankind under this one mark of biological difference. However, sexual liberation as a sign of political liberation needs to be seen in its historical context. For Carolee Schneeman, in her performance *Interior Scroll* (1975), rupturing the sealed container of the female body by drawing out of her vagina a paper scroll on which was written a diatribe against the male-dominated art establishment was a necessary act of defiance against the marginalisation of the female artist. Rosemary Betterton describes this as a process of 'making the invisible visible'. The female body was once viewed by Freud as a 'dark continent', an unknown site of sexual difference, neither understood nor spoken about,[18] but now this mysterious interior space of the female body-vessel was to be illuminated by the authority of a feminine voice, expressing a politics of liberation.

Deconstruction

The early feminist emphasis on vaginal symbolism was to be viewed as dangerously reductive, biologically determinist and even racist from the perspective of 1980s theories of deconstruction, which gave it the pejorative label of 'essentialism'. The physicality of the female body began to disappear under the weight of its own history in the early 1980s, becoming almost a taboo subject for image-makers because one would add to the overwhelming pile of objectified and stereotyped representations in the dominant culture. As its physical representation became increasingly problematic, the female body dissolved into a flux of shifting signifiers and tangential references. It became more photographed than physically present – for example as the empty silhouettes of Ana Mendieta's body imprint on the landscape; as the absent maternal body of Lacanian 'lack' in Mary Kelly's *Post-Partum Document*; and in the external masquerade of Cindy Sherman's alter egos.[19] What mattered was to deconstruct its ideological meanings, the interrogation of signs across its surface.

As feminist politics became increasingly pluralistic in the 1980s, there was no longer one feminist movement based on universal oppression, but a range of different perspectives based in differences of race, class, sexuality and disability. A central issue was how to represent the female body differently, challenging the dominance of the idealised and objectified white heterosexual body from a number of different political viewpoints.

In this context, Helen Chadwick's autobiographical reframing of the female nude in the form of photographic installations was both bold and politically controversial. In *Ego Geometria Sum* (1982–4), Chadwick's starting-point was the neoplatonic idea of the correspondence of the perfectly proportioned (male) body to regular geometric forms. Chadwick feminises this idea by projecting her own body on to minimalist geometric solids derived from her own childhood experience, such as a pram, a piano and a trunk. Drawing on the medieval tradition of *vanitas* painting in *Of Mutability* (1984–6), Chadwick now critiqued the perfect body with the imagery of putrefaction and decay. The *vanitas* image of the artist, nude and admiring her own image in a round mirror, was offset by the column of rotting vegetation entitled *Carcass*, a stark reminder of the physical processes of the body. The installation was subtitled 'Before I was bounded, now I've begun to leak', making reference to those aspects of the female body abjected from the image of the closed, idealised body of the female nude in representation.[20]

Perfection and abjection

When Lisa Tickner wrote about reclaiming the female body in 1978, there was not yet a theoretical language with which to analyse it, whereas Lynda Nead's book *The Female Nude* (1992) reflected the development of a sophisticated toolkit of theory developed over the previous decade.[21] In particular, Nead drew on the purity/pollution structures proposed by the anthropologist Mary Douglas in 1966 and developed by the French psycho-analyst Julia Kristeva in 1982. It was Mary Douglas who first recognised how the categories of clean (on the side of order and social control) and unclean (on the side of disorder and danger to the social order) were projected on to the female body and used symbolically as a means of exercising control over women in different ways in different cultures. Kristeva realised the signifi-cance of these ideas with regard to the maternal body, outlawed and rendered monstrous by the social order. She recognised the denied power of the mother in the fundamental mapping of the clean and proper body in the early stages of a child's socialisation, before the development of language.

Lynda Nead extended these ideas to the high-art representation of the female nude which she describes as a sealed container, 'a kind of magical regulation of the female body, containing it and momentarily repairing the orifices and tears'. This patriarchal idealisation and control of the female body and its insidious pervasiveness in the fashion, food and advertising industries is a fundamental issue. Almost perforce, the feminist artist must pit herself against the boundaries of this definition, and transgress the boundaries of the clean and proper body. The process of 'redrawing the lines' and bringing to visibility other forms of and perspectives on the female body is described by Nead in geographical and spatial terms. In *Monster*, from the series *Narratives of Dis-ease,* Jo Spence uses humour to bring the disabled body into visibility. She mockingly contrasts a pair of 'perfect' breasts, in the form of a 'booby prize' of baked biscuits, with her own 'imperfect' body marked by cancer. A similar irony underscores Della Grace's *The Three Graces* which subverts the classical canon of beauty by portraying Venus's handmaidens as stylish contemporary nudes with bald heads and Doc Martens.[22]

The 'Sensation' exhibition and the female body in the 1990s

How do we connect these historically related issues and iconographies of the female body with the installation work of the 'Sensation' exhibition? A leap of faith is required to situate the postmodern table piece *Two Fried Eggs and a Kebab,* a self-portrait by Sarah Lucas, into this evolving feminist critical discourse about the nude (Figure 2.1). Lucas's work appears shockingly untheorised, as well as unashamedly mainstream and populist. Lucas creates a reclining nude out of a kitchen table, two fried eggs for breasts and a kebab in pitta bread for a vagina. There are conspicuous references to the modern masters, for example to Magritte in the menucard face, and the installation as a whole has a careless ready-made look declaring its Dada and Surrealist 'found-object' heritage, and yet the depth of its irony has a feminist edge. Lucas has no fear of vaginal iconography. With irreverent bravura, she reappropriates feminist icons of the 1970s such as the fried egg breasts that adorn the ceiling of the Womanhouse kitchen and the vaginal plates of Judy Chicago's *The Dinner Party.* The central image of consuming the female body as food, also a metaphor for sexual consumption, is underlined in the confusion of orifices between mouth and vagina, a motif already canonised in Meret Oppenheim's *Fur Breakfast* and in *The Dinner Party.* Whereas Chicago's aim was to recuperate and honour women consumed by history, Lucas draws attention to the continuing consumption of the female body, like fast food,

Figure 2.1 Sarah Lucas, Two Fried Eggs and a Kebab, *1992. Photograph, fried eggs, kebab and table 76.2 × 152.4 × 89cm. The Saatchi Gallery. © the artist; courtesy of Sadie Coles HQ, London. Photograph by Stephen White reproduced with permission.*

by the sex and media industries in the 1990s. Lucas also acknowledges the seminal influence of Andrea Dworkin's writings on pornography.

Two Fried Eggs and a Kebab is pair to the more disturbing *Bitch*, a savagely misogynistic back-view nude with melons for breasts and a kipper for a vagina. *Bitch* is precisely in the pose of Allen Jones' *Table* (1969) a highly fetishised sculpture of a woman as a coffee table, which was the subject of a feminist demonstration at the ICA in 1978. One can conclude therefore that these installations, which look so deceptively casual, resonate as much with an Old Mistress iconography as an Old Master one.[23]

While it is possible to reappropriate Lucas's work for a feminist agenda, this is certainly not her declared intention. The predominant weapons in her arsenal are pastiche and irony. She plays a dangerous game of satirising the misogyny of media constructions of female sexuality and the routine chauvinism of unthinking masculinity by outshocking. With her snookered headless bunny girls and brutal sexual innuendoes, she outlads the lads while virtually appearing to be one of them. The impact of her work is made possible by her position: as a female peer of a conventionally male-dominated avant-garde, her position still brings with it some of the loading of marginalisation and othering which Griselda Pollock argues for in *Old Mistresses*. Both Lucas and Tracey Emin carry and exploit a feminist-derived 'bad-girl' image that encompasses butch heterosexuality and excessive behaviour in public and controversial artworks which operate in the gap between art and life, between public and private spaces.

Figure 2.2 Detail of Deep Throat.

Figure 2.3 Mona Hatoum, Deep Throat, *1996, 74.5×85×85cm, table, chair, tablecloths, glass, plate, fork, knife, water, glass, monitor, video disc and player. Photograph by Phillip Schönborn.*

Uncanny interior

Opposite Lucas's *Two Fried Eggs and a Kebab* in the 'Sensation' exhibition was another tablepiece: Mona Hatoum's more austere *Deep Throat* (1996), another self-portrait. The plain, unassuming place-setting on the white cloth is no preparation for the strange endoscopic vision of the artist's pulsating larynx projected on to the dinnerplate (Figures 2.2 and 2.3). Once again there are strange echoes of Judy Chicago's *The Dinner Party*, but this time we are invited into the unknown interior of the artist's body.

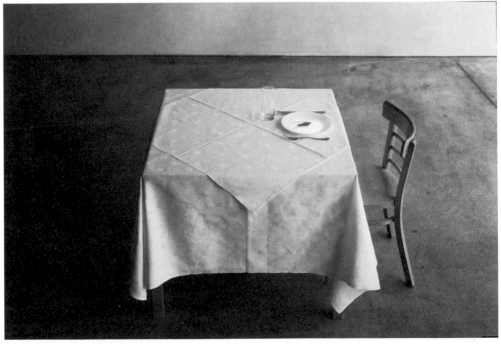

With voyeuristic brutality, the ultimate mystery of this interior space is laid bare using medical technology.

The 1990s saw a renewed preoccupation with the physicality of the gendered body, but now it had been irrevocably reshaped and atomised by the impact of AIDS and by developments in medical science. The female body became opened up as an internal space to be invaded and dissected by the eyes and instruments of science, down to the microscopic detail of its very cells. Contemporary artists such as Orlan, Helen Chadwick and Mona Hatoum investigated the issues raised by body-altering procedures such as cosmetic surgery, *in vitro* fertilisation and fibre-optic photography. Yet, the more the female body is revealed, the more its 'otherness' seems to be reinforced.

The dining-table context of *Deep Throat* emphasises an iconography of food, voyeurism and consumption, reinforced by the self-mocking title's associations with pornography and spying. The issues raised by *Deep Throat* need to be discussed in combination with her earlier and more architectural installation *Corps Etranger*, exhibited at the Turner Prize shortlist show of 1995. Using a panoply of medical technology (endoscopic and coloscopic examination of the full tract of the digestive system), the artist invites the spectator to travel through the inner channels of her body on a sort of poltergeistian inquisition of the interior. The French title, meaning 'foreign body' is ambiguous – is it a reference to the foreignness of the artist's Palestinian background? Or is it the familiar object of the gaze, the female body estranged by a new form of voyeurism, surveillance on the inside, the final deconstruction? The contradictions abound.

Hatoum's imagery is rooted in the atmosphere of oppression and surveillance of her Palestinian background, and her involvement in Britain with black and feminist politics. More recently, she has returned to an art school interest in bodily processes and the abject. Her preoccupations come together in the two projection pieces, and Hatoum enjoys the ambivalence of these images, commenting on the 'wonderful paradox between woman portrayed as victim and woman as devouring vagina'.[24] She recognises the ambiguity of the image and the subjectivity of the viewer's position. Is the image controlling or controlled?

Perhaps most significantly, Hatoum is commenting on the inside of the female body, and the fact that the looking-at, the voyeurism, is on the inside too. There is no outside to this female body – the threshold has been breached. The 'dark continent' is tamed by technology, yet the symbolic power of its abjection continues to disturb. The route whereby the inside of the artist's gendered body is explored is the alimentary canal, the route along which food passes through the body. As Rosemary Betterton points out, food straddles the borderline between the edible and the polluting, and thus carries an ambivalent resonance of the 'unclean', disturbing the accepted differences between what is properly 'inside' and 'outside' the body.[25] In the monstrousness of the image, we are confronted with a recognition of the transgressive power of the abject, as the displaced power of the mother and the feminine, to challenge and overwhelm the conventions of representation.

The visual power of *Corps Etranger* derives from the fact that its effect is unnerving, 'uncanny'. Freud's classic definition of this word – *unheimlich* in German – draws out its deepest meaning of 'unhomely/strange'.[26] He links the disturbing character of the *unheimlich* to, among other things, the castration complex, viewing the sight of the female genitalia as uncanny, and he explains that it is characterised by taking familiar objects and making them unfamiliar – like the womb, which is both known and unknown.

Maternal metaphor

Uncanny associations and references to the maternal body are also to be found in another work from the 'Sensation' exhibition: Jane Simpson's furniture-piece *Sacred*, yet another female body fetishised as a piece of furniture. Again, there is a confusion of sex and food. This shapely cabinet, painted white and faintly mottled like the skin of a cow, seems to be an inside-out refrigerator, and ice forms like a thin layer of milk on its top.[27] Is it a cupboard for Mother Hubbard? Is it woman as provider, the ever-open refrigerator door? What is it that is sacred? Is it the female body as sacred cow? Or is the pregnant maternal torso equated with a fridge, dispensing milk just as a fridge might? Perhaps there are also ecological references to the dangers to the ozone layer of recycling refrigerators and the hazards of eating beef? The female body becomes a surface upon which society can project both its anxieties and desires.

Domestic monuments

The references to the maternal body begin to proliferate but are always elliptical in using metaphors of feeding, nurturing, consuming, and engulfing. Scattered throughout the 'Sensation' exhibition was the monumental, formally rigorous work of Turner prizewinner Rachel Whiteread. Like Louise Bourgeois, Whiteread deals in interiors, but whereas Bourgeois's rooms resonate with passion, Whiteread's are cool. Whiteread's geometric spaces have the inertia of the materials in which they are cast, mausoleums of plaster or moulds of viscous, synthetic jelly. The human presence is implicit but absent. Whatever is recognisable is peeled away, leaving only its residue. Yet the perspective is feminine: these are domestic spaces and objects, which resonate like Bourgeois's stage sets with the emotions and memories of early childhood. Gaston Bachelard, the author of *The Poetics of Space*, described the first experience of space as the house we were born in, which is 'physically inscribed in us'.[28] The space of the house is imprinted with the body of the mother. Whiteread's castings record childhood experiences of the inside and underside of furniture, congealing the spatial experiences of memory. *Ghost* is the cast of a whole room, including the fireplace. It is the apotheosis of Berthe Morisot's domestic interior, literally made concrete but also strangely eroticised. The concrete body of *House* reveals the invisible space of the house's interior space, the domestic suburban space of the feminine stripped of its outer skin. Bartomeu Mari discusses how Rachel Whiteread's sculpture connects public with private, and claims that the artist investigates the space of domesticity as a kind of 'personalised architecture'.[29] The dichotomy of public and private is breached by Whiteread's transformation of domestic space into a monument to itself. Private emotions and memories acquire public and collective meanings when *House* is seen as a symbol of homelessness. Whiteread's success as a public artist making monumental sculpture hinges on her gendered interpretation of domestic space.

Conclusion

As we have seen, a number of themes can tie the installation work by women artists shown at the 'Sensation' exhibition to both feminist debates and the historical development of women's art since the mid-nineteenth century, if we choose to read them in that way. In making connections between works, I have tried to explore aspects of the relationship between the female body and the gendering of exterior and interior spaces. It is evident that not only is there a mapping of the geography of domestic spaces onto the female body, but that the female body itself is seen via the feminist project as a space to be decolonised and remapped both externally and now, more recently, internally as well. Women artists have been engaged in a radical reinvention of the representation of the female body from within. This has meant breaking open the sealed and deodorised confines of the objectified and fetishised female body, in order to expose issues of commodification and exploitation and to challenge our lived dichotomy between clean and unclean. It appears that this process of analysis and reconstruction is reiterated in new ways and from different perspectives in each generation.

Notes

1. Adams, Jardine, et al., *Sensation*.
2. H. Reitmaier, 'Off the Agenda and in Disguise' and M. Mancio, 'Superlass', *make*, no. 71, August–September 1996.
3. Pollock, *Vision and Difference*, pp. 54–63.
4. A. Higonnet, *Berthe Morisot* (Berkeley, Los Angeles and London: University of California Press, 1995), p. 171.
5. A. Elsen, *Pioneers of Modern Sculpture* (London: Hayward Gallery, 1973), p. 8.
6. Harriet Hosmer, quoted in A. Garrihy and P. G. Nun, 'Women, Sculpture and Heroism in the Nineteenth Century', *FAN* (1985) vol. 2, no. 2.
7. M. Cliff, 'Object into Subject, Some Thoughts on the Work of Black Women Artists' in F. Bonner, *Imagining Women* (Cambridge: Polity Press, 1992).
8. W. Chadwick, *Women Artists and the Surrealist Movement*, pp. 119—23.

9. J. Withers, 'The Famous Fur-lined Teacup and the Anonymous Meret Oppenheim', *Arts* (1977) 52 no. 3, p. 90.

10. A. Wagner, 'Miss Hepworth's Stone is a Mother' in *Barbara Hepworth Reconsidered* (Liverpool: Tate Gallery, 1996).

11. L. Lippard, *Eva Hesse* (New York: New York University, 1976).

12. Lippard, *From the Center*, pp. 238–50.

13. Bernadac, *Louise Bourgeois*, p. 8 and pp. 23–8.

14. Lippard, *From the Center*, p. 56.

15. Broude and Garrard, *The Power of Feminist Art*, p. 51.

16. L. Tickner, 'The Body Politic: Female Sexuality and Women Artists Since 1970' in Parker and Pollock, *Framing Feminism*, pp. 266 and 272.

17. Betterton, *An Intimate Distance*, ch. 6 and especially p. 138.

18. M. Whitford (ed.), *Irigaray Reader* (Oxford: Basil Blackwell, 1991), p. 39.

19. M. Kwon, 'Bloody Valentines: Afterimages by Ana Mendieta' in C. de Zegher (ed.), *Inside the Visible* (Cambridge, MA and London: MIT Press, 1996), p. 169.

20. H. Chadwick, *Enfleshings* (London: Secker and Warburg, 1989).

21. Nead, *The Female Nude*, pp. 7, 31–2 and Part II.

22. Parveen Adams, *The Emptiness of the Image* (London and New York: Routledge, 1996), ch. 9.

23. Jan Van Adrichen, 'Things That Have to Come About' in *Sarah Lucas* (Rotterdam: Boymans Museum, 1996).

24. Interview with Hatoum in Archer, Brett and de Zegher, *Mona Hatoum*, especially p. 71.

25. Betterton, *An Intimate Distance*, pp. 139–44.

26. S. Freud, 'The Uncanny' in Freud, *Art and Literature* (Harmondsworth: Penguin, 1985), vol. 14, p. 368.

27. Kent, *Shark Infested Waters*, p. 85.

28. Fiona Bradley, *Rachel Whiteread, Shedding Life* (Liverpool: Tate Gallery, 1997), pp. 61–71.

29. Bartomeu Mari, 'The Art of the Intangible' in Bradley, *Rachel Whiteread, Shedding Life* (Liverpool: Tate Gallery, 1997).

Bibliography

Adams, Brooks, and Lisa Jardine et al., *Sensation: Young British Artists from the Saatchi Collection* (London: Royal Academy of Arts, 1997).

Archer, M., G. Brett, and C. de Zegher, *Mona Hatoum* (London: Phaidon Press, 1997).

Bachelard, Gaston, *The Poetics of Space* (Boston: Beacon Press, 1989).

Bernadac, Marie-Laure, *Louise Bourgeois* (Paris: Flammarion, 1996).

Betterton, Rosemary, *An Intimate Distance: Women, Artists and the Body* (London: Routledge, 1996).

Broude, Norma, and Mary Garrard, *The Power of Feminist Art* (New York: Harry Abrams, 1994).

Chadwick, Whitney, *Women Artists and the Surrealist Movement* (London: Thames & Hudson, 1985).

Jones, Amelia, *Sexual Politics: Judy Chicago's Dinner Party in Feminist Art History* (Berkeley and London: University of California Press, 1996).

Kent, Sarah, *Shark Infested Waters* (London: Zwemmer, 1994).

Lippard, Lucy, *From the Center, Feminist Essays on Women's Art* (New York: Dutton, 1976).

Nead, Lynda, *The Female Nude: Art, Obscenity and Sexuality* (London: Routledge, 1992).

Parker, Rozsika, and Griselda Pollock (eds), *Framing Feminism: Art and the Women's Movement 1970–1985* (London: Pandora, 1987).

Parker, Rozsika, and Griselda Pollock, *Old Mistresses: Women, Art, and Ideology* (London: Routledge, 1981).

Pollock, Griselda, *Vision and Difference, Femininity: Feminism and Histories of Art* (London: Routledge, 1988).

Chapter 3

Performance art

Helen Potkin

IN THE 1970S, MANY women artists rejected traditional art practices in favour of forms less burdened with history, such as installation and performance art, forms which seemed to offer potential for experiment and subversion. This chapter focuses on performance art as a site of feminist intervention, exploring a range of practices, issues and debates from its inception to today. The discussion highlights practice in Britain, and concentrates on particular issues and themes, rather than attempting to be a comprehensive survey of feminist performance.[1] I will begin by outlining debates about agency, the body and documentation, before considering feminist performance art in 1970s and 1980s. Analysis of contemporary practice is conducted in terms of issues of subjectivity, identity and difference which bear witness to critical shifts in feminist theory. The final section considers the implications of the intersection of performance with video art and engages with broader notions of performativity. The discussion considers both live performance and its documentation, inter-woven with themes of presence and absence, visibility and marginality.

Performance art may be understood as a practice in which the body of the artist is central or is the medium itself. Staged on the street, in a room or in an art gallery, performance takes place in time and space and may involve sound or voice. It may be experienced as a live ephemeral event or in a more permanent documented form such as text, photography, film or video. It is rooted in the radical and experimental anti-art gestures of the avant-garde in the early twentieth century.[2] For many, performance is a hybrid form, drawing on diverse practices from theatre to installation, film to music, visual arts to dance. It is also a practice that disrupts and disturbs boundaries and is 'an ever evolving and shifting area of live cultural practice'.[3]

Performance consciously positioned itself outside of and antagonistic to mainstream practice, and its emergence as an important practice for women in Britain is founded in the conception of performance as an alternative site. Mona Hatoum has commented, 'Performance is very attractive to me because I saw it as a revolutionary medium, setting itself apart from the gallery system and the art establishment.'[4] Implicit in this position is a rejection of modernist forms of practice and systems of power perceived as masculine and a resistance to established hierarchies and the notion of art as commodity.[5] Its ephemeral nature, its focus on the body of the artist, on action, and on speaking rather than on traditional concerns of production of an object are the basis on which such claims are made.

Performance art by women can also be understood as a response to art politics, which marginalised women as artists and manipulated the body of 'woman' in representation, and women performance artists have sought to insert the female self into art practice. Performance foregrounds the role of the artist as woman and as such, it is claimed, operates as a critique of traditional notions of subject/object within art.[6] The notion of woman 'gaining a voice' is important to an understanding of feminism both politically and culturally, as are notions of reclaiming the body. In her seminal article, Lisa Tickner discussed the idea that the female body is a 'colonised territory' that must be reclaimed from masculine fantasy. She indicated the potential for the production of radically different art produced by women based on the different nature of their experience.[7]

Through the restaging of the female body, performance art by women has sought to dismantle dominant constructions of women. It is claimed that performance's speaking, moving subject resists the assumption of the passive female, and challenges the patriarchal gaze.[8] However, as Lynda Nead has pointed out, interpretation is not solely in the hands of the performer and the 'female body can be re-appropriated for meanings quite other than those originally intended.'[9] Lucy Lippard has suggested that performance by women is also open to accusations of narcissism.[10] Performance has also had to negotiate other traditions of women on the stage – such as the stripper – and connotations of objectification of the female body. Sally Potter has referred to performance by women as being on a 'knife edge of the possibility of joining this spectacle of women', and has problematised the use of the very term 'performance' in this context.[11] Recently, Catherine Elwes has recalled performing in the dark by torchlight 'for fear of giving the chaps what they wanted.'[12]

The idea of performing in the dark implies disappearance and evokes notions of feminist performance as an invisible practice. Katherine Meynell has recently remarked that despite the long history of woman and performance, there is still a severe lack of knowledge and information about it.[13] This situation relates to the nature of a practice rooted in the live event and experience. Performance art by women occupies a curious position that aims at visibility of the producer within a specific context, yet remains invisible without sustained analysis or a written history (particularly in a culture that is so reliant on secondary sources). Many writers, including Elwes, see performance as direct and unmediated, viewing the practice as the only form guaranteeing the artist's presence and authentic experience. The influential American writer Peggy Phelan has written, 'Performance's only life is in the present. Performance cannot be saved, recorded, documented, or otherwise participate in the circulation of representations of representations: once it does so, it becomes something other than performance.'[14] Writing about performance appears problematic, particularly if it 'becomes itself through disappearance'.[15] Not being there, not witnessing the event in these terms is a disadvantage. If writing about performance alters it, how am I to proceed? What status do forms of documentation have? What status does this text and its selected images have?

Amelia Jones has recently countered such privileging of the live event, 'while the experience of viewing a photograph and reading a text is clearly different from that of sitting in a small room watching an artist perform, neither has a privileged relationship to historical "truth"'. She refutes the possibility that a direct 'unmediated relationship to any kind of cultural product, including body art' exists. Through the performance, the body of the artist is still re-presented to us. Jones asserts that the body in performance 'is not self-sufficient in its meaningfulness but relies not only on a authorial context of "signature" but on the receptive context in which the interpreter or viewer may interact with this body'.[16] Despite appearing to be more direct in its relationship with the audience, the live performance may also be an exclusive experience since many performances take place in front of small and selected audiences. It is only through documentation that it receives wider circulation.

Two works completed in 1979 demonstrate the differing roles of live performance and documentation. Catherine Elwes' *Menstruation II* was a three-day performance coinciding with her menstrual period, in which the artist could be seen bleeding and writing in a white, glass-fronted box. Photographic documentation of the performance shows Elwes in the act of performing and recalls the live performance. Susan Hiller foregrounds the process of documentation itself in a piece called *10 Months* that records her pregnancy. The work consists of photographs showing a sequence of images of the swelling body. Much work of the 1970s and 1980s focused on the mother/child relationship and sought to provide positive models of women that related to 'real' women's lives and experiences, for example Shirley Cameron and Tina Keane involved their children in their works. Important in this context was the idea of women's private experience made public, with the focus on subjectivity seen as a critique of male formalist art. Reclaiming tradition, as in Hannah O'Shea's *Litany for Women Artists* performance in 1977 and the collective practice of groups such as Fenix, were important in raising consciousness and reaffirming the role of women within art. Many of these practices were criticised for universalising female experience, and in their essay, 'Textual Strategies: the Politics of Art Making', Judith Barry and Sandy Flitterman situated performance art that valorises women's experience and the body, as essentialist (the notion of female essence residing somewhere in the body) as opposed to anti-essentialist or deconstructive strategies of feminism.[17] Discussing the work of Gina Pane and Hannah Wilke, their influential analysis positioned performance as retrograde, and this position privileged the production of text-based, or scriptovisual work as exemplified by the work of Mary Kelly.[18] Nevertheless, women have continued to employ their own bodies in their work, and such binary oppositions (essentialist/anti-essentialist, body/theory, and so on) have been challenged by recent commentators as inadequate.[19]

The profile of women's performance art was raised by the

'About Time' exhibition in 1980 which consisted of performance and time-based work, and was organised by Catherine Elwes and Rose Garrard in conjunction with Sandy Nairne.[20] The works were selected in order to 'indicate the artist's awareness of a woman's particular experience within patriarchy'.[21] The show included a range of work that engaged with women's lives and experience: the mother/daughter relationship, as in Elwes' work; notions of domesticity, as in performances by Sylvia Ziranek and Bobby Baker; and concepts of beauty and femininity, as evident in the work of Roberta Graham. The show was hailed as a 'major breakthrough',[22] and Rozsika Parker and Griselda Pollock suggested that time-based practice and performance in particular had become an important area for feminist work.

It was at this time that writers began to map out histories of performance and the role of women within it.[23] RoseLee Goldberg remarks that by the mid-1980s performance had reached a peak of acceptance.[24] The 1980s saw a proliferation of festivals, publications, and an increase in the number of promoters presenting performance, and performance was now funded by the Arts Council under a separate category of live art. The pamphlet *Live Art Now*, published in 1987, reveals the range of performance practice being supported in the 1980s, and makes specific mention of the feminist practices of Hatoum, Garrard and Rose Finn-Kelsey. There was a touring exhibition of Garrard's work in 1984–5, and Ziranek, O'Shea and Rose English were included in the Tate Gallery's performance art season in 1985. This work was seen within the mainstream gallery context, but some feminist work continued to occupy countercultural sites, as Shirley Cameron and Evelyn Silver's *Brides Against the Bomb* performance at Glastonbury in 1983 attests. The limited success and visibility of performance by women needs to be read against the promotion of traditional forms of production such as painting and the dominance of practice by men in the 1980s.

Throughout the period under discussion, several artists have maintained a commitment to feminist performance. For example, in 1994 Rose Garrard documented her own history within performance from 1969 onwards. Bobby Baker began making performances in the 1970s and returned to practice in the late 1980s after a break to have children; her work of the 1980s and 1990s deals with cultural coding around the notions of woman, artist, mother, wife. Rose English has continued to redefine and explore multiple personae and to confront stereotypes of gender.[25]

Issues of gender, identity and difference are addressed in much recent performance art by women. For Judith Butler, identities are performative and transitory, constantly being remade through repetition and reiteration.[26] The notion of performativity has various implications for the current discussion of performance art, particularly in terms of the display and staging of the body. Recent critical shifts in feminist theory have focused on the body not as a biological entity but as socially and psychically constructed. The body has been seen as 'a place where the marking of sexual difference is written' and, as such, is reinvested as a critical site of feminist intervention.[27] Although the use of the female body is problematic in masculine culture, Janet Wolff has argued for reinstating corporeality and 'a cultural politics of the body, based on a recognition of the social and discursive construction of the body, while emphasising its lived experience and materiality'.[28] In this context, subjectivity may operate as a strategic and provisional articulation of identity.

Metamorphosis, transformation and shifting identities are themes that run through the work of Rona Lee. In her performances, she acts upon objects, altering them and leaving upon them traces of her presence. Andrea Phillips remarks, 'Lee herself, becoming visible then vanishing, leaves us to complete the picture'.[29] Like Ana Mendieta, Lee's work negotiates the complexities of the 'absence' of the body of woman within art practice.[30] In her 1996 work *Shrinking the Miniature* (Figure 3.1) and project for *Disorders,* she has centred on the bed as a site of symbolism through which connotations of the domestic, the uncanny, and female desire and destruction are explored.

The meanings of objects and their relationship with history and colonialism are examined in the work of Susan Lewis. In *Ladies Falling* (1994), she uses symbols of tea, sugar and rum 'to map out a counter history which discloses the different "value" of similar objects in differing cultures'.[31] Her work emphasises the black female body and its absence from visual discourse. Employing choreographed movement, performance, costume, sound and film, the work can be seen as a way of examining issues of marginality and female suppression. Su Andi makes use of the autobiographical and personal experience in her performance, through narrative and

Figure 3.1 Rona Lee, Shrinking the Miniature, *1996. A First Site commission. Photograph by Graham Rose.*

story-telling. The idea of reclaiming language, or 'claiming a voice', is seen as central to the process of decolonisation.[32] The performances of Dorethea Smartt, Shirlee Mitchell, Vaishali Londhe, Maya Chowdry, Chila Kumari Burman and Nina Edge also point to the legacies of colonialism and issues of race and gender within British culture. In this context, performance is understood as a site of opposition and cultural resistance.

Challenging the expectations of the viewer and resisting stereotypes of the body inform the work of Anne Whitehurst and Mary Duffy. Both confront their invisibility as disabled women, but they do so in very different ways. Whitehurst is concerned specifically with contesting the impersonality of bureaucracy and raising awareness of issues around disability and access. She set up the Disability Research Unit which operated as a 'real' office in which the 'audience' is encouraged to participate. We might understand her work as intervention or live action but with none of the connotations of theatricality evident in the term performance art. Awareness-raising also informs the practice of Mary Duffy, which focuses on the tactical display of her own body. She says, 'I wanted to hold a mirror to all those people who have stripped me bare previously'.[33] She seeks to challenge the audience's expectations of what a body looks like, and rejects the conception that it is incomplete, politicising the role of visibility itself.

The explicit or transgressive body in performance has been the subject of much recent writing, and these ideas can be situated within wider contexts in the history and meanings of the body. In the USA, the practice of Karen Finley, Annie Sprinkle and Holly Hughes, among others, confronts issues of sexuality, pornography, and obscenity. In Britain, Tessa Boffin has staged sexually explicit works in gay clubs, and presents gender as drag, performing in various identities. Appearing as lesbian boy and queer dyke, she is seen to 'ride the edge of gender-fuck'.[34] Lewis and Horne have written, 'Tessa's masquerade performance of lesbian drag offered both the materiality of her body and denied any attempt to make a single truth of it.'[35] The assertion of sexuality is seen as central to lesbian identity. However, pornographic imagery has been, and still is, problematic within feminism, and Jill Dolan points out that the anti-sex morality of the anti-porn movement 'threatens to render lesbians not only marginal to feminism, but totally invisible'.[36] Like Boffin, Annie Sprinkle, an

American sex worker turned performance artist, confronts issues of pornography and art in her performances. The notion of the transgressive, of erotic excess, may be seen as offering potential for subversion, and Sprinkle has said, 'I think women just choosing to be filmed having sex is a feminist act. Women are not supposed to enjoy sex openly and freely so just to suck and fuck on camera is a feminist act.'[37] Sprinkle's performances reconfigure debates about female pleasure and desire and push the audience/viewer to confront their curiosity and voyeurism, and we might understand such performances as straining the 'sacred frontier' between high culture and vulgarity.[38] However, the transgressive can be problematic, and Marsha Meskimmon suggests that at times, such practices have become dangerously close to the very objectifications they have sought to dismantle.[39]

The work of the French performance artist Orlan, seen in Britain in 1994 and 1996, appears to transgress the boundaries of art practice and of the body itself. Orlan's ongoing transformation of self through plastic surgery confronts notions of beauty, identity, control and technology. The self is reconstructed by working on the flesh, targeted as the link between inner and outer. Under local anaesthetic, she directs the performance, destabilising her audience, and it is they, not her, who seem to experience pain and horror. This appears to be the case whether audiences witness it live, through live broadcast to a gallery, or through visual forms of documentation. Her work blurs the boundaries between art and life, between performance and being. She declares, 'This is my body . . . this is my Software' and reincarnates for herself what has been described as a cyborg identity.[40]

Several artists who began in live performance have now moved into new media and technology as the basis of their practice rather than as a document of it. In a culture filtered and reflected through the screen of mass media, in which technology is affordable, video art has become a more dominant mode and has taken up many of the concerns of performance art, such as issues of identity and particularly the exploration of the relationship between artist and audience. Much of Mona Hatoum's early work consisted of live performance in which she investigated identity and oppression. In a recent work, *Pull* (1995), Hatoum examined issues of present-ness and presence through an exploration of the boundaries of performance and video. The piece consisted of a television screen showing the face of Hatoum upside down, and beneath the screen a plait of hair hung down. The visitor was invited to pull the hair, and in doing so brought an expression of pain to the face on the screen. Most viewers/participants assumed that the effect was simulated, but in fact the hair belonged to the artist, who was 'actually' present behind the screen. The work engages in dialogue with spectator, challenging the distance of the television image, and it confronts the confusion between the real and the representation, confounding our expectations of the screen, the nature of experience, and of notions of reality itself. Recent video work, such as Sam Taylor-Wood's 1998 installation *Atlantic* (Figure 3.2), may be seen to 'contain traces of sensibilities explored by performance artist over the past two decades'.[41] Such work with its wraparound narrative and display of intense emotion which may be acted or real, implicate the viewer in a similar way to live performance. Certain tendencies within video art may be seen as performative, even theatrical. In Gillian Wearing's video *Dancing in Peckham* (1994), it is the artist herself who is seen performing for the camera, staging herself as both subject and object, complicating and confusing boundaries of space and spectatorship. Performativity may be seen as operating in the contemporary context – through the staging of self not only within practice but also through those forms in which the artist herself is mediated: the photograph and interview.[42]

At the turn of the century, feminist performance has to continue to negotiate issues of visibility and marginality. Organisations such as Locus+ and Hull Time Based Arts have been important in funding and promoting a range of interventionist projects in the public domain. However, Lois Keidan points out that very little live performance has been seen within the gallery space recently, and suggests that this may relate to artists stating 'their position as existing outside the parameters of existing structure' as well as the problems of accommodating live art practice.[43] The expansion of the field of live art so that performance has to compete for funding with installation and time-based practices using new technologies may partially explain why feminist performance is receiving little critical attention at the start of the new century. It continues to slide in and out of sight, continually encountering its own ephemerality, its alternative positioning and its complex relationship with documentation.

Figure 3.2 Sam Taylor-Wood, Atlantic, 1997, three laser discs for three projections. Photocredit: courtesy of Jay Jopling, London.

Notes

1. No history of feminist performance has yet been written. Rozsika Parker and Griselda Pollock document work up to 1985 in *Framing Feminism*, while more recent publications (Schneider, *The Explicit Body* (1997), Jones, *Body Art* (1998), and Goldberg, *Performance: Live Art* (1998)) have tended to focus on practice in the USA rather than the UK.
2. RoseLee Goldberg, *Performance Art* (London: Thames & Hudson, 1988).
3. Lois Keiden, 'Showtime: Curating Live Art in the 90s', *Art & Design*, vol. 12, Jan/Feb 1997, p. 38.
4. Interview with Michael Archer in *Mona Hatoum* (London: Phaidon, 1997), p. 9.
5. Lynn MacRitchie, 'About Time – Historical Background' in Elwes and Garrard (eds), *About Time*, unpaginated.
6. For example, Linda Klinger suggests that the identity of woman as producer is crucial to feminist practice. See Linda S. Klinger, 'Where's the Artist? Feminist Practice and Post-structural Theories of Authorship', *Art Journal*, vol. 50, Summer 1991 pp. 35–47.
7. Lisa Tickner, 'The Body Politic: Female Sexuality and Women Artists Since 1970', *Art History*, vol. 1, no. 2, June 1978 (reprinted in Parker and Pollock, *Framing Feminism*, p. 226).
8. See Elwes and Sally Potter in Elwes and Garrard (eds), *About Time*.
9. Nead, *The Female Nude*, p. 68.
10. Lucy Lippard, 'The Pains and Pleasures of Rebirth: European and American Women's Body Art' in *From the Center: Feminist Essays on Women's Art* (New York: Dutton, 1976), pp. 123–5.
11. Elwes and Garrard (eds), *About Time*.
12. Catherine Elwes, 'In Video Veritas: a Feminist Perspective on Women's Video across Two Decades', *Make* 81 Sept/Nov 1998, p. 9.
13. Ibid. p. 10.
14. Phelan, *Unmarked*, p. 146.
15. Ibid. p. 146.
16. Amelia Jones, ' "Presence" in Absentia: Experiencing Performance as Documentation', *Art Journal*, vol. 56 Winter 1997, pp. 11–18.
17. Reprinted in Parker and Pollock, *Framing Feminism*, pp. 313–15.
18. Kelly also critiqued performance as unsophisticated and idealist. See Mary Kelly, 'Re-Viewing Modernist Criticism', in B. Wallis (ed.), *Art After Modernism: Rethinking Repre-*

sentation (New York: New Museum of Contemporary Art in association with Davide R. Godine, 1984).

19. Janet Wolff, 'The Artist, the Critic and the Academic: Feminism's Problematic Relationship with "Theory"' in Deepwell, *New Feminist Art Criticism*.

20. Held at the Institute of Contemporary Arts (ICA) in London, as part of the Festival of Women's Art.

21. Introduction to Elwes and Garrard, *About Time*.

22. Parker and Pollock, *Framing Feminism*, p. 39.

23. For example, Elwes, 'Floating Femininity', and Goldberg, *Performance Art*.

24. Goldberg, *Performance Art*, p. 210.

25. Rose Garrard, *Archiving My Own History: Document of Works 1969–1994* (London: Cornerhouse/South London Gallery, 1994). Baker and English are discussed in Childs and Walwin, *A Split Second of Paradise*.

26. Judith Butler, *Gender Trouble: Feminism and the Subversion of Identity* (London and New York: Routledge, 1990); and Judith Butler, *Bodies That Matter* (London and New York: Routledge, 1993).

27. Pollock, *Generations and Geographies*, p. 6.

28. Wolff, *Feminine Sentences*, p. 138.

29. Katherine Wood, *Rona Lee* (Colchester: Firstsite, 1996), p. 53.

30. Miwon Kwon, 'Bloody Valentines: Afterimages by Ana Mendieta' in Catherine de Zegher (ed.), *Inside the Visible* (Cambridge, MA and London: MIT Press, 1996).

31. Ugwu (ed.), *Let's Get It On*, p. 68.

32. bell hooks, 'Performance Practice as a Site of Opposition' in Ugwu (ed.), *Let's Get It On*, p. 212.

33. Quoted in Nead, *The Female Nude*, p. 78.

34. Cherry Symth, 'Dyke! Fag! Centurian! Whore! An Appreciation of Tessa Boffin' in P. Horne and R. Lewis, *Outlooks: Lesbian and Gay Sexualities and Visual Cultures* (New York and London: Routledge, 1996), p. 111.

35. P. Horne and R. Lewis, *Outlooks: Lesbian and Gay Sexualities and Visual Cultures* (London and New York: Routledge, 1996), p. 7.

36. Quoted in Christine Tamblyn, 'No More Nice Girls: Recent Transgressive Feminist Art', *Art Journal*, vol. 50 Summer 1991, p. 54.

37. Quoted in Marsha Meskimmon, *The Art of Reflection: Women Artists' Self-Portraiture in the Twentieth Century* (London: Scarlet Press, 1996), p. 111.

38. Nead, *The Female Nude*.

39. Marsha Meskimmon, *The Art of Reflection: Women Artists'*

Self-Portraiture in the Twentieth Century (London: Scarlet Press, 1996), p. 111.

40. See Parveen Adams, *The Emptiness of the Image: Psychoanalysis & Sexual Differences* (London: Routledge, 1996).
41. Goldberg, *Performance: Live Art*, p. 181.
42. Fran Lloyd, 'Bad Girls: In Bed with Madonna', *Contemporary Art*, Winter 1995/6, pp. 39–42.
43. Lois Keiden, 'Showtime: Curating Live Art in the 90s', *Art & Design*, vol. 12, Jan/Feb 1997, p. 42.

Bibliography

Childs, N. and J. Walwin, *A Split Second of Paradise* (London: Rivers Oram Press, 1998).

Deepwell, Katy (ed.), *New Feminist Art Criticism* (Manchester: Manchester University Press, 1995).

Elwes, Catherine, 'Floating Femininity: A Look at Performance Art by Women', in S. Kent and J. Morreau (eds), *Women's Images of Men* (London: Pandora, 1990), pp. 164–93.

Elwes, Catherine and Rose Garrard, *About Time* (London: ICA, 1980).

Goldberg, RoseLee, *Performance Art* (London: Thames & Hudson, 1988).

Goldberg, RoseLee, *Performance: Live Art since the 60s* (London: Thames & Hudson, 1998).

Jones, Amelia, *Body Art, Performing the Subject* (Minneapolis: University of Minnesota Press, 1998).

Nead, Lynda, *The Female Nude: Art, Obscenity, and Sexuality* (London: Routledge, 1992).

Parker, Rozsika and Griselda Pollock (eds), *Framing Feminism: Art and the Women's Movement 1970–1985* (London: Pandora, 1987).

Phelan, Peggy, *Unmarked: The Politics of Performance* (London: Routledge, 1993).

Phillips, Andrea, *Out of Time* (Hull: Hull Time Based Arts, 1997).

Pollock, Griselda (ed.), *Generations and Geographies in the Visual Arts: Feminist Readings* (London and New York: Routledge, 1996).

Schneider, Rebecca, *The Explicit Body in Performance* (London and New York: Routledge, 1997).

Ugwu, Catherine (ed.), *Let's Get It On: the Politics of Black Performance* (London: ICA, 1995).

Warr, Tracey (ed.), *Live Art Now* (London: Arts Council, 1987).

Wolff, Janet, *Feminine Sentences* (Cambridge: Polity Press, 1990).

Chapter 4

Multicultural discourses

Pauline de Souza

THIS CHAPTER DISCUSSES SOME of the manifestations of multiculturalism, as they appear in a recent work by the black artist Sonia Boyce. It explores the significance of postmodernism for the art practice of black people and demonstrates how this relates to the postcolonial and multicultural dimensions of contemporary culture. One aspect of multiculturalism comes from the recognition of the autonomy of cultural identities and histories, and this gives rise to an art practice which respects this recognition. Another definition of multiculturalism stems from the concepts of internationalism and globalism that are used in theories of postmodernism.

Sonia Boyce's work is very much part of a discourse that questions an ethnic self living within political structures, which define black art in Britain today. Boyce uses an explicit relationship to political subject-matter to challenge the formalism that is, arguably, still the dominant aesthetic of modern art in Europe and the culture of the West. Some of the political issues that inform her subject-matter are those of domesticity and of the interface of the racial and sexual taboos that persist in a society which considers itself liberal and tolerant. Boyce's work also refers to debates from the past thirty years of feminist visual art practice, and explores how these might relate to the newly emergent multiculturalism that informs the work of many contemporary black artists. I aim to show that Boyce's recent work *Afro-Blanket* enables us to develop a rich relationship of theory to practice in a way that is both contemporary and relevant.

Sonia Boyce's *Afro-Blanket*

Sonia Boyce made *Afro-Blanket* (Figure 4.1) in 1994, at a time when the use of the term 'Afro' immediately evoked a political dimension. Its name alone identified it as political art transgressing the boundaries of formalist aesthetics, and this was the first element that characterised it is a radical work. The second element of radicalism is that it evokes the black subject without depicting the black body, using hair metonymically to refer to the 'blackness' of its subject matter. It thereby separates the signifier from the referent, locating the work within a modern idiom. Located at both centre and margins of the discourse of modern art, it successfully creates an ambivalent space from which to contest the boundaries of existing discourse.

The piece is made of thirty-seven Afro wigs which are put together loosely to form a blanket. The meanings generated by this apparently simple piece are subtle and complex, and are also woven loosely together to make a text that reveals as well as concealing and clothing. *Afro-Blanket* has much in common with the characteristics of post-minimalist art: the pliable materials, the reference to the body, the element of chance that preserves the work from having a predetermined closure are all aspects of this. But Boyce uses these in a way that makes the meanings generated by the piece work towards an assemblage that is unlike most apolitical post-minimalist art. The work has an 'edge' that provides information about its own history and cultural placing.

A third level at which Boyce's piece contests the boundaries of art practice is in its challenge to the concept of the linear continuity of history. The historical referent of 'Afro' is shown to be multiple and discontinuous, with history doubling back on itself and having a multiplicity of layers within a moment in time. 'Afro' has meanings which refer simultaneously to many historical moments. For example, 'Homo Afer' is a legacy of the European, eighteenth-century, Linnean classification of species, according to which the 'racial' differences between different populations of humans can be determined from visible signs. It relates to one historical moment in which racism became fixed within the knowledge/power dynamic described by Foucault. More recently, in the twentieth century, 'Afro' refers to the hairstyle adopted by radical North American blacks in the Civil

Figure 4.1 Sonia Boyce, Afro-Blanket, *1994. Photocredit: National Touring Exhibitions.*

Rights and Black Power movements of the 1960s, when this 'untamed' hairstyle was a bodily statement of defiance against the conventions of dress, personal grooming and appearance that were felt to be vestigial remains of nineteenth-century colonial control. The stereotype of black people as being sexual and too physical was seen as a legacy of slavery, and black people claimed their African ancestry as an alternative to being defined by colonial slavery. The freedom of the hair became a metaphor for the freedom sought from political oppression.

In Boyce's piece, the sexual connotation of hair is also used in a powerful but subtle way. The articulation of maternal domesticity which is contained in the blanket's associations with security and comfort, and the more sexual and fetishistic aspects of body hair create an ambiguous set of meanings that refuse closure and cannot be controlled or bounded by words.

An additional level of ambiguity is provided by the layering of the historical meanings of the hair. The wigs were created by Boyce from hair gathered at hairdressers' salons, they are taken from 1990s Britain, but nostalgically recreate a fancy-dress parody of an imaginary America of the 1960s, which in turn was harking back to a Utopian past in an imaginary Africa of freedom and authenticity. If black people were thought to be more 'natural' than white, then the levels of artificiality which *Afro-Blanket* reveals demonstrate that the history of black femininity is created out of culture's artifice of nature. The mythic simplicity and nature of black femininity is a transparent naturalness that is even more opaque and artificial because it is a construct designed to hide something shameful in white European history.

The fourth way in which *Afro-Blanket* challenges modernism is in the way it transforms the meanings of gender and sexuality. As I have noted above, the associations of a blanket evoke security, warmth and protection, all of which create a signifying chain that leads to fantasies of home, the maternal and domesticity. As Claire Doherty notes, 'home' is both a fiction, created by the stereotypes that circulate in the mass media, and simultaneously a lived reality.[1] In Lucy Lippard's essay 'Household Images in Art',[2] there is a discussion of works by female artists that raise questions about domesticity as a social subjectivity and an identity comprising a complex articulation of pleasure, desire, fear and pain. And as Griselda Pollock and Rozsika Parker note, textiles have traditionally been considered women's work.[3] However, the significance of *Afro-Blanket* as an African blanket adds a deeper level of meaning that evokes white people's fear of the nakedness and 'animal' nature of the colonial primitive savage that they set out to conquer, tame and control in the last quarter of the nineteenth century. The need to clothe and conceal a primitive nakedness as a colonial impulse is well documented in the histories of Christian missionaries. If nakedness is associated with a shameful proximity to nature. it must be concealed by clothing the body, an ambivalent act in which the need to control masquerades as a desire to protect. It symbolises the duplicity of the coloniser who thinks the act of power is an act of civilisation.

The substance of the blanket is not fibres from other species, such as cotton plants or animal wool, it is unwanted, rejected human hair made into synthetic hairpieces. Here we find more associations with femininity and the need for female beauty or desirability to be expressed in terms of physical and bodily sexual power. Again, a deeper level of meaning emerges as the postcolonial meaning of black femininity is represented. White people's fantasies of the eroticism they imagined to be the core of the exotic are here made plain in this collection of false identities that can be donned for weekend parties or discos by anyone wanting to masquerade as that fantasy of black femininity. More troubling associations of Afro hair relate to the curiosity that the texture of the hair evokes for a culture whose idea of feminine hair is Eurocentric. The exoticism of the tight curls and darkness of Afro hair unconsciously symbolises the sexuality of adult pubic hair. The shock of untamed Afro hair lies not only in the assertion of blackness as a positive cultural identity, of untamed anger, but also because it seems, to Eurocentric eyes, to connote an indecent shamelessness by not differentiating between hair that is cultivated and styled for visual display – hair on the head – and hair that should be considered unsightly and shameful – pubic hair. It doubly signifies an indifference to Eurocentric values, an indifference to the two taboos that are most fundamental to European definitions of femininity: the taboo on aggression and the taboo on visible sexuality.

In lifting the boundary that opposes maternal, domestic values and those of sexual femininity, *Afro-Blanket* represents another transgression, and this is deeply challenging to discourses on Western art.

Multiculturalism and postcolonialism

In the 1980s, the concept of postmodernism began to be widely used in art, and theories of postmodern culture began to circulate. Among the key concepts of postmodernism was that of 'globalisation', a term used by Frederic Jameson to describe the new international structure of capitalism, the impact of new communication technologies and the migration and movements of ethnic populations. These factors not only make national identity problematic, but they make it impossible to think of ethnic identity in terms of simple location. Globalisation also refers to the changing relationship between 'global' and 'local' scale in culture. This concept is of great interest to those who question the relevance of national identity, such as people whose relation to their own national or ethnic identity is affected by colonial history and politics. The concept of a postcolonial society is useful for anyone thinking about the endurance of colonial history and the new strategies which have been deployed to ensure the continuance of domination and control.

Figure 4.2 Anwar Jalal Shemza, The Wall, *painting, catalogue cover for 1989 Hayward Gallery exhibition 'The Other Story'. Photocredit: John Webb. Courtesy of the Hayward Gallery.*

Multiculturalism in one sense is part of postmodernism, while in its other sense it can be differentiated from the latter's internationalism; it indicates the emergence of plural and ethnically various populations and cultures coexisting within dominant cultures such as the 'art world'. In the 1980s a shift from global to multicultural identities became discernible, and this offered opportunities for black artists to explore new forms and practices in their work (Figure 4.2).

One mainstream exhibition to focus on the discourse of identity was 'Mistaken Identities', held in 1993 at the Corcan Gallery, Washington D.C., which defined multiculturalism as a response from the postcolonial world to the effects of global migrations on the culture of modernity, leading to an acknowledgement of the diversity of cultural histories that coexist in contemporary urban communities. Abigail Solomon-Godeau writes in the catalogue to the exhibition, 'If artists of color can legitimately be discussed

The Other Story

apart from other artists situated within the cultural space of postmodernism, it is because they acknowledge the limits and possibilities of postmodernism's analysis of material and institutional power.'[4] From this perspective, art from diverse cultures is considered to be of equal intellectual and cultural value, and the question of identity is placed within a common, shared culture. However, the transformations characterised as postmodern have not radically changed the discourses of art, most of which repeat the familiar structures of modernism. They still deploy the critical concepts of Western and especially European aesthetics and history which perpetuate their own values and judgements and celebrate Western achievements.

A conference, held at the Tate Gallery, London in May 1999, on museums of modern art and the 'end of art history', explored the importance of multiculturalism and modernism and recapitulated the arguments on the need to recognise and respect the difference of other cultures at the same time as suggesting that Western modernism and its critical dialogues are of greater significance. Contributing to this conference, Stuart Hall argued that black art and black cultural studies are incompatible with postmodernism. However, many black artists are fully engaged with the debate on postmodernism and find it a dynamic one.

The idea of 'sameness' is a useful concept congruent with theories of postmodernism, and has been used by Judith Wilson to think about art in her essay 'Will the New Internationalism be the Same Old Story? Some Art Historical Considerations'. Wilson argues that postmodern internationalism can reproduce familiar ideological biases alongside social and economic disparities. The concept of multiculturalism recast as a postmodern internationalism evokes the critique of ethnicity and postcolonialism offered by Rasheed Araeen in his 1987 essay 'From Primitivism to Ethnic Arts'. There he argues that British political structures have organised new conceptual and administrative frameworks to control non-European peoples by labelling them as ethnic minorities. His theories of British politics is informed by a Foucauldian concept of subjectivity which he applies to the history of Western colonialism. He shows that institutional discourses on 'other' peoples and their culture resulted in the stereotyping of non-European people. According to Araeen, new political and administrative systems developed from nineteenth-century colonialist frameworks, and these he calls postcolonialism. He argues that these systems exerted power over black culture, with great detrimental effects. In 'Preliminary Notes for a Black Manifesto', published in the journal *Black Phoenix* in 1975, Araeen argues that postcolonialism suppresses indigenous culture by refusing to acknowledge its history and its cultural productivity.

In Britain in the 1980s, the term 'black' still had negative connotations, denoting the displacement of non-European people but also being used implicitly to criticise those people. It became used by 'black' artists in order to confront and challenge these negative connotations, so that Asian, Central and South American and Oriental artists also defined themselves as 'black'. This successfully removed any realist nomination from the term as a biological, social or cultural description. The signifier was successfully severed from its signified. In the USA, the term 'people of color' was being used, and this refers to the history of black Americans being similarly labelled as 'colored'. Histories of exile and displacement were described as diaspora, and the shift from concepts of ethnicity to definitions of 'blackness' had an empowering effect on many communities. For example, in 1980 the Wolverhampton Young Black Artists Group, formed by the artist Eddie Chambers, initiated a radical alternative art practice, exploring the political struggle of the black community in Britain. In May 1982, at the Ethnic Arts Conference, organised by the Greater London Council's Ethnic Sub-Committee, discussions were held on the possibility of finding alternative names to signify the difference of non-European people. By 1985, the term 'black' was being used for events involving black artists and cultural theorists, such as the 'Vision and Voice, Black Visual Arts' conference. Exhibitions such as 'The Essential Black Art' in 1988 emphasised the black experience of racism and imperialism.

In work by Rasheed Araeen and Eddie Chambers and by Paul Gilroy, 'blackness' is considered an essential quality, as a metaphysical condition or state of the soul, accessible to everyone regardless of cultural difference and accessible to those visiting the exhibition.[5] The term 'blackness' was becoming a frame for a critical dialogue. In 'Black Art: A Discussion', Araeen suggests that it is important that black artists have an open dialogue with western modernism provided that they maintain a critical distance enabling them to translate modernist practice and objects into work that can be critical of postcolonialism.

Kobena Mercer emphasises that the representation of the black diaspora relies on the restructuring of existing philosophical sources and the processes of gathering and re-using.[6] Cornel West explores this new form of multiculturalism, based on hybridity and appropriation, in his essay 'The New Cultural Politics of Difference'.[7] West discusses new forms of intellectual and social consciousness created by black artists and critics, which function to destroy the monolithic historical flow of Western culture. The distinctive characteristic of new cultural difference is its multiplicity and heterogeneity.

These models of political struggle are based on the Marxist theories of Antonio Gramsci. According to Gramsci's views of society, the objective of ideological struggle is to examine the structures and past conceptions of a social system. Where there are spaces, new cultural images, as well as meanings, can be articulated. Striving to be a British and a black artist requires a double consciousness, in which cultural assemblages deal largely with the articulation of nationality, ethnicity and authenticity.

Expressions of authenticity are rooted in cultural traditions that have been invented and institutionalised, and symbolic objects are used to describe certain values and types of behaviour. The construction of tradition can lead to an unprecedented interest in a particular culture whose objects can then be reinterpreted – Sonia Boyce's *Afro-Blanket*, with its layering of meanings attributed to the symbolic objects used in the work, is an example of this.

The black body

One aspect of postmodernism circulates around the concept of a fragmented body, a metaphor for the decentred subject. The latter concept comes from Foucault's ideas of 'knowledge' and 'power'. Knowledge comprises the production of discourses which may then be used for political ends to dominate or to subvert. Although Foucault suggests that all subjectivity is decentred, being the product of discourses and structures of power, his ideas have especial significance for black artists since the structures of postcolonialism cause particular alienation and depersonalisation, and mean that the black self is in perpetual struggle to actualise itself.

In his pioneering book *Black Skins, White Masks*, Frantz Fanon discusses the psychological and subjective effects of colonisation on the black self. He observes the ways in which the coloniser projects distorted fears, desires and fantasies onto the idea of a black body in a way that leads to the fragmentation of the black experience of self. The black body, deprived of its history and its 'original' identity, remains the 'other'. Fanon notes that this otherness expresses a difference which means that the idea of the black body is used for the projection of white culture's fears. He investigates the distortions that a postcolonial history exerts on black masculinity and black femininity, and he also discusses the tendency that white hegemony has to sexualise and eroticise the 'exotic'.

In the radical reconstruction of black identity, the fragmented or whole body has to remain within the centre of discourse. If we consider Frederic Jameson's essay 'Postmodernism and Consumer Society', the breakdown of temporal continuities makes room for new experiences and multiple identities. The human subject or its signifier is given over to separate visions that enable the new meanings of existence to coexist. It is this shift back to a centred subject on which black identity relies. This doubling of the subject provides a space between the moments of being, a space where the self is created, which is ambivalent. The presence of a fragmented body disrupts temporal normality and it is within this space that new objects begin to redefine culture. Jameson's model of postmodern multi-identities is accessible to all artists: in collecting different cultural objects to create new identities, artists are described as 'ethnographers'. Artists such as Boyce whose work is based on political transformation remains on the margins of a discourse of art which cannot contain or integrate the contradictions and challenges that it proposes.

Black feminism

If Boyce's work does refrain from identifying itself with the postmodern internationalism that reduces art to the same, and if it does raise questions that move away from a black centrality, then the alternative centralities it makes possible create new problems for black artists and critics who dislike black art having any relationship with mainstream art. For example, Cornel West in 'The New Cultural Politics of Difference' is concerned about the fragmentation of black art when the social differences of class, gender and sexuality are all acknowledged.[8] He suggests that when black artists identify with other minority groups that have a different political and social agenda, to challenge 'Western oppression', this undermines the strength of black art and alters its identifiable position within the margins of art discourse. In *There Ain't No Black in the Union Jack*, Paul Gilroy consistently claims that the legitimacy of black culture lies in a political and social unity among black people and not in an identification with fragmented groups who want to discuss sexuality and gender. He writes, 'the assimilation of Blacks is not a process of acculturation but of cultural syncretism. Accordingly their definitions and cultural expressions draw on a plurality of black histories and politics.'[9] For Gilroy, the reconciliation and formation of new black identities through the process of globalisation is a central issue. However, his critical formation has its own tensions and contradictions: he acknowledges the struggle of black British people as they transcend the formal division of class, and his emphasis on cultural production moves his theory away from classical Marxism. Instead, he thinks within a Gramscian theory of hegemony, according to which minority groups give or withhold their consent to the cultural leadership of dominant or emergent class and cultural factions.

Over the last decade, black feminism has been generally sympathetic to the ideas of Cornel West and Paul Gilroy. There was experience of racism on the part of 'white' feminism towards non-European people, and the problems and dilemmas of black feminism were linked to 'white' feminism's ambition to achieve the same degree of power that exists in a patriarchal system. In the case of black feminism, the attack on materialist feminism is crucial. Materialist feminism in the 1970s recognised gender as a political issue only in relation to the gender division of labour and in terms of class division; it did not view cultural differences as a 'primary' contradiction. Black feminism, on the other hand, set out to redefine class and cultural differences within the feminist movement. As bell hooks puts it:

Class is much more than Marx's definition of relationship
to the means of production. Your experience [determined
by your class] validates how you are taught to behave, what
you expect from yourself and from others . . . It is these
behavioural patterns that middle class woman resist
although they are willing to accept class in Marxist terms,
(but they) avoid really dealing with class behaviour.[10]

Materialist feminist theory began to use the term 'oppression' to
define the common bond among all women. 'The rebirth of
feminism coincided with the use of the term "oppression" [which]
refers back to a choice, an explanation, a situation that is
political.' writes bell hooks.[11] The real significance of cultural
and 'ideological' differences was discovered by feminism in the
1970s, through the Lacanian readings of Freud that led Juliet
Mitchell to write 'Psychoanalysis and Feminism'.[12] Subjectivity,
rather than relations of production, became a new focus of
attention, and the dynamics of gender and sexuality were understood as central. Black feminists believed that this alternative way
of constituting meaning still reflected the values of postcolonial
society. Using poststructuralist theories of relating power, knowledge, deconstruction and invisibility, black feminists argued in
the 1980s and 1990s that within Western institutions there
existed new, unprecedented disciplines of control directed against
the black body. Black feminism was concerned to construct a
feminist ideology that would fit into a political and social framework. The aim was to rearticulate a pre-existing black women's
view and recentre the language of existing discourses of visual
imagery in order to be able to represent black history. The
political significance of black womanhood was to assign central
importance to black cultural identity. Lubaina Himid wrote,
'Positive conception of the ethnicity of the margins [leads to] a
recognition that we all speak from a particular place, out of a
particular history, out of a particular experience, a particular
culture without being contained by that position'.[13] Black feminists criticised colonial ideas of black sexuality as promiscuous,
following Fanon's view that the 'other' is found in the psychological uncertainty of the colonial self. The 'other' occurs when
the non-European and the coloniser are observing each other, and
it is the coloniser who is able to assign attributes to the black body

that emphasise cultural differences. The identity of the black person becomes confused because there are conflicting identities and the black person is unable to discover the true identity of the black self.

Notes

1. Doherty, *Claustrophobia*, p. 12.
2. Lucy Lippard, 'Household Images in Art' in Lippard, *From the Center*.
3. Parker and Pollock, *Framing Feminism*.
4. Abigail Solomon-Godeau, Catalogue for 'Mistaken Identities', Corcan Gallery, Washington, 1993, p. 26.
5. Araeen and Chambers, 'Black Art: A Discussion'; Gilroy, 'Cruciality and the Frog's Perspective' and 'It Ain't Where You're From'.
6. Mercer, 'Black Art and the Burden of Representation'.
7. Cornel West, 'The New Cultural Politics of Difference' in Ferguson and Minh-Ha (eds), *Out There*.
8. Ibid.
9. Gilroy, *There Ain't No Black*, p. 155.
10. hooks, *Feminist Theory*, p. 3.
11. Ibid. p. 5.
12. Juliet Mitchell, 'Psychoanalysis and Feminism' in Parker and Pollock, *Framing Feminism*.
13. Lubaina Himid, 'New Ethnicities' in Hall (ed.), *ICA Documents 7*, p. 29.

Bibliography

Araeen, Rasheed, 'Preliminary Notes for a Black Manifesto, *Black Phoenix*, 1975.

Araeen, Rasheed, and Eddie Chambers, 'Black Art, a Discussion', *Third Text*, Winter 1988/9.

Couzens-Hoy, David, *Foucault: A Critical Reader* (Oxford: Blackwell, 1991).

Doherty, Claire, *Claustrophobia* (Birmingham: Ikon Gallery, 1998).

Fanon, Frantz, *Black Skin, White Masks* (London: Pluto Press, 1991).

Ferguson, Russell and Trinh T. Minh-Ha, *Out There: Marginalism and Contemporary Culture* (Port Townsend, Washington: MIT Press, 1983).

Fisher, Jean (ed.), *Global Visions: Towards a New Internationalism in the Visual Arts* (London: Kala Press, 1994).

Foster, Hal, *The Anti-Aesthetic: Essays on Postmodernist Culture* (Port Townsend, Washington: MIT Press, 1983).

Gilroy, Paul, 'It Ain't Where You're From, It's Where You're At, The Dialectic of Diasporic Identification', *Third Text* (Winter 1990).

Gilroy, Paul, *There Ain't No Black in the Union Jack* (London: Thames & Hudson, 1992).

Gilroy, Paul, 'Cruciality and the Frog's Perspective: an Agenda of Difficulties for the Black Arts Movement in Britain', *Third Text*, Winter 1989/90.

Hall, Stuart (ed.), *ICA Documents 7: Black Film, British Cinema* (London: ICA, 1988).

Hiller, Susan (ed.), *The Myth of Primitivism* (London: Routledge, 1991).

hooks, bell, *Feminist Theory: From the Margins to the Center* (Boston: South End Press, 1984).

Jameson, Frederic, 'Postmodernism and Consumer Society' in Foster, Hal, *The Anti-Aesthetic: Essays on Postmodernist Culture* (Port Townsend, Washington: MIT Press, 1983).

Lippard, Lucy, *From the Center: Essays on Women's Art* (New York: Dutton, 1977).

Mercer, Kobena, 'Black Art and the Burden of Representation' in *Third Text*, Winter 1989/90.

Oliver, Kelly (ed.), *The Portable Kristeva* (New York: Columbia University Press, 1997).

Parker, Rozsika, and Griselda Pollock, *Framing Feminism: Art and the Women's Movement 1970–1985* (London: Pandora, 1987).

Chapter 5

Photography

Jessica Evans

SUMMARISING THE RELATIONSHIP OF feminism and photography presents a significant challenge since the relationship between a political and social movement and the study of a visual medium is not a straightforward one. There is now a venerable body of work on the politics of representation and the visual image, based variously in feminist film theory, photography and art history, and cultural and media studies.[1] However, this work has tended to privilege *textual* investigations based in the rhetoric of the image, drawing out the *effects* of representation in terms of ideology and power. Accordingly, the politics of representation often turns out to be the same politics, regardless of whether the kind of object under investigation is, for example, a film, painting, advertisement, or television programme.

I raise this issue in order to highlight the problem of the conditions under which we define something as a photograph. In the realm of the profane, advertising or the 'representations of women in the media' have, for example, been a key staple of cultural and media studies analysis, but rarely are the images under consideration disaggregated as *photographs*. The products of photographic work are often regarded as visual constructions, as texts, like any other. Although it may appear that photography is only the effect or product of a set of determinations that are logically prior, it is important to realise that the institutions of advertising and journalism would not exist as we know them without photography. The person of the 'photographer' is also at stake here. Thus, the fine artist is never a 'photographer', but, as can be seen in monographs and exhibition catalogues, an artist-who-happens-to-use-photography. The object we wish to apprehend in this essay – photography – seems to slip away under the weight of other appellations. In this case, photography and art are viewed as antinomies, the term 'photographer' detracting from the ability of the artist to transcend the machine of the camera and thus achieve full human agency and subjectivity. This indicates that photographers are largely of low status, bound by pre-given aesthetic and commercial codes and adhering to a primarily institutionalised and instrumental ethos. But it is with these lowly and prosaic areas that the most important feminist interventions and analyses have been concerned. Of course, there is still much work to be done in rescuing previously disregarded female photographers and recognising their achievements and contributions to photographic history.[2] However, this by itself would seem to do no more than confirm the values of the hallowed accounts of the 'history of photography', which present us with a story based on a roll-call of isolated photo-pioneers, each struggling to establish their own 'unique visions' of the world, overcoming the technical limitations of previous generations and 'revealing' their insights to an abstracted, unspecified audience. These are fundamentally romantic and individualist accounts, tending often to the metaphysical. They have as their central conceit the idea of a self-created artist who uses photography as a medium to express a heightened subjectivity but combines this, often contradictorily, with a capacity to penetrate the hitherto undiscovered secrets of reality.

Therefore, anyone writing photographic history must address the established historiographic approach to their subject, an approach that is based almost entirely on the tropes of traditional art history. It is clear that the implications of this for photographic studies are far more disturbing than for art history even: photography as art, or fine art photography, counts for only a small portion of all photographs in use; photography cannot be assimilated under the category of art. But if we consider the debates in art history, where the richest debates on historiography have taken place, there is no justification from a feminist point of view for continuing to study only the 'significant', the 'better', the more 'aesthetically satisfying or sophisticated' objects.[3] So, in terms of photographic history, the challenge is to do more than putting the historical record straight in terms of admitting females into the canons of photographic history. First, there is a need to pay close attention to what women photographed and how they photographed, in order to observe the previously unnoticed and taken for granted limits of a genre – in terms of what it does and does not show, and what it can and cannot say. Studies of this kind may indicate that a genre's definitions have so far been set through the activities of a well organised community, based on the partial knowledge and interests of masculine experience. Val Williams, for example, has shown how in the sphere of photo-journalism, photographers such as Grace Robertson specialised in picture stories which brought childbirth, child-rearing and working mothers into the public domain via the publication *Picture Post.* [4]

Second, the study of photography means that photographs other than those identifiable by an individual, named photographer must necessarily be studied. There are a whole host of photographic practices made and used as documents in the private, unpublished domain which largely exist below the thresholds of authorship and other forms of official accreditation. One of the elusive features of photographs is that they are spliced into the everyday practices of our lives, practices that are routine to the extent that they exist largely below the threshold of consciousness.

The question posed in this chapter, then, is to what extent it is possible to think about the specificities of a medium, its conditions of production, distribution, consumption and practical use, without subsuming them under a more universalising assumption that since its products are 'representations', this is only what we must analyse. When we are thinking about photography, we should keep in mind the way it is often discursively put to use in order to make appearances equate with reality; to reduce the field of what can be known to what is observable; to entice us with 'evidence' for which viewers are interpolated as 'witnesses'. We should be wary of claims to 'see clearly' and without distortion, for these are always entangled with power relations and with *a priori* frameworks that regulate the relationship of seeing to knowing.

As we will see, the suspicion of the visible and a concern with what the process of making visible might in fact be hiding is certainly manifested in much feminist use and analysis of photography, which at times has taken on shades of an iconoclastic attitude. But the first historical moment of feminist cultural analysis did not cast aspersions on the visual field itself. Laura Mulvey has usefully set out the two successive historical moments of feminist film analysis, but they can be adapted well to the successive moments of intervention in critical-radical photography circles from the 1970s to the 1980s.[5] First, there was a period marked by the effort to change the content of cinematic and photographic representation, in order to develop realistic images of women, to record women talking about their real-life experiences, to investigate and represent women's experiences and problems, or to present 'positive images of women'. A good example of this is the work of the Hackney Flashers feminist photography collective which documented women's invisible labour in Hackney, London.[6] A period characterised by a mixture of 'consciousness-raising and propaganda', its focus was to *improve* current forms of representation, so as to produce accurate and fair representations of women rather than the idealised or distorted images of the media.[7] While it was concerned with what had previously remained hidden, it advocated a democracy of the seen, a fair crack of the whip so that everything could be brought into the sphere of the visible. It was assumed that it was possible to attain direct knowledge of, and therefore visually represent, real 'women', a stable and unproblematic category of knowledge.

In the second period, an emphasis on the language of representation became dominant, and the 'fascination with the cinematic process' led film-makers and critics to become interested in, and use, the aesthetic principles and terms of reference provided by the avant-garde tradition'.[8] It was assumed that 'foregrounding the process itself, privileging the signifier, necessarily disrupts aesthetic unity and forces the spectator's attention on the means of production of meaning'.[9] The specific inflection of this in the critical avant-garde and the feminist photographic practice that burgeoned in both the UK and the USA in the 1980s was a highly academic and feminist practice largely based in a combination of poststructuralist theory. Specifically, this was an admixture of psychoanalysis and structural linguistics derived from the work of Althusser, Lacan, and Saussure; the strategies of European, modernist avant-garde practice; and an appropriation of the visual rhetorics of popular cultural forms such as advertising.

Its main theme was the countering of the aesthetic of realism and illusionism with its link to bourgeois ideology's pretensions to 'show things as they are' and the embracing of formalism, inter-textuality, pastiche, and Brechtian techniques such as distancia-tion. Femininity could be shown to be a 'masquerade', something that had to be endlessly performed and reinvented. Made out of material signifiers which marked sexual difference, woman could be demonstrated to be a sign and feminine identity achieved in and through identifications with discursive rhetorics.[10] But the distinctiveness of this work – in terms of its underlying philoso-phical position rather than its visual style – lies in what I would characterise as its suspicion of positive knowledge. In part a product of the iconophobia mentioned earlier, it was, and is, particularly intense in critical/feminist photographic practice in contrast to all the other arts, because of the unique claim that photography appears to have on the real. For positivists, the indexical nature of the photographic sign means that the photo-graph slavishly holds to the full material presence of the object, so that, it is argued, it posits nothing beyond what is presented to it as the idolater of that-which-is. The realism of photography seems, therefore, to justify the essentialist assumptions of mascu-line forms of institutionalised knowledge. This becomes possible because the whole apparatus of sexual difference, as with racial difference, appears to be uniquely based on the centrality of 'vision', of what can be *seen*. These differences are made to seem 'real' and therefore 'true' – and unchangeable – because the differences we can 'see', the biological differences between men and women's bodies, appear to ground their 'truth' beyond history, in what is naturally so, in Nature.[11]

Therefore, underpinned by the deconstructive impetus of post-structuralism, the radical way forward in one wing of feminist photography practice (and criticism) was to problematise the category of 'woman' in its entirety, making it opaque rather than transparent in a refusal of the Enlightenment assumption that more knowledge of objects equals progress. Accordingly, 'wo-man' became something that could not be 'known' nor repre-sented, and for many, the model of 'representation' became impossible. The effect of this strategy of refusal was, as Griselda Pollock puts it in her account of the important exhibition 'Dif-ference: On Representation and Sexuality',

to make the viewer conscious of how much she desires to
find within a work of art a secure locus of meaning whether
in a woman about whom a story is being told or in one
telling the story. We scan the work for that identity around
which our fantasies can be permitted to develop.[12]

Mary Kelly illustrates this well in her work *Interim*, a project
which addressed women's public and private identities as they
confront the ageing process. The work used objects as a 'trace',
standing in for the presence of a woman, and thereby also
evoking the workings of the public discourses of fetishism in
which masculine anxiety is allayed through the fixing of the gaze
onto part-objects.[13] More broadly, many feminists and progres-
sive/left photographers of the early 1980s encountered a situation
in which the act of photographing someone had become so
analysed as a relation of power that representation of persons
became embargoed.[14] Jo Spence and her colleagues were reduced
to photographing dolls,[15] and she and many others turned to self-
representation as the politically acceptable way out – although
there are additional explanations for the widespread movement in
the late 1980s to work on the self and identity.

So far, I have considered feminist interventions into photogra-
phically produced art, but the academic analysis of photographic
practices has also been concerned with what does and does not
enter into the sphere of visibility – with, therefore, the regulation of
the scopic. The best way of defining the specificity of this approach
is via a suggestive distinction embedded in various works by
Michel Foucault. In his often visual accounts of events, for example in his historical analysis of the modern penal system as
embodied in the model of the panopticon,[16] Foucault did not focus
on *how things are made to look like in representation*. Instead, his
analyses grapple with the question of how things *came to be
considered appropriate* for codification as visual 'data' in the first
place; with how knowledge could be founded upon 'sight'; and
with how things were 'shown to' knowledge and power.[17]

Let us explore how this insight from Foucault can help contextualise feminist approaches to photographic practices. Pierre
Bourdieu, in his introduction to *Photography: A Middlebrow Art*,
writes, 'One might say of photography what Hegel said of
philosophy: "No other art or science is subjected to this last

degree of scorn, to the supposition that we are masters of it without ado." [18] For, unlike the more technically demanding artisanal modes of drawing and painting, photography 'presupposes neither academically communicated culture, nor the apprenticeships and the "profession" which confer their value on the cultural consumptions and practices ordinarily held to be the most noble, by withholding them from the man in the street'. [19] The fact that the very means of *producing* photographic images is not regulated in a legally and economically restricted or centralised manner (in contrast to the institutions of the 'mass' media) is, in part, why photography has often been considered as *the* medium of democratisation. It accounts for the ease with which it appears across public and private domains and for the sense that it is a medium in which we can all take part, a medium that has no status, class, or serious financial barriers to access. That this is so is due largely to the basic division of labour which lies at the heart of mass amateur photography – between the camera operator and the process of developing and printing the photograph, a separation that persists today. In the words of George Eastman, whose Kodak Box Brownie was the first camera to embody this principle, and thus to industrialise photography to the extent that for the first time lower-middle-class and working-class people could own and make images of themselves:

> The principle of the Kodak system is the separation of a work that anyone can do in making a photograph, from the work that only an expert can do. We furnish anybody, a man, woman, or child, who has sufficient intelligence to point a box straight and press the button. It can be employed without any preliminary study, without a darkroom, without chemicals. [20]

The logic of Kodak snapshooting is one in which technical skill and knowledge of the making of pictures is removed from the activity of the photographer; Don Slater has commented on the paradox it embodied: 'the very means by which the power to represent was democratised also rendered it impotent'. [21]

Accordingly, we cannot simply assume that the ease with which anyone can, indeed, 'take' their own pictures means that power and its relations have evacuated the sphere of representation. One of the central operations of power that impinge on photographic practice in order to impoverish its wider use can be located in the high-pressure mass marketing of photographic equipment consonant with the logic established by Kodak.[22] Indeed the institutionalised difference at the level of consumption between 'taking' and 'making' – so essential to the distinction between the identity of, on the one hand, the snapshooter and, on the other, the serious amateur and especially the art photographer – points to the limits of mass amateur practice. This, combined with the ideologies of familiarism which dominate the private sphere, as perhaps Jo Spence was the first to point out, impacts directly upon the domain of the most ordinary, everyday and taken-for-granted practices of representation, the most apparently private and localised practices of the amateur snapshooter photographer. It is here that the most stultified and stereotyped repertoire of composition, subject-matter and style resides.

A provocative and influential feminist analysis has identified the profoundly important gendered dimension in the construction of the amateur photographer.[23] The culture of the snapshooter is entirely different from that of the typically male 'serious amateur': in industry terms this bread-and-butter mass market is deeply feminised; indeed the majority users are women and come from a wider socioeconomic range than the serious amateurs. Products and services for this group are described as 'foolproof' and it is assumed that photographers have low expectations and few technical competencies – in this way, 'the camera compensates for the lack of skills and confidence of the user'.[24] The photographer's interest in photography is limited to its use as a record of family and leisure activities, which is specified right down to the illustrations on the wallet in which the developing and processing company send back prints.[25]

What amateur photography did, from its inception in the early years of the twentieth century, was to associate the private use of the camera with leisure activities. At the same time, the family itself, as the linchpin of social relations in the private sphere, was emerging as a primary site of leisure consumption. The reinvention of the family in the postwar years as a haven, as the opposite of work and as the primary source of emotional strength; the ethos of demonstrative and active parenting; the increasing informalisation of private life during the twentieth century; and the related predominance of ideals of self-expression over those of obligation and duty – all these changes in the social field are refracted in photographs of the family. It is the family at play and at recreation and those moments in which family members mark their rites of passage and their sense of continuity in the form of births, birthdays, weddings and holidays, that have a privileged place in the use of photography in the private sphere.[26] Jo Spence, in a number of pioneering works from the late 1970s onwards, investigated the complex ways in which family life is carefully orchestrated for the camera according to a set of largely taken-for-granted conventions which dictate *what* and *how* things can be photographed. What could enter into the sphere of the visible, and what operations of power are at work? Spence showed how the family album is an operation on family memory, that what lies at the heart of the selection of idealising moments for the telling of the family story are the very mechanisms for forgetting. What is omitted from the family album? Whose memories are represented in family albums? We do not think of taking cameras into the workplace, on shopping trips, or on visits to the doctor: what more indication is needed of the mental connection between the use of the camera and a private sphere underpinned by the idea of innocent and spontaneous recreation? Spence and others argued that within the realm of personal life, photographs of angry children, divorcing and rowing parents, sickness or sibling rivalry – in short, the representations of the pain and conflict that are a part of family life – either do not get taken or are discarded. It is largely *parents'* wishful thinking and 'memories' that are represented by family pictures, although they are offered as children's own. Moreover, as Spence pointed out with reference to her own family album, photography is firmly integrated into the ways we all manage our identities and have them managed for us. There can be few who have not attempted to regulate the image of themselves by constructing their pose for a camera, or tearing up the photograph that makes them feel uncomfortable or ugly.[27]

In a short article, 'Woman in Secret', written just before she died, Spence drew attention to the secrets that most of us carry around for years out of fear of shame, terror or stigmatisation and the need to maintain integrity by protecting the idealised parts of ourselves which are often bound up with parental ideals.[28] In fact, Spence's work was consistently been concerned with how social conventions of class, culture and taste regulate what can be said in public and what has to be hidden from view. Often accused of 'hanging her dirty washing out in public' – an apt metaphor for someone who increasingly played on grotesque imagery in a deliberate attempt to transgress these boundaries – Spence developed a phototherapeutic practice in which her body becomes a theatrical performance.[29] Her work in this area, particularly in the years subsequent to contracting cancer, is traversed by a basic assumption that to reveal is cathartic (Figures 5.1 and 5.2). In work such as this, feminist thinking about the image reverts to a full, even exaggerated naturalism based in a desire to fully expose to the witness of the camera the murky and repressed events and activities of ageing, scarring, sex, eating, defecating – activities all replete with characteristics that are coded as female. Spence borrows for her visual tropes from the traditions of the carnivalesque, the tradition of licensed subversion in which hierarchical rank and prohibitions are suspended via vulgar humour, profanities, and costumes and masks.[30] Mary Russo has indicated how the female grotesque, the key figure of the carnivalesque, is associated with 'making a spectacle out of oneself', connoting an embarrassing loss of control and boundaries.[31] Indeed, we can observe in Spence's photographs the attention to the marks and protuberances that lie on the surfaces of the body, as if the boundary between self and other is fragile, as if the various parts of the personality cannot be held together. The viewer is likely to feel both fascinated and repelled. Perhaps not unlike Frida Kahlo, about whose work it has been said that, 'The unclothed body is not a 'self' but a socialised body, a body that is opened by instruments, technologised, wounded, its organs displayed to the outside world',[32] Spence reveals her body as the site *where others have made their mark* (Figure 5.2), and the site where she can 'write-back' (Figure 5.1). For Spence, the act of photographing was a direct way of creating a sense of agency; in the context of her cancer, it was absolutely necessary in order to fight the infantalising process of being a patient. As she remarked, 'It's not part of patients' rights that you can take photographs in hospital'.[33] When a doctor walked up to Spence on the hospital ward and marked her breast with a cross (Figure 5.2), saying, 'This is the one that's coming off', she felt branded as if she were an animal being led to the slaughterhouse.[34] The capacity to think while under fire was nurtured with a camera.

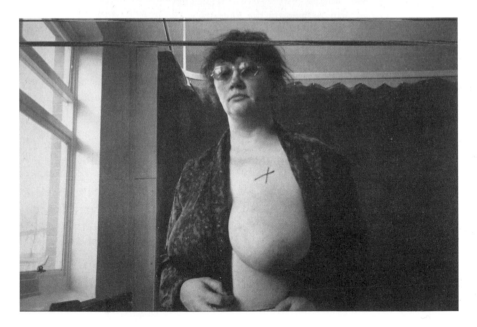

Notes

1. See, for example, Betterton, *Looking On,* and Coward, *Female Desire.* For a more recent collection, see Evans and Hall, *Visual Culture.*
2. See Williams, *Women Photographers.*
3. Parker and Pollock, *Old Mistresses*; Pollock, 'Feminist Interventions in the Histories of Art' and 'Vision, Voice and Power'; Broude and Garrard, *Feminism and Art History.*
4. Williams, *Women Photographers.*
5. Mulvey, 'Feminism, Film and the Avantgarde'; see also Pollock, 'Missing Women: Rethinking Early Thoughts on Images of Women'.
6. Spence, *Putting Myself in the Picture,* pp. 66–77.
7. Mulvey, 'Feminism, Film and the Avantgarde', p. 6.
8. Ibid. p. 7.
9. Ibid. p. 175.
10. The work of Mary Kelly, Barbara Kruger, Cindy Sherman, Marie Yates, and Yves Lomax is typical, as is that of Victor Burgin and Ray Barrie, all of which reached a peak of prominence in the mid-1980s. For writings on these artists, see the catalogue for the high-profile and definitive exhibition 'Difference: On Representation and Sexuality', edited by Linker; Owens, 'The discourse of others'; Solomon-Godeau, 'Winning the Game When the Rules have been Changed'; and Wolff, 'Postmodern Theory and Feminist Art Practice'. In 'Screening the Seventies', Pollock makes the link between Brechtian strategies and deconstructive feminist photography. Williamson, 'Images of Woman' is a useful account of Cindy Sherman's work.
11. It has been remarked that psychoanalytic theory's account of the process of identification, and the relation to the 'other' through which biological individuals become 'subjects', is pervaded by metaphors of scenes and looking relations, from Freud's famous 'primal scene' and castration complex – which is founded on what can and cannot be seen and therefore what the woman is seen to lack (the penis) – to the 'mirror stage' of Lacan. For Freud, the very desire to know had sexual origins, and was rooted in a fraught and highly conflicted relationship between seeing and knowing, as evidenced in his concepts of voyeurism, exhibitionism, and narcissism (see Rose, 'Sexuality in the Field of Vision').
12. Pollock, 'Art, Art School, Culture', p. 62.
13. In similar fashion, Barbara Kruger is quoted as saying, 'I see

my work as a series of attempts to ruin certain representations, to displace the subject and to welcome a female spectator into the audience of men', in Wolff, 'Postmodern Theory and Feminist Art Practice', p. 95. For Kruger's work, see her exhibition catalogue *We Won't Play Nature to Your Culture*, which also has an excellent contextualising essay.
14. See Evans, 'Camerawork – An Introduction', pp. 26–9.
15. For example, the cover of Holland et al., *Photography/Politics Two*.
16. Foucault, *Discipline and Punish*.
17. See also Foucault, *The Birth of the Clinic*, and 'The Eye of Power'; and the discussions in Rajchman, 'Foucault's art of seeing', and Evans and Hall, *Visual Culture*.
18. Bourdieu, *Photography: A Middlebrow Art*, p. 5.
19. Ibid. p. 5.
20. Kodak advertising copy, 1898.
21. Slater, 'Marketing the Medium', p. 173.
22. Ibid. p. 173.
23. See Spence, *Putting Myself in the Picture* and *Cultural Sniping*; Porter, 'Trade and Industry'.
24. Porter, 'Trade and Industry', p. 46.
25. See Wells, ' "Sweet It Is to Scan . . ." Personal Photographs and Popular Memory', pp. 136–7.
26. See Spence, 'Beyond the Family Album' and *Putting Myself in the Picture*; Williamson, 'Images of Woman'; Slater, 'Domestic Photography and Digital Culture'. Market research surveys suggest that just under three-quarters of the adult population own a camera, and in 1989, 88 per cent of 25–34-year-olds owned cameras. 'Family occasions' are frequently quoted as one of the principal reasons for camera ownership. See the discussion in *Cultural Trends*, pp. 43–5.
27. Spence, *Putting Myself in the Picture*.
28. Spence, 'Woman in Secret'.
29. See Spence, *Cultural Sniping*. For further discussion of Spence's work, including her phototherapy and her photographic response to her health crisis, see Evans, 'An Affront to Taste? The Disturbances of Jo Spence'.
30. Bakhtin, *Rabelais and his World*.
31. Russo, 'Female Grotesques'.
32. Franco, *Plotting Women*, p. 107.
33. Spence, 'Body talk?', p. 25.
34. Spence, *Putting Myself in the Picture*, p. 171.

Bibliography

Bakhtin, Mikhail Mikhailovich, *Rabelais and his World* (Bloomington: Indiana University Press, 1984).

Betterton, Rosemary (ed.), *Looking On: Images of Femininity in the Visual Arts and Media* (London: Pandora/RKP, 1987).

Bourdieu, Pierre, with Luc Boltanski, Robert Castell, Jean-Claude Chamboredon, and Dominique Schnapper, *Photography: A Middlebrow Art* (first published in France in 1965 as *Un Art Moyen*) (Cambridge: Polity Press, 1990).

Broude, Norma and Mary D. Garrard (eds), *Feminism and Art History* (New York: Harper and Row, 1982).

Coward, Rosalind, *Female Desire: Women's Sexuality Today* (London: Paladin, 1984).

Cultural Trends, 1990. 8 London: Policy Studies Institute.

Evans, Jessica 'Camerawork – An Introduction' in Evans (ed.), *The Camerawork Essays* (London: Rivers Oram Press, 1997).

Evans, Jessica, 'An Affront to Taste? The Disturbances of Jo Spence' in Evans (ed.), *The Camerawork Essays* (London: Rivers Oram Press, 1997).

Evans, Jessica and Stuart Hall (eds), *Visual Culture: The Reader* (London: Sage/Open University, 1999).

Foucault, Michel, 'Panopticonism' in *Discipline and Punish* (Harmondsworth: Penguin, 1977), also extracted in Evans and Hall, *Visual Culture: The Reader*.

Foucault, Michel, *The Birth of the Clinic* (London: Tavistock, 1973).

Foucault, Michel, 'The Eye of Power' in Gordon (ed.), *Michel Foucault: Power/Knowledge* (Brighton: Harvester Press, 1980).

Franco, Jean, *Plotting Women: Gender and Representation in Mexico* (London: Verso, 1989).

Hirsch, Julia, *Family Photography: Context, Meaning and Effect* (Oxford: Oxford University Press, 1981).

Holland, Patricia, Jo Spence, and Simon Watney (eds), *Photography/Politics Two* (London: Photography Workshop/Comedia, 1986).

Kruger, Barbara, *We Won't Play Nature to Your Culture* (London: Institute of Contemporary Arts, 1983).

Linker, Kate (ed.), *Difference: On Representation and Sexuality* (New York: The New Museum of Contemporary Art and ICA, London, 1984).

Mulvey, Laura, 'Feminism, Film and the Avantgarde', *Framework*, vol.10, Spring 1979.

Owens, Craig, 'The Discourse of Others: Feminists and Postmodernism' in Foster (ed.), *Postmodern Culture* (London and Sydney: Pluto Press, 1984).

Parker, Rozsika and Griselda Pollock, *Old Mistresses: Women, Art and Ideology* (London: Routledge, 1981).

Pollock, Griselda, 'Missing Women: Rethinking Early Thoughts on Images of Women' in Squiers (ed.), *The Critical Image: Essays on Contemporary Photography* (London: Lawrence & Wishart, 1990).

Pollock, Griselda, 'Feminist Interventions in the Histories of Art: An Introduction' and 'Vision, Voice and Power: Feminist Art Histories and Marxism', in *Vision and Difference: Femininity, Feminism and Histories of Art* (London: Routledge, 1988).

Pollock, Griselda, 'Screening the Seventies: Sexuality and Representation in Feminist Practice – a Brechtian Perspective', in *Vision and Difference: Femininity, Feminism and Histories of Art* (London: Routledge, 1988).

Pollock, Griselda, 'Art, Art School, Culture' in Bird, Curtis, Mash, Putnam, Robertson, Stafford, Tickner (eds), *The Block Reader in Visual Culture* (London: Routledge, 1996).

Porter, Gaby, 'Trade and Industry', *Ten 8 International Photography Magazine*, 35, Winter 1989/90.

Rajchman, John, 'Foucault's Art of Seeing', *October*, 44, Spring 1988, pp. 88–119.

Rose, Jacqueline, 'Sexuality in the Field of Vision' in *Sexuality in the Field of Vision* (London: Verso, 1986).

Russo, Mary, 'Female Grotesques: Carnival and Theory', in de Lauretis (ed.), *Feminist Studies/Critical Studies* (London: Macmillan, 1988).

Slater, Don, 'Domestic Photography and Digital Culture', in Lister (ed.), *The Photographic Image in Digital Culture* (London: Routledge, 1995).

Slater, Don, 'Marketing the Medium: an Anti-marketing Report' in Evans (ed.), *The Camerawork Essays* (London: Rivers Oram Press, 1997).

Solomon-Godeau, Abigail, 'Winning the Game When the Rules have been Changed: Art, Photography and Postmodernism', in *Screen*, vol. 25, no. 6, Nov–Dec 1984.

Spence, Jo, 'Beyond the Family Album', *Ten 8*, 4, Spring 1980.

Spence, Jo, *Putting Myself in the Picture* (London: Camden Press, 1986).

Spence, Jo, 'Body Talk? A Dialogue between Ros Coward and Jo Spence', in Holland, Spence, Watney (eds), *Photography/Politics Two* (London: Photography Workshop/Comedia, 1986).

Spence, Jo and Patricia Holland (eds), *Family Snaps: the Meanings of Domestic Photography* (London: Virago, 1991).

Spence, Jo, *Cultural Sniping* (London: Routledge, 1995).

Spence, Jo, 'Woman in Secret', in Spence and Stanley (eds), *What Can a Woman Do With a Camera?: Photography for Women* (London: Scarlet Press, 1995).

Watney, Simon, 'On the Institutions of Photography', in Evans and Hall (eds), *Visual Culture: The Reader* (London: Sage/Open University, 1999).

Wells, Liz, ' "Sweet It Is to Scan . . ." Personal Photographs and Popular Memory', in Wells (ed.), *Photography: a Critical Introduction* (London: Routledge, 1997).

Williams, Val, *Women Photographers: The Other Observers 1900 to the Present* (London: Virago, 1987).

Williamson, Judith, 'Images of Woman – the Photographs of Cindy Sherman', *Screen*, vol. 28, no. 2, Spring 1987.

Wolff, Janet, 'Postmodern Theory and Feminist Art Practice' in *Feminine Sentences: Essays On Women and Culture* (Cambridge: Polity Press, 1990).

Part II

Design

Hide-A-Bed Sectionals can be used for corner or wall arrangements with lamp table in between or can be put together for an extra-long sofa. In charcoal tweed. Also in green, russet, olive and old gold. $239 each.

Lawson style Hide-A-Bed $299.50 as shown in blue floral matelassé. Also in red, gold, dark green, gray and sage (see swatches below). This model as little as $239.00 in other fabrics.

Modern channel arm Hide-A-Bed in attractive metallic tweed. Choice of colors—old gold (shown above). Also available in green, brown and charcoal. $299.50 full size. $289.50 twin size.

Only Hide-A-Bed® offers the extra value of a Simmons mattress

at no extra cost!

Hide-A-Bed sofa and Beautyrest mattress made only by SIMMONS the greatest name in sleep

Remember this! The Hide-A-Bed sofa, an invention of Simmons, can be imitated . . . *but never equalled.*

No other sofa-bed offers a choice of Deepsleep* mattress . . . or famed Beautyrest* only $20 more. *Both* are longer, wider, thicker than the usual sofa-bed mattress.

Don't risk quality. Get Hide-A-Bed, the best investment for your money. Thirty styles. Many sizes and fabrics.

Only Hide-A-Bed sofa can offer you all these features !

Wide choice of colors. Model at upper left in these shades of floral matelassé. Just one of more than 100 decorator fabrics!

Longer, wider seating space than the usual sofa-bed. Choice of famous Beautyrest innerspring or foam rubber seat cushions.

Easy as opening a bureau drawer. Just as easy to close. Folds away, bedding and all, ready for another night's restful sleep.

All-steel frame. Some sofa-beds have a wood frame built only for a time. Hide-A-Bed has an all-steel frame built for a lifetime!

Easy to clean. Tilt forward and hard-to-reach places are right at hand. No pulling and tugging to clean behind the Hide-A-Bed sofa.

*Trade-Mark Reg. U. S. Patent Office. Copr. 1954 by Simmons Co., Mdse. Mart, Chicago, Ill.

Issues in feminist design

Claire Pajaczkowska

AS DESIGN IS ONE of the newer professions in visual culture and is associated with the modern movement that coincided, in many ways, with early twentieth-century feminism, it is often thought to be immune to the irrationalities of sexual and gender difference. The ideals of international modernism articulated complex strands of politics, philosophy and techniques of making. In the Bauhaus, for example, the politics of democracy, socialism and feminism were combined with a rationalist neo-classical minimalism to produce the ethics and aesthetics of the designs based on a 'truth to materials'. This early form of material practice of structuralism can be seen to have originated in the Soviet formalist design schools of the 1920s, with their even more radical combination of revolutionary communism and experimental modernism, and their pioneering feminist designers such as Popova and Stepanova, the 'Amazons' of textile, ceramic, graphic, fashion and theatre design.

So how is it that, some seventy years after these idealistic origins of modern design, contemporary practitioners find themselves working in a profession that is fraught with sexual and political contradictions inseparable from what seem to be ideologically neutral questions of style, function, materials, colour, form and innovation? There may be some specificity to the British situation that inflects it with a particular history. In the manufacturing industries of the nineteenth century, Britain's assimilation of the technological rationalism that underlies modernism took place within a fundamentally unchanged social structure. The origins of the British modern movement have been traced to 'pioneers' such as William Morris and the Arts and Crafts movement, and these present a very different tradition from the more revolutionary and collectivist tradition of European modernism. In Britain, professional designers traditionally work within either a system of industrial production or a slightly romantic individualist 'pre-industrialist' ideal such as the Arts and Crafts workshops, the Glasgow School or the Omega workshops. Individual interior designers, such as Syrie Maugham and Eileen Gray, could establish themselves, like 'signature' architects, as professional designers by working on commissions from wealthy patrons, or by virtue of a private income that underwrote their design practice. Some of the more famous woman, such as Gertrude Jekyll, whose garden design is now an integral part of Hampstead Garden Suburb and who influenced the conception and planning of other British garden cities, became designers whose work exists within the liminal space of both 'authored' and 'anonymous' design.

For women designers today, this remains a contradictory predicament. The definition of industry is now, of course, very different from the manufacturing industries of the nineteenth century, which created the prevalent idea of the designer as 'product designer', and is more likely to be based within the service industries, cyberculture, the mass media, or in advertising and merchandising. However, the options for working as a designer still depend on choosing between, or combining, professional practice in industry, or in more autonomous collective organisations, or as a self-employed freelance designer and often craftsperson, working with commissions. As many contemporary career pathways are based on sequential combination of these forms of employment, with different short-term contracts in a range of enterprises and sometimes a range of countries, there is a dynamic between the potential for innovation and tradition that each predicament offers. Similarly, for designers working within a project where there is great scope for innovation, there is a dynamic between the ratio of the 'authorship' and 'anonymity' of the innovation.

Another contradiction lies in the fact that whereas a partnership consisting exclusively of male designers – which is common among architects for example – is considered unremarkable, the all-women partnerships in graphic design and architecture described here by Teal Triggs and Sarah Chaplin seem to be pointedly political rather than equivalent to their male counterparts. Again, the irrationality that enables masculinity to be ascribed a bounded identity and autonomy, while women are ascribed an adjectival function, is evident in the contradictory way that authorship is ascribed in collaborative projects in which men and women work together. The partnership between Charles and Ray Eames, architects and furniture designers, is often reduced to simple single authorship in his name; and in the partnership between Le Corbusier and Charlotte Perriand, designs that were exclusively hers have often been wrongly attributed to his more canonical oeuvre. There is, in conventional design history, great resistance to acknowledging the significance of female creativity within design practice. Sarah Chaplin explores the relationship between the conventions of modernism in architecture and the idealisation of the masculine author of a work, and goes on to discuss the contemporary practice of a feminist architectural collective.

As Sarah Chaplin notes, the emphasis on, and even fetishisation of, authorship in the methods and concepts of conventional design history has been maintained by overlooking the significance of the reception and use of design. This is a methodological issue of interest not only to feminism, and it is currently emerging as a new area of research and interest in design practice in general, where greater curiosity is now focused on the object-user interface, and on the processes of 'consumption' through which objects are customised, recycled, possessed, endowed with personal significance, classified and otherwise 'incorporated' into daily life.

This dialectic between feminist designer as producer and as user of objects is also explored by Rebecca Arnold and Janis Jefferies who analyse the debates on gender in the fashion industry and in textile art practice. While women are anonymously placed as consumers of fashion, they are often the equally anonymous designers of their own style through home dressmaking, knitting, adapting paper patterns and customising bought clothes. In this case, the debate centres on the conventional distinction that is made between professional design and 'crafts': a hierarchical distinction in which the traditional association of textile production with female crafts has not been qualitatively changed by the industrialisation of

textile production. If crafts are defined by their basis in artisanal modes of production, this definition is overdetermined by
ideological meanings which are generated by the multiple,
contradictory and heterogeneous forms of craft practice in
contemporary culture.

Janis Jefferies discusses the history of feminist textile art,
noting how issues of women's role as employees in the textile
industry, as well as the association of crafts such as sewing,
embroidery, darning and mending textiles in the home with
'housework' and maternal labour, have been addressed and
represented by feminism. The range of forms taken by the
politics and the poetics of cloth in the work of feminist textile
artists over the last thirty years gives an account of the 'rich
tapestry' of the history of the postwar women's movement in
Britain.

Rebecca Arnold discusses the work of Miuccia Prada and the
professional practice of women as fashion designers. Because
clothing is closely associated – both literally and metaphorically – with the body and with the sense of the tactile, it is
ranked low in the hierarchy of cultural forms. If scientific
abstraction and thought occupy the higher ranks of culture,
along with the sense of vision as associated with knowledge
and distance, the bodily registers of taste and smell are associated with the lower arts of cooking, and the tactile sense with
its associative cultures of texture and textiles is not ranked
much higher. There is, of course, a gendered axis to these
associations and to the critical value and hierarchical distinctions that govern their cultural meaning. This makes the
juxtaposition of textile art and fashion design particularly
anxiogenic and apparently contradictory within conventional
design history – witness the ambivalence condensed in the use
of the name 'rag trade' for clothing industry and design, and
the slightly contemptuous classification of textile design as 'soft
furnishing'. It is also interesting that the celebration of 'weak
thought' by postmodernists seeking an alternative to the 'grand
narratives' of modernism have led philosophers to textile
metaphors for conceptualising alternative perspectival systems
such as the baroque 'folding' transformation of the Renaissance grid.

There are similar debates within the culture of ceramics. Cheryl

Buckley describes the history of women's employment within the ceramics industry, as designers and as 'paintresses', before detailing the work of two twentieth-century women designers who explored innovations in the form and decoration of industrial ceramics.

Chapter 6

Architecture

Sarah Chaplin

ARCHITECTURE FORMS A PART of visual culture that is
dominated by men and still has a predominantly masculinist
outlook producing overtly gendered practices: most practitioners
are male, and its discourse has since time immemorial been driven
by patriarchal imperatives. However, feminism has had a significant impact on architecture in this century – in terms of the
way it is both practised and theorised – and it has called into
question on many fronts the logical positivism and instrumental
rationality of the 'master builder'.

Today, as in many other fields, the practical effects of feminism
within architecture are numerous, giving women new opportunities and new means to contribute to the development of the
profession. Women now hold many positions of authority within
schools of architecture and professional institutions such as the
Royal Institute of British Architects.[1] Access for women, particularly mature women, to study architecture has been enhanced
in the UK with government-supported foundation courses, and
opportunities for part-time study have been widened to enable
those with family commitments to participate more fully in a
professional education. Research has been carried out in schools
of architecture to examine pedagogy and to determine whether or
not certain styles of studio teaching and public critique unfairly
advantage male students.[2] Recent gender-orientated architectural
conferences have opened up debates about feminism and architecture and generated fresh insights into the issue of feminist
design practice and education, revealing inherent patriarchal
ideology and dogma which had long been unchallenged.[3]

However, the real work of feminism in relation to architecture
has been in the area of history and theory, where feminist re-

evaluations of architectural discourse and, in particular, the canon of architecture have irrevocably changed the way architecture is interpreted and received. Issues of gender, sexuality, spatiality and design have generated a considerable amount of new writing, constituting what amounts to a feminist architectural discourse. This has forced a reconsideration of the relationship between the production and consumption of architecture, of traditional readings of spaces and cities, and of the ways in which architecture is legitimised, and it has also given rise to new forms of architectural practice foregrounding concerns that were previously neglected.

In this brief overview of feminism and architecture, I will explore three aspects. First, I will present a schematic historiography of the ways in which women's contributions to the production of architecture have been represented over the past 100 years, in order to contextualise the struggles of female architects to foster their own methodology and attain recognition for their efforts. In so doing, I will outline recent work by feminist architectural historians which asserts women's role and challenges historical omissions and misrepresentations. This process has been described as 'compensatory feminism' by Gerda Lerner, informed by a desire to attribute work more accurately to the authors concerned and restore women to their rightful place in history. Obviously, within this project, there is the contentious issue of authorship as a masculinist criterion for selection. Lerner has argued that what is needed instead is a women-centred analysis of history and culture, so that ultimately the discipline of history itself is not defined purely in terms of men's experience, but rather that 'All history as we now know it, is, for women, merely prehistory.'[4]

Secondly, I will look at a range of theoretical positions which have been employed to mount a feminist re-assessment of the criteria by which architecture is theorised and the way in which practice is problematised, with reference to key texts. Thirdly, I will look at the issue of language in relation to the representation and experience of architecture, and present a few proposals made by feminist architectural writers and practitioners as to how best to achieve the kind of future that they envisage for architecture.

Why have there been so few women architects?

It is difficult to construct a broad-brush overview of the changing role that women have played in architecture, not least because this necessarily involves a simultaneous reconsideration of the criteria by which architecture is judged. This therefore makes loose periodised categorisations and the naming of 'exceptional' female figures in architecture problematic at best and, at worst, meaningless. However, I offer this tentative schema as a means to demonstrate the underlying shifts in the way that women have been allowed a place in the masculinist discourse of architectural history. This is by no means a universal depiction of changing circumstance, and only applies to a European/North American context; and, even then, it is in only the most generalised terms.

Women's role in the field of architecture in the nineteenth century has been represented as relatively marginal within the classic historical accounts of the period, that give only brief details of the work of figures such as Margaret Macdonald (the wife of architect Charles Rennie Mackintosh), and other women involved in the decorative arts and the Arts and Crafts movement. In many ways, the role of the woman at this time has been depicted as that of muse, inspiring but not instigating artistic innovation. Where women did play a part in the design process, their contribution has typically been acknowledged only as producing handcrafted items which were used to decorate the interiors of the houses that their male counterparts designed.

A step forward from the representation of women designers in this ancillary role can be perceived in the commission for the Schröder House, built in 1924 and considered a landmark of early modernist design (Figure 6.1). Truus Schröder, recently widowed and keen to develop new ideas about the appropriate spatial circumstances in which to bring up a young family, engaged the services of Gerrit Rietveld, a furniture designer, to build her a house on the edge of Utrecht in the Netherlands. This shift towards a more active and participatory role in the design process transformed the historical representation of woman in architecture from muse into the role of enlightened client: Truus Schröder's ideas were directly incorporated and gave rise to an ingenious open-plan interior which is still much emulated. Among contemporary historians there has been considerable debate as to the extent of Truus Schröder's contribution to the design of the house. In a paper entitled 'Not a Muse' Alice Friedman argues that, 'The Schröder House and other houses built for women clients reveal the narrowness of conventional approaches to the history and design of domestic architecture.'[5] She draws attention to the fact that many women have contributed to the development of modern architecture through their role as clients and collaborators, and issues a charge to feminist historians and critics: 'To reveal, through research that begins with individual lives and choices, the cultural conditions in which buildings are produced, and to confront the relationships of power that structure the physical environment and produce the socio-psychological conditions in which the lives of men and women are lived.'[6]

The 1930s have also been the source of much historical reconsideration, and while traditional accounts tend to situate the woman as guru's assistant in terms of architectural design, feminist scholarship has delved into the archives to produce evidence to the contrary. Thus, whereas the work of Charlotte Perriand and Eileen Gray has been traditionally presented as inferior and subordinate to the master architect, Le Corbusier, recent research – in particular that of feminist historian Beatriz Colomina – shows that Le Corbusier was in fact envious of Gray's talents, and that he sabotaged and defamed her work through damning correspondence and vandalising murals at Gray's house at Cap Martin. Colomina methodically considers the context of Le Corbusier's involvement with Gray's work and this house in particular, documenting his erotic obsession with Algerian prostitutes as evidence of his attitude towards women, and she concludes that, 'Le Corbusier's architecture depends in some way on specific techniques of occupying yet gradually effacing the domestic space of the other.'[7]

Historical accounts of the 1940s, 1950s and 1960s reveal a growing acknowledgement of women in architectural history, under the auspices of the husband-and-wife team. The joint efforts of Ray and Charles Eames, Alison and Peter Smithson, and Robert Venturi and his wife Denise Scott Brown feature prominently during this period. Their work as double acts has been praised and canonised, and tension only emerges in architectural history when the precise nature of the wife's work, as

Figure 6.1 Gerrit Rietveld, Schröder House, Utrecht. *Photograph by Sarah Chaplin.*

distinct from her husband's is defined. Scott Brown has been the most vocal among this group in speaking out about the problems of misattribution in connection with her work. Venturi and Scott Brown's office even invented a system of issuing information sheets on each project, detailing the contribution of different members of staff, but this did not prevent their critics from lumping all their work together under Venturi's name. Interestingly, Scott Brown comments, 'Although I had been concerned with my role as a woman years before the birth of the [women's] movement, I was not pushed to action until my experience as an architect's wife.'[8] Writing at the end of the 1980s, she admits somewhat wryly, 'To the extent that gurus are unavoidable and sexism is rampant in the architecture star system, my personal problem of submersion through the star system is insoluble. I could improve my chances of recognition if I returned to teaching or if I abandoned collaboration with my husband.'[9]

The 1970s saw the emergence of all-women practices, steeped in post-1968 feminist philosophy and a commitment to forms of practice that were political and empowering, not just for women but for other minority constituencies. Not surprisingly, this revolutionary period in women's contribution to architectural production and the reshaping of cities has received little attention within standard architectural histories. Media treatment at the time made the work of organisations like Matrix and the Women's Design Co-operative seem too extreme in its approach to furthering the cause of women's liberation. Furthermore, the effect of deliberately effacing the single architect-author by means of these organisations' generic names meant that critics and historians alike could not pin the work onto the master individual, rendering their own historical methodologies ineffectual. In 1984, Matrix published their views on architecture in *Making Space: Women and the Manmade Environment*, a book which attempted to change standard approaches to domestic and urban design issues.

The conservative Thatcher-Reagan era brought another kind of empowerment to a generation of female architects in Britain and North America, and the 1980s can justifiably be identified as the period when female superstars emerged in the field of architecture. Zaha Hadid gained notoriety through teaching a studio at the Architectural Association in London and through high-profile competition entries, which showed an allegiance to the forms and aesthetics of Russian constructivism, even if they lacked its revolutionary political intent. It was work male critics could approve of, and Hadid had a fierce personal reputation for which she was also held in esteem by male counterparts. In Japan, Itsuko Hasegawa was the first woman architect to be taken seriously by the establishment, and worked on several substantial commissions that attracted media attention worldwide. Both women now receive top billing at architectural events around the world, but it is difficult to see this without a hint of tokenism: their popularity is not entirely a ringing endorsement of the women's talents as designers, but is more an indication of what the profession currently deems creative and fashionable.

While the 'star system' has given some women the opportunity to gain public recognition for their work, it is a myopic patriarchal system of approval which neglects to value the real contribution of architects to society. Reacting to this situation, the 1990s witnessed the emergence of many 'enigmatic' post-feminist practices, particularly in the UK, which are critical of the complacency of the architectural profession, the construction industry, and architectural education, and are capable of manipulating the media to put across a more polemical position. One example of this type of practice is developed as a case study at the end of this chapter, where it can be seen that co-operative MUF is more interested in challenging and subverting the status quo than signing up to its definition of success.

Blurring the binaries

Much of the historical and theoretical work in terms of a feminist approach to rethinking architecture has been informed by Marxism, psychoanalysis, semiotics and deconstruction, although feminism has in fact been critical of all these approaches. Marxist theory offered scope for considering the implicit relationship between architecture and property, and the ways in which the architect is complicit with a capitalist, patriarchal structuring of society. Marxism also made visible the way in which architectural discourse had become naturalised as inherently masculine. The relationship between systems and spaces of production and reproduction also became apparent in the separation of the domestic sphere from places associated with work, prompting a re-evaluation of town planning and a move towards more integrated policies. Publications such as Jane Jacobs' *The Life and Death of Great American Cities* issued a strong polemic to city planners of the day, whose allegiance to a functionally segregated urban realm kept apart the spaces of production and reproduction and generated landscapes of fear, incarceration, and disillusionment for large numbers of women. Jacobs argued for mixed communities, orientated around streets where pedestrians and activity at street level could bring neighbourhoods to life.

In the domestic sphere, feminists have also turned their attention to the early twentieth century when the woman's realm suffered a male invasion in order to rationalise and scientise its working processes. The kitchen formed a particular focus for this activity, where industrial systems of production invented by men were imposed so as to improve efficiency within the home, thereby applying capitalist principles of managing time and enhancing productivity. Feminists have shown, however, that the time-saving devices that were introduced invariably created more work and served to undermine a woman's control over central aspects of her life.[10]

Psychoanalysis has brought new insights to feminist architectural discourse and generated a considerable body of work which relates quite closely to film theory. Chief among these is the notion of the gaze, which, as Laura Mulvey has shown in her work on narrative cinema, is constructed as masculine. This is no different in architecture, in that the gaze of the designer purports to be objective and distanced, and whereby pleasure in the architecture is to be derived from the act of looking from a masculinist perspective. As Jos Boys has stated, 'The knowledge base of architecture perceives the world through the limited frame of masculinist rationality, a way of seeing which assumes the architect as objective observer and the building as the transparent expression of that gaze.'[11] The architectural object of this gaze is frequently shown to be female and is moreover fetishised, in that it is decontextualised and heightened by the conventions of architectural representation and by the isolating gaze of critical appraisal.[12] Furthermore, psychoanalysis has been engaged to explain the phallocentrism of classical architectural forms, and to answer the charge of 'effeminate' in architectural terms, interpreted within feminist writings as a form of deviance and perversion in relation to what is considered architecturally acceptable.[13]

Psychoanalytic scholarship has also examined the tendency among late nineteenth-century/early twentieth-century historians to classify architecture according to whether or not it displayed masculine or feminine characteristics and to choose a suitable 'gender' for a particular building typology. The work of Louis Sullivan seems to be ambiguously valorised in this respect: regarded as the most pre-eminently masculine work of its time, in retrospect his embroidered surfaces seem to betray his sexuality.[14] Psychoanalysis has also enabled a detailed questioning within feminist writings of the tendency to accommodate and differentiate the sexes spatially, and this had led to a re-examination of many architectural exemplars, such as the Farnsworth House by Mies van der Rohe, the Glass House at New Canaan by Philip Johnson,[15] and the Josephine Baker House by Adolf Loos,[16] all of which were designed for wealthy single women. All three designs have been shown to construct domestic space as an exaggerated outcome of a masculine gaze, voyeuristically witnessing the presence of these women as they occupy their houses.

In terms of deconstruction and feminism, the work of philosophers such as Gayatri Chakravorti Spivak and Elizabeth Grosz has been influential, prompting a radical reconsideration of the domestic, the decorative, the everyday, the between, and the excluded, as well as opening up a range of debates around the spacing of ethnicity and alterity. As far as architectural discourse is concerned, the key binary pairs to have been deconstructed are: architecture/building; architecture/the everyday; public/private; art/craft; eye/body; form/surface; and word/image. Karen Burns has discussed the opposition between architecture and building as the gap between sameness and difference, describing the building as 'the naive other that does not know what it means or does.'[17] Mary McLeod counterposes the avant-garde in architecture with the neglected realm of the everyday, which has more to offer the designer by way of radical new ideas than the notion of abstraction or newness for its own sake.[18] Jane Rendell has argued that the paradigm of 'separate spheres', which keeps public and private apart needs to be challenged, and she sets up a feminist/ Marxist/deconstructionist methodology that establishes new meaning for the marginal of the pair, rendering it beyond binary distinctions.[19] Sherry Ahrentzen suggests that the sanctity of the designer-guru can only be overcome if architecture is promoted as a craft rather than an art.[20] Deborah Fausch argues that to overthrow the dominance of the male gaze requires that the importance of the body, in terms of understanding and conceiving of architectural form, is asserted.[21] Catherine Ingraham invokes Derrida and talks about the image and the word, equating women and writing in relation to architecture: 'women, like writing, are in an always already fallen position with respect to architecture'.[22] Andrea Kahn employs a mix of psychoanalysis and deconstruction to articulate a position which shows how the building site is traditionally configured as a lack, and that conventional site analysis treats this lack as something to be overcome, to be marked, where the site is feminine, awaiting colonisation. Kahn proposes that site analysis is a pseudo-rational, pseudo-scientific myth, and should be replaced by 'site construction': that is, rather than treating the site as a blank sheet awaiting the genius of the individual architect to be visited upon it, site construction would instead take up existing cues presented by the site, and work with it in a more provisional and responsive manner.[23]

In search of a feminist language of architectural representation, Kahn's approach is indicative of a shift within architectural practice towards 'contextual feminism', and the application of gender-sensitive ways of designing and working with the built environment. Feminist writers have shown the possibilities for new ways of using language to go beyond the essentialism which hampers feminist architectural discourse, and to begin the next phase which is to allow for and account for difference.[24] In architecture, language necessarily takes many forms, and is not simply text-orientated. It is about the language of built form, which needs to determine new definitions of pleasure that are not gendered and do not revolve around the gaze. It is about the language of architectural drawings, which needs to discover other means beyond the masculinist strictures of orthography to represent design intentions, or what Ingraham calls the 'burdens of linearity'.[25] It is about the language of architectural education, which needs to embody a richer, more gender-neutral set of values in order to foster a different kind of creativity, wherein projects are 'mothered' over a longer period of gestation rather than 'fathered' or conceived in a single act of creative procreation.[26] It is about the language of public critique, where there is a Deleuzian libidinal economy at work which values the process of reaching different plateaux in design, in contrast to the prevailing emphasis on the orgasmic end-product, or what Akis Didaskalou has called the ejaculatory mode of the design masterclass.[27] It is about a renewed sensitivity to the language of materials, which can provide us with a rich tactile environment that goes beyond the experience of the visual, and sustains the earth's resources rather than exhausts them.[28] Finally, it is about paying attention to the language of the user, who through her speech acts, appropriates and assigns unanticipated meaning to the lived spaces of everyday life, even finding ways – tactics – through her occupation of space to resist the strategies of hegemonic power and the imposition of heterosexual authority as articulated in the built environment.[29] Architects are often unfamiliar with these other languages – metaphorical, physical or otherwise – and are more concerned to invent private, elitist languages of their own, which only their (masculine) peers can appreciate.

Nevertheless, there is evidence to suggest that inclusive, hybrid, contingent models of architectural practice are being adopted. This has often been interpreted by male architectural critics as some sort of postmodern crisis within architecture, a loss of direction, or a sign of the growing emasculation of the architect at the end of the twentieth century.[30] Even so, the closed exclusivity of the profession is starting to give way to a new kind of creative network of loose affiliations and interdisciplinary working. Monologue is slowly being replaced by dialogue,[31] in the form of exhibitions, debates, documentaries and a general open-door policy, as the success and popularity of recent events and new institutional contexts in Britain have shown: Open House, City of Architecture, Architecture Centres, the Architecture Foundation, *Building Sites*, the *Late Show* and so on. In this respect, feminism's greatest contribution is to bring about an increased understanding of the consumption and consumers of architecture, where before only its production and producers seemed to count.

Despite ongoing problems such as the day-to-day problems of balancing part-time working and childcare, dealing with a culture of obligatory unpaid overtime, and confronting the elements of sexism that still remain within the profession, female architects today find themselves in a powerful liminal position, according to Francesca Hughes, in that they are both insiders and outsiders: 'It is precisely this diversity, this ability to be central and marginal simultaneously that will allow women to expand the territory of architecture.'[32] If women architects can find ways of benefiting from this position – not merely personally (this would only amount to an achievement for 'corporate feminism') but also from the point of view of opening up the political debate about the future role of architecture – then feminism's project to effect change can be realised.

Jos Boys has written at length on the subject of rethinking the relationships between architecture and gender, and proposes a series of 'alternative disruptions' to the masculinist model of architectural knowledge, which include: a refusal to conceptualise architecture as the mirror of society; the adoption of a more neutral gaze which does not profess to sustain its own moral high ground, proper language or universal truth; a refusal to attach fixed categories of meaning to architectural ideas; an acceptance of architecture as a deep social process which needs to re-engage with contemporary issues such as free market, ethics and professional roles; and a basic commitment on the part of architects to be explicit about their approach and more attentive to economic and political processes affecting built form.[33]

Case study: MUF

Figure 6.2 Katherine Clarke and Cathy Hawley, MUF design group. Proposal for Pleasure Garden of Utilities, *Hanley, Stoke-on-Trent.*

Jos Boys' aspirations for feminist design practice to be a deep social process may be seen to operate in the work of MUF, which, as one article put it 'stands for Modern Urban Fabric, Militant Urban Feminists, or something a shade saucier, depending which rumour you believe.'[34] MUF is an all-female group of designers and artists which has over the past few years worked on a wide range of interdisciplinary projects including films, parks, events, exhibitions, small interiors, and large-scale urban regeneration schemes (Figure 6.2). They quip that at client meetings they take along a token man,

who does not say anything, like a crash test dummy. This attitude has not endeared MUF to some sections of the establishment, and belies the gentle rigour of their innovative approach which involves extensive on-the-ground research and listening to local people before embarking upon any design ideas. This socially and culturally grounded methodology has won the support of local authorities and government ministers alike, but MUF were recently sacked from their role as one of the designers for the New Millennium Experience, because their idiosyncratic design process was not seen to produce anything their clients deemed 'stunning'. This entrenched position in the establishment with regard to the importance of maintaining a strong visual impact in projects like the Dome is hardly likely to steer MUF away from their way of working: it serves to strengthen their commitment to a process which radically reframes notions of 'good' design, and actively celebrates plurality and diversity. It remains to be seen how the work of MUF and other similar practices will be presented and contextualised historically, and to what extent it furthers the underlying ambitions of the women's movement.

Notes

1. For example, the posts of RIBA Director of Education, RIBA Director of Architecture Centre, Head of UNL School of Architecture, and Head of Brighton University School of Architecture, are all posts currently held by women. Latest figures show that 9 per cent of registered architects in the UK are women.
2. Akis Didaskalou, 'Making Love/Making Architecture', in McCorquodale, Rüedi, Wigglesworth (eds), *Desiring Practices*, pp. 116–31.
3. For example, 'Desiring Practices' symposium, RIBA, autumn 1995.
4. Gerda Lerner, extract from 'The Majority Finds Its Past', reprinted in Humm (ed.), *Feminisms: A Reader*, p. 330.
5. Alice Friedman, 'Not a Muse: the Client's Role at the Rietveld Schröder House', in Agrest, Conway, Weisman (eds), *The Sex of Architecture*, p. 229.
6. Ibid. p. 230.
7. Beatriz Colomina, 'Battle Lines: E 1027', in Hughes (ed.), *Reconstructing Her Practice*, p. 22.

8. Denise Scott Brown, 'Room at the Top? Sexism and the Star System in Architecture', in Berkeley, McQuaid (eds), *Architecture – A Place for Women*, p. 240.
9. Ibid. p. 243.
10. See Susan Henderson, 'A Revolution in the Women's Sphere: Grete Lihotsky and the Frankfurt Kitchen', in Coleman, Danze, Henderson (eds), *Feminism and Architecture*, pp. 221–53.
11. Jos Boys, 'Neutral Gazes and Knowable Objects', in McCorquodale, Rüedi, Wigglesworth (eds), *Desiring Practices*, p. 34.
12. Francesca Hughes has commented that, 'Casting architecture as feminine renders its muse female and consequently induces a necessary crisis of identity for the female architecture maker' in Hughes (ed.), *Reconstructing Her Practice*, p. xi.
13. See Adrian Forty, 'Masculine, Feminine, Neuter?', in McCorquodale, Rüedi, Wigglesworth (eds), *Desiring Practices*, pp. 140–55.
14. For other work on Louis Sullivan, see Clare Cardinal-Pett, 'Detailing', in McCorquodale, Rüedi, Wigglesworth (eds), *Desiring Practices*, pp. 88–105.
15. See Christine S. E. Magar, 'Project Manual for the Glass House', in Coleman, Danze and Henderson (eds), *Feminism and Architecture*, pp. 72– 108.
16. See Beatriz Colomina, 'The Split Wall: Domestic Voyeurism', in *Sexuality and Space*, pp. 73–130.
17. Karen Burns, 'Architectural Discipline/Bondage', in McCorquodale, Rüedi, Wigglesworth (eds), *Desiring Practices*, p. 77.
18. See Mary McLeod, 'Other Spaces and Others', in Agrest, Conway, Weisman (eds), *The Sex of Architecture*, pp. 15–28.
19. See Jane Rendell, 'Subjective Space, a Feminist Architectural History of the Burlington Arcade', in McCorquodale, Rüedi, Wigglesworth (eds), *Desiring Practices*, pp. 216–33.
20. Sherry Ahrentzen, 'The F Word in Architecture: Feminist Analyses in/of/for Architecture', in Dutton, Mann (eds), *Reconstructing Architecture*, p. 72.
21. See Deborah Fausch, 'The Knowledge of the Body and the Presence of the Body – Toward a Feminist Architecture', in Coleman, Danze, Henderson (eds), *Feminism and Architecture*, pp. 38–59.
22. Catherine Ingraham, 'Losing IT in Architecture', in Hughes (ed.), *Reconstructing Her Practice*, p. 157.
23. See Andrea Kahn, 'Overlooking', in McCorquodale, Rüedi, Wigglesworth (eds), *Desiring Practices*, pp. 174–85.

24. See writings by Luce Irigaray and Hélène Cixous. Deborah
    Fausch makes a case for essentialism as a tool to think with
    for feminism, in Coleman, Danze, Henderson (eds), *Femin-
    ism and Architecture*, p. 39.
25. See Catherine Ingraham, 'The Burdens of Linearity', in
    Whiteman, Kipnis, Burdett (eds), *Strategies in Architectural
    Thinking*, pp. 130–47.
26. See Judi Farren Bradley, 'Architecture and Obstetrics: Build-
    ings as Babies', in McCorquodale, Rüedi, Wigglesworth
    (eds), *Desiring Practices*, pp. 46–59.
27. See Akis Didaskalou, 'Making Love/Making Architecture',
    in McCorquodale, Rüedi, Wigglesworth (eds), *Desiring
    Practices*, pp. 115–31.
28. See Brenda Vale, 'Gender and an Architecture of Environ-
    mental Responsibility', in McCorquodale, Rüedi, Wiggles-
    worth (eds), *Desiring Practices*, pp. 264–73.
29. See Nancy Duncan (ed.), *Bodyspace* for essays on the queer-
    ing of public space.
30. Katerina Rüedi, 'The Architect: Commodity and Seller in
    one', in McCorquodale, Rüedi, Wigglesworth (eds), *Desiring
    Practices*, p. 239.
31. Sherry Ahrentzen describes architectural discourse as really a
    monologue; see 'The F Word in Architecture', in Dutton,
    Mann (eds), *Reconstructing Architecture*, p. 76.
32. Hughes (ed.), *Reconstructing Her Practice*, p. xv.
33. Jos Boys, 'Beyond Maps and Metaphors: Rethinking the
    Relationships between Architecture and Gender', in Ainley
    (ed.), *New Frontiers of Body, Space and Gender,* pp. 203–17.
34. Andy Beckett, 'You Can Be Too Cool', *The Guardian,* 6
    February 1999.

Bibliography

Agrest, Diana, Patricia Conway, Leslie Kanes Weisman (eds), *The
Sex of Architecture* (New York: Harry Abrams, 1996).
Ainley, Rosa (ed.), *New Frontiers of Body, Space and Gender*
(London: Routledge, 1998).
Berkeley, Ellen Perry, Matilda McQuaid (eds), *Architecture – A
Place for Women* (Washington, DC: Smithsonian Institution
Press, 1989).
Coleman, Debra, Elizabeth Danze, Carol Henderson (eds), *Fem-
inism and Architecture* (New York: Princeton Architectural
Press, 1996).

Colomina, Beatriz (ed.), *Sexuality and Space* (New York: Princeton Architectural Press, 1992).

Duncan, Nancy (ed.), *Bodyspace: Destabilising Geographies of Gender and Sexuality* (London: Routledge, 1996).

Dutton, Thomas, Lian Hurst Mann (eds), *Reconstructing Architecture: Critical Discourses and Social Practices* (Minneapolis: University of Minnesota Press, 1996).

Fausch, Deborah , Paulette Singley, Rodolphe EI-Khoury, Zvi Efrat (eds), *Architecture in Fashion* (New York: Princeton Architectural Press, 1994).

Grosz, Elizabeth, *Space, Time and Perversion* (London: Routledge, 1995).

Hughes, Francesca (ed.), *Reconstructing Her Practice* (Cambridge, MA: MIT, 1996).

Humm, Maggie (ed.), *Feminisms: A Reader* (London: Harvester Wheatsheaf, 1992).

Jacobs, Jane, *The Life and Death of Great American Cities* (New York: Random House, 1961).

Lorenz, Clare, *Women in Architecture* (London: Trefoil Publications Ltd, 1990).

Matrix, *Making Space: Women and the Manmade Environment* (London: Pluto Press, 1984).

McCorquodale, Duncan, Katerina Rüedi, Sarah Wigglesworth (eds). *Desiring Practices: Architecture. Gender and the Interdisciplinary* (London: Black Dog Publishing, 1996).

Mulvey, Laura, 'Visual Pleasure and Narrative Cinema', *Screen* 16:3:1975.

Spivak, Gayatri Chakravorti, 'Who Claims Alterity?', *Remaking History* (Seattle: DIA Art Foundation Discussions in Contemporary Culture, No. 4, 1989).

Torre, Susan (ed.), *Women in Architecture* (New York: Whitney Library of Design, 1977).

Whiteman, John, Jeffrey Kipnis, Richard Burdett (eds), *Strategies in Architectural Thinking* (Cambridge, MA: MIT, 1992).

Chapter 7

Graphic design

Teal Triggs

GRAPHIC DESIGN IS ALL around us; it is an inherent part of the contemporary visual landscape. We are constantly bombarded with information that demands our attention as we walk down the street encountering billboards, posters and timetables at bus shelters; as we read magazines and newspapers; or as we sit in front of the television or surf the Internet. Both men and women who work in the field of graphic design have played an important role in defining this visual culture, yet throughout the history of graphic design, the contributions made by women have remained essentially invisible. As one maps women's contributions from the early days of book and job printing to the present, it becomes increasingly apparent that women have often been omitted from the history books. Whether or not unwittingly, this process has presented an unrepresentative and distorted notion of women's contributions to the design profession. The aim of this chapter is to make explicit the particular problems of writing the history of graphic design. At the same time, I will raise certain questions in order to prompt consideration of how a framework of inquiry might be established to readdress this present imbalance. Central to this discussion is an investigation of the ways in which feminist theory might be employed to help to redefine and integrate a 'women's history' within graphic design. I will also present a case study of the Women's Design Research Unit (WD+RU), which indicates how criticism and practice can be combined.

Profiling women

'The design activity stands between us and our material existence, affecting not only our visual and physical environment but a sense of ourselves as well.'[1]

'As women start to enter the canons of art history, hopefully we won't enter them the same way the guys have.'[2]

'The initial task of feminist art history is therefore a critique of art history itself.'[3]

When I first started working as a graphic designer in the late 1970s, only a handful of women had been recognised for their achievements within the profession. For the most part, those found at the forefront were often identified with American-based design studios or were established as educators within academic institutions. Within the last twenty years, however, the number of women working in design has increased dramatically. I know of many more colleagues and design bodies that are ready to readdress gender issues within the profession. It is apparent that more conference organisers are asking female designers to participate, and that more women have been elected as officers of professional design groups and councils.[4] At the same time, the international design press has increased its coverage of women graphic designers.

But despite such indicators, women are still underrepresented in the industry. This is particularly true of women working in Britain, where a recent report compiled by the Institute of Practitioners in Advertising (IPA) indicated that out of 1,074 art directors working in Britain, only 158 are listed as being women. Even more disturbing is the indication that most key positions of power in advertising agencies are held by men: the report statistics showed that under the category of 'Agency Management', for example, 422 men were employed as opposed to 114 women.[5]

In addition, women in design still face obstacles caused by the 'glass ceiling', unequal pay, inadequate childcare, stereotypical representations, and prejudice within the workplace.[6] The situation in the USA, on the other hand, seems slightly better, and the American Institute of Graphic Arts survey in 1990 indicated that more female designers were entering the profession.[7] What the report failed to demonstrate, however, was that despite this increase, women were still unable to find a 'collective voice'. The design writer Moira Cullen has suggested that a 'parallel industry of accessible talent' has emerged with women working at home as freelancers or running businesses as sole proprietors. As a result, change has been slow in coming. Cullen suggests that 'there are two different measurements: one a passive statistic of what is, the other an active assertion of will'.[8] Today, a traditional imbalance of power remains where for women, 'majority . . . is no guarantee of influence'.[9]

At the same time as patriarchy assigns women their status, value and roles within the design profession, its written history reflects the process. Michael Rock and Susan Sellers have remarked that, 'While most design history and criticism claims to be non-ideological and value-neutral, it is in fact that design has been controlled and produced by men'.[10] In 1992, Bridget Wilkins pleaded for 'no more heroes' in graphic design history writing, criticising the idea of singling out individuals, which merely tends to emphasise the 'designer not as a communicator but as a personality'.[11] Unfortunately, only a few design historians have taken note, reinforcing an 'askewed patriarchal Who's Who of graphic design'.[12]

The fact that women are all too frequently relegated to the margins of graphic design history is compounded by the general lack of published 'critical biographies' in graphic design.[13] There are a number of books on the work and careers of male typographers and graphic designers, including biographies about the contributions of Paul Rand, Paul Renner and Lester Beall. Monographs form another category displaying the work of, for example, Neville Brody and David Carson, as do the self-promotional studio publications of Fuel and Tomato. While these designers have played important roles in design practice and in design education, critics and publishers have failed to recognise women designers who have made equal contributions to the development of the profession. Critical accounts of the work and contributions of women designers, writers and educators such as Beatrice Warde, Marie Neurath, Bea Feitler, Muriel

Cooper, Elaine Lustig Cohen, Sheila Levrant de Bretteville or Katherine McCoy might give us further insight into the profession and its working practices. With this in mind, the historian Martha Scotford called for a review of Roger Remington and Barbara Hodik's biographical account of *The Nine Pioneers of American Graphic Design*. In light of the fact that the book only contains the work and biographies of selected male 'pioneers', Scotford laments the omission of the late *Mademoiselle* and *Glamour* art director Cipe Pineles. By measuring Pineles' work against the criteria by which Remington and Hodik included the other nine, Scotford is able to demonstrate that Pineles' work earns her a place as the 'tenth pioneer'.[14]

However, Nanette Salomon cautions that the use of women's biography 'underscores the idea that she is an exception; they apply only to her and make her an interesting individual case'.[15] This reinforces the notion of biography as a form of marginalisation in which a spurious history is promoted, and this is where history becomes problematic. There is a danger that female designers are no longer integrated into an overall picture of design history but rather separated out and glorified as individual, special cases. The reverse is also true: presentation of positive role models may help to break down gender stereotypes and, in doing so, help to establish a more productive, discursive space.

In either case, in order to locate women within a changing visual landscape and establish their impact upon it, we need to question the way in which historical knowledge is produced.[16] Graphic design is comprised of a set of complex and culturally diverse relationships which necessitate an understanding of audience, sociopolitical contexts and communicative processes. Graphic designers mediate between these relationships and, in doing so, become part of the process that shapes tastes and perceptions. Graphic design can no longer rely on a discourse that merely emphasises aesthetics. It is imperative that any analysis of graphic design should endeavour to develop a clearer understanding of communication and its social significance.[17]

For example, for some female artists and designers, the motivation for creating visual artefacts often comes from the need to share concerns about a variety of issues such as health or sexual politics, or to generate a discourse or comment upon broader social, economic and political issues as they relate to women's experiences. Suzanne Lacey, a past member of the Feminist Studio Workshop at the Woman's Building in Los Angeles, reflects that 'private experience could be revealed through art [design] in order to influence cultural attitudes and transform stereotypes'.[18] The 1970s feminists' view the 'personal is political' formed the basis for much of the early political work produced by female graphic designers. While some of the messages were overtly political in nature, other works sought to extend the feminist discourse into the public arena. In the process, as Veronique Vienne has suggested, 'graphic communication represents a chance to develop a powerful voice without having to speak up in public'.[19] In keeping with the practices of graphic communication, feminist designers share a concern for the audience – particularly in terms of issues of effectiveness and evaluation, and 'an understanding of how to reach it'.[20]

Sheila Levrant de Bretteville, Barbara Kruger, Laurie Haycock Makela, and the Women's Action Coalition (WAC) are examples of designers who have used their skills as visual communicators to raise awareness about issues that concern themselves as well as other women. Much of their work has been viewed in public spaces in the form of community-based projects, fly poster or placard campaigns, or in art galleries. These spaces have provided opportunities for designers to work collaboratively, and to re-examine personal experiences while at the same time reinforcing feminist notions of social interactivity. Here, graphic design is a collaborative process that uses multifarious juxtapositions of images and texts to address, persuade, and inform its target audience, and depends upon an understanding of cultural codes and visual languages.

A critique of women in graphic design becomes a critique of graphic design itself. Steve Baker proposes, in his analysis of graphic design criticism, that through an acknowledgement of sexual differences, history might be opened up 'rhetorically' to a 'more inquiring attitude'.[21] New spaces are made discernible (for example, the domestic sphere) and acknowledged as being of equal importance to the understanding of a women's history. Moreover, the graphic design historian should be able 'to reconsider an understanding of the most fundamental ordering of social reactions, institutions and power arrangements within the society we study'.[22] Any historical narrative of graphic design must include an understanding of how women have been positioned within the institutional or patriarchal frameworks of design: it must not only 'restore' women to the annals of history but also recognise that, in the process of documentation, specific attention must be paid to the role of gender.[23] It must also take into account how the female experience in design is measured within these parameters.

(Re)reading history

'Compared with other areas of design, graphic design has been given the short shrift by historians.'[24]

Only recently have there been significant contributions to graphic design criticism that acknowledge a feminist perspective. Despite the fact that they have been overshadowed, it is worth highlighting their basic themes. While patriarchy is problematic as a defining set of ideas, it may be argued that a study of its structure has presented feminist historians with a starting-point for an examination of women's roles.[25] This is made evident in the writings of art historians including Griselda Pollock, Lisa Tickner, and Lucy Lippard. While raising awareness of women artists, their writings have equally questioned the nature of how history is written within their discipline. As Pollock has commented: 'Demanding that women be considered not only changes what is studied and what becomes relevant to investigate but it challenges the existing disciplines politically'.[26] Much of this work has grown out of early feminist writings on the history of women artists, including Linda Nochlin's seminal 1971 article 'Why Have There Been No Great Women Artists?'[27] Nochlin observed that in order to reveal any 'biases and inadequacies', a 'catalyst' was required to question basic assumptions of the discipline of art history. Her response was to employ a 'feminist critique'[28] suggesting that this would allow for more than just raising women to higher levels by using their 'criteria of greatness'.[29]

Nochlin's influence is evident in design history, most notably in the work of Cheryl Buckley and Judy Attfield. While Attfield proposes that 'feminism is a political position which seeks changes in the interest of women', it is Buckley's work which is of greater significance to us here, in particular her article 'Made in Patriarchy: Toward a Feminist Analysis of Women and Design'.[30] Here, Buckley writes that feminist theory seeks to understand 'patriarchy and the construction of the feminine'.[31] Traditional art and design histories are often written as linear narratives, highlighting events chronologically through the work of individuals or stylistic movements. Feminist history challenges the 'centrality of the individual as agents of history and the focus on professional structures and modes of activity'.[32] It is this aspect that is most pertinent to any study of graphic design whose history has been written with modernism's often dogmatic viewpoint in mind, resulting in the absorption into history of a single (male) voice of authority. Martha Scotford concurs and calls for a similar feminist approach to be considered for writing about graphic design history. In Scotford's essay, 'Messy History vs. Neat History: Toward an Expanded View of Women in Graphic Design', she explores the reasons behind existing imbalances of male and female representation in design writing. According to Scotford, one reason for this might be the difficult task of breaking down perceptions of women and their roles within public and private spheres. Like Buckley,[33] Scotford demonstrates that certain design roles held by women have been constructed through the context of patriarchy and its corollary value systems. For example, woman have always had less access to vocational or technically-orientated work such as typesetting and printing because these were occupations considered to be 'physically strenuous' and, as a result, 'unsuitable' for women.[34]

In order to better understand the conditions in which women have been (de)valued, Scotford proposes an analytical model that questions conventional history and history writing. Her intent is to create a typology of women in graphic design by which historians may be better able to 'conceptualize the inclusion and significance of women'.[35] Scotford defines women's involvement in graphic design by categories which broadly include women practitioners, women in education, women as critics, historians and theoreticians. Her subtypes encompass independent designers and studio owners, employees and workers, as well as collaborations that occur between design partners or spouses. While assembling a typology is one valid method of analysing women in graphic design, the historian must be aware of the potential problems of analysis: women can become 'fixed' within these categories which are constructed and defined by specific moments in time.[36] Yet, Scotford's approach is worthy of consideration as an alternative model for the study of design and one which attempts to revalue women's experience.

(Re)claiming territory

To date, the literature concerning women's professional roles and their contributions to the development of graphic design has been sparse, and even fewer books have made some attempt at contextualising these experiences. Ellen Mazur Thomson, for example, is one historian who explores the conditions which promoted sexual divisions of labour in the printing industry and graphic arts at the turn of the century. In her book, entitled *The Origins of Graphic Design in America 1870–1920*, Thomson devotes an entire chapter to how women participated in the early developments of the American graphic design profession as printers, typesetters, book designers and advertising artists, and through her re-assessment of historical documentation, brings into graphic design history an account of female contributions. Equally relevant is Pat Kirkham's book, *Charles and Ray Eames: Designers of the Twentieth Century*. This book and other articles on the Eames are significant in that they highlight the importance of collaboration, as well as signalling problems of attribution, between this husband and wife team. While the Eames' American studio is probably best known for its innovation in furniture design, they also completed a plethora of work for film, exhibitions, catalogues and multi-screen, all of which have been an important source of inspiration for many graphic designers.

Isabella Anscombe's *A Woman's Touch: Women in Design from 1860 to Present Day*, published in 1984, was one of the first books to claim attribution for those women working within the professional arena, and it was followed by Liz McQuiston's book *Women in Design: A Contemporary View* (1988). Both Anscombe and McQuiston have been criticised by feminist historians, such as Cheryl Buckley and Susana Torre, for adopting a 'women-designer' biographical approach. Despite this criticism, it may be argued that both writers brought forward the names of many women who have made significant contributions to the crafts, design and architectural professions. More recently, McQuiston has gone on to develop and contextualise women's roles in graphic design through the documentation of political activity in the form of posters. In *From Suffragettes to She-Devils: Women's Liberation and Beyond*, she investigates the visual language of graphic expression found in the work prompted by various moments in the history of the women's struggle.

However, other books on design, such as *Essays on Design 1: AGI's Designers of Influence* published by the international graphic design organisation Alliance Graphique International (AGI), tend to reflect the inherent problems of gender imbalance within the profession: out of the 240 elected members of the AGI, forty-six designers have writings reprinted in the collection, and out of those forty-six, only three are women. Ironically, one of those three is Paula Scher, a partner in Pentagram Design in New York, who takes issue with the adoption of a feminist stance. She laments in her essay 'The Boat' that she has 'ambiguous feelings about women's issues in relationship to design'.[37] But it is in this reprinted exchange of letters with Julie Lasky, managing editor of *Print* magazine, that she voices concerns shared by many women designers at the top of their field: although there is an increase in the presence of women as speakers at conferences, judges for design competitions, or as subjects for magazine interviews, these places are often filled by the same small group of 'notables'. Scher also proposes that, in her experience, women are frequently invited not on the basis of their achievements as designers but through 'tokenism'.

In general, any substantial work applying a feminist critique of graphic design is in the form of articles published in specialist journals and magazines such as *Visible Language*, *Zed*, *Eye*, and *Emigre*. For example, 'Underground Matriarchy', a fax dialogue between Laurie Haycock Makela and Ellen Lupton, first appeared in *Eye* magazine in 1994. This short piece is important in that it defines the current roles of American women in design and argues for a canon of matriarchs that is not 'a closed set but an open one'.[38] Likewise, Janet Fairbairn presents an extract from an independent project at Yale University in 'The Gendered Self', in which she canvassed the opinions of women and asked them how design, cultural traditions, education, and the feminist movement influenced their work. In the piece, she concludes that the 'question of gender difference challenges us [women designers] to think about our lives in ways we may not have considered'.[39]

One woman who appeared as part of Fairbairn's study was the graphic designer Sheila Levrant de Bretteville, whose own work as a feminist and practitioner has successfully crossed the boundaries between theory and practice, between community art and graphic design. De Bretteville's early 1973 essay 'Some Aspects of Design from the Perspective of a Woman Designer', published in Icographic 6, is a particularly significant contribution to this field. By providing personal insights into her own community-based work, de Bretteville outlines how feminist theory may be applied to graphic design. She discusses, for example, her designs for a special issue of Everywoman, an American feminist newspaper, and describes how she integrated her interests in feminism into a design which visually created a structure encouraging 'participating, non-hierarchical, non-authoritarian relationships'.[40] Many of these ideas about design were taken forward by de Bretteville in her teaching at the Women's Design Program at the California Institute of the Arts in the early 1970s. The aims of the programme were also published in Icographic 6, along with a selection of projects completed by students on the course. Through the curriculum, de Bretteville sought 'to embody feminist principles into a course of study' but also encouraged women to 'discover the design implications of the reawakening of feminism'.[41] Her work then, as it does today, provides one way forward in building a framework of enquiry where, for example, community assumes a central role in the communication process.

As more historians write about the subject of women working in graphic design, new ways of presenting and analysing their work and professional careers are being explored. As part of this process, there will be a move away from relying solely on conventional biographical methods toward one in which due consideration will be given to women in relationship to patriarchy, as well as economic, social, cultural and political contexts, individual and collective practices, the nature of audience, and personal and gendered experiences. It is important to recognise that the female experience brings new 'content' to graphic design as well as new voices and perspectives on female representations and means of empowerment.

(Her)stories and WD+RU

'Feminism is an ideology, a value system, a revolutionary strategy, a way of life.'[42]

'We must be able to change the present by means of how we re-present the past.'[43]

'They [WD+RU] aim to talk to women in all walks of life, but the first step is to initiate a debate that will politicise designers and prompt them to address gender issues through their work.'[44]

So where does that leave us? How can the observations of these feminists and women critics be built upon to useful effect? For the moment, it is worth considering how feminism might alter our thinking about graphic design and, in what ways it may be applied directly to design practice. There are three main aspects to consider when talking about women in graphic design. First, discussion can focus upon women working professionally by tracking career progression within the industry, and upon issues such as equal pay and workplace prejudices, childcare provision and design education. The second aspect is how women have been represented in general, that is how roles have been constructed through sexual stereotyping in design and advertising.[45]

The third aspect is how graphic design may also serve as a tool for women to explore and comment upon women's issues. This may include, for example, issues surrounding women's bodies (such as the work of April Greiman, Diane Gromala and Lucienne Roberts), community (Sheila Levrant de Bretteville), language (WD+RU), social, political and economic structures, (Women's Action Coalition, Class Action) or even women and technology (Danielle Eubank). I will now explore this third aspect of feminist activity by looking at the work produced by some of these designers and, more specifically, the Women's Design Research Unit (WD+RU).

WD+RU began its life in 1994 as a response to the male-dominated platform of speakers for the London FUSE '94 conference on typography. While featuring work of type designers from FUSE – the interactive publication for innovative typeface design – the conference organisers unwittingly highlighted the problem of exclusion. While all the speakers were highly regarded typographers, it became apparent that the profession was not accurately represented in terms of women. The conference, and the publication itself, led WD+RU to question why type designers such as Zuzana Licko, Carol Twombly, Margo Johnson, Freda Sack, Cynthia Hollandsworth and Sibylle Hagmann were noticeably absent.[46]

WD+RU took its name from the first British design consultancy team set up in 1942 by Misha Black, Milner Gray and Herbert Read, called the Design Research Unit.[47] The organisational structure of WD+RU is based upon the idea of flexibility and aims to enable its members to respond effectively to changing professional and personal circumstances. The unit focuses on the development of self-initiated projects which, in most cases, fall outside the constraints of client-based activities, and only those members who are interested or have the time will work collaboratively as a project team to achieve the proposed results. Its remit was, and still is, to raise awareness about women working in the field of visual communication while also addressing corollary issues such as those affecting women in design education. Above all, WD+RU is an inclusive organisation welcoming men and their contributions.

One of the main concerns of WD+RU has been communication and finding a way to make women's voices heard. Lucy Lippard has written that women in the arts have always been interested in 'expressing oneself as a member of a larger unity, or community, so that in speaking for oneself one is also speaking for those who cannot speak'.[48] While modernism established a measure of the 'universal', feminism has celebrated the diversity of many 'voices'. While it may be suggested that women's 'lived experiences' are different from each others', they often find their situations defined by culture as well as the way in which they are 'located within complex social relations'. And as women share in a general 'cultural understanding of what it means to be a woman', they may find a common voice.[49]

For WD+RU to capitalise on these observations, it first had to ask what impact they had in visual terms. For graphic designers, messages are conveyed through the conjunction of word and image and carried by any number of different vehicles and formats. The poster, for example, has proved to be an effective medium for women who want to take personal issues to a wider public audience. This is partly due to an ease of access, for example the visual immediacy of a boldly stated message as well as the access of production afforded its author. Posters can be produced cheaply in any scale, they can use different printing techniques, and they can be created in multiples or as one-offs. The poster has carried the messages of women from the fight for women's voting rights at the turn of the century up to more recent awareness-raising campaigns produced for the Breakthrough Breast Cancer and Age Concern charities, and its versatility has made it popular with women's political activists. At the same time, the poster format presents visually a shared viewing experience, and Lucienne Roberts, a British graphic designer, has commented that 'posters pull together the like-minded . . . you feel part of a collective movement looking at them'.[50]

However, feminism advocates more than simply conveying a message. One of WD+RU's more successful projects was a collaboration in 1997–8 with a group of second-year graphic design students at the London College of Printing, with contributions from schoolgirls aged 14–16 who were enrolled in programmes in the local catchment area (Figure 7.1).[51] The area in question has a rich, ethnic mix and is one of the less affluent boroughs of London. With this in mind, the aim of the project was to develop a poster campaign that would encourage girls to consider design as a career option. More importantly, the objective was to initiate a dialogue between the graphic design students and the schoolgirls (and, on a secondary level, with the careers officers responsible for advising students about their future job options) in order to raise an awareness on both sides about issues affecting career opportunities in design. The final result was a series of posters which were returned to careers officers to post in the corridors of their schools.

Like feminism itself, WD+RU is interested in promoting 'an element of outreach',[52] which occurs in the form of making connections beyond the graphic object itself. The graphic designer must engage the audience through the work and, at the same time, actively involve the reader in the construction of the intended message. The designer must be 'responsive' and willing to explore avenues of discourse through visual images. This is best illustrated by Sheila Levrant de Bretteville's 1973 poster project entitled *Pink*, which still resonates today as one of the best examples of how feminist intent and visual communication strategies can be combined to create an effective forum for an interactive dialogue. While the intent of *Pink* was to question conventional categories of 'woman', it simultaneously explored aspects of the design process – that is, it investigated the poster as a communication vehicle as well as questioning who the audience might be and what 'participation looks like'.[53] 'The *Pink* poster was posted along the streets of Los Angeles, and as part of her underlying intent to 'reveal assumptions' about women, de Bretteville also handed out three-inch squares to people in the street asking them to write down what 'pink' meant.[54] De Bretteville has commented that by encouraging 'thinking audiences', interactivity is produced, and consequently she recommends that 'mass media' should include visual contradictions within its messages. She writes, 'Were its images to contain suggestions rather than statements, the viewer could make an effort to bridge the gap, to interpolate, extrapolate, participate'.[55] This thinking, while highly original at the time, has today become virtual orthodoxy among the avant-garde design community. In many respects, feminism has achieved its goal in bringing forward values and approaches which are now shared by both men and women, but it may be argued that a male modernist design establishment still dominates.[56]

Figure 7.1 Project team: Women's Design Research Unit and second-year graphics students, London College of Printing, example from a series of posters intended to educate schoolgirls about careers in graphic design.

WD+RU has always believed that the modernist concept of 'one image to fit all' is no longer appropriate to today's thinking audience. As de Bretteville's work demonstrates, the postindustrial audience can no longer be considered as a single homogenous entity. While modernism often encourages the oversimplification of its message, reducing images and ideas to a universal language, graphic design today acknowledges the culture of the individual. One option is to create a reading of 'ambiguity, choice and complexity', which invites the viewer to actively participate in constructing the message. As Ann Tyler suggests, one method to activate the audience as a 'dynamic

ARE YOU REALLY SITTING COMFORTABLY?

If not, a career in
design would give
you an opportunity
to make a difference

A fair society is one in which women have an equal presence

For more information,
contact your local
Career's Officer

participant' is by using rhetoric.[57] By this she means that the message should be provocative, setting up an argument within the piece itself. The ensuing discussion between the client/designer/audience generates the message. Tyler also realises that, in order to initiate a discussion, designers need to recognise the needs of the individual reader – that is, an awareness that an audience has particular interests, visual and verbal vocabularies, and so on. The design critic Richard Buchanan suggests that if this approach is adopted, designers 'would no longer be viewed as individuals who decorate messages, but as communicators who seek to discover arguments by means of a new synthesis of images and words'.[58]

Nevertheless, WD+RU recognises that it cannot design with an 'aesthetic object' in mind. Instead it proposes that both male and female designers must take an approach that rejects the notion of addressing a homogenous audience in favour of addressing the individual. This is particularly true in the case of how the media (for example, advertising) represents and categorises men and women into preconceived roles that do not necessarily reflect those offered by any real experiences. One way in which feminist criticism has been useful to designers is that it challenges the iconography of sexual stereotyping. Equally, it can question how women can bring a different understanding to the design of the graphic object. Feminism attempts to break away from images which 'focus on the way men are often represented as modern, rational, cultured subjects within the context of modernity and women as traditional, irrational, "natural" objects'.[59] Establishing such defining characteristics ultimately generates a hierarchical ordering of meaning as well as uneven institutional structuring.[60]

One of the first WD+RU projects was the design of a typeface called 'Pussy Galore' in 1995, which questioned conventional stereotypes, both positive and negative, as portrayed through images or words (Figure 7.2). Commissioned by FUSE magazine, the typeface was the result of discussions which had taken place with the editor over concerns about the lack of women represented in the publication and at the FUSE '94 conference. The typeface was created as a form of 'propaganda' making evident through the technological capabilities of the computer, the cultural baggage which is brought to bear by its user. Pussy Galore

Figure 7.2 Women's Design Research Unit, 'Pussy Galore' typeface: the word 'woman' spelled out in lowercase and uppercase, demonstrating how alternative meanings may be constructed.

woman

WOMAN

played with the notion of accessibility and used the immediacy of the communication form in its development of commonly used words and isotype forms such as the male and female figures on toilet signs. WD+RU wanted to create a typeface which was interactive, prompted the user to (re)consider his/her 'political' position and, at the same time, allowed them to enjoy playing with the medium.[61]

Conclusion

Lucy Lippard has written that 'the goal of feminism is to change the character of art [design]'.[62] It may be argued that graphic design has the greatest potential to effect change. Its responsiveness to change has as much to do with its ephemeral state as with its access to highly visible communication networks. The strategies and skills associated with graphic design make it a key means by which feminist interventions can be made. It is a political act and is integral to the establishment of a contemporary visual culture. A new canon of graphic design history must make history accountable not only to contributions drawn from the mainstream but also to those which have traditionally fallen outside convention. It should present a critique of history initiating change; provide a framework which recognises the everyday in terms of objects and women's experiences; and constantly review the relationships and challenged positions of male-dominated culture, notions of female and male representation, and the established categories of culture.

If conventional historiographical practices continue to be condoned, the implication is that women cannot be considered as agents of social change, and are therefore unable to participate fully in defining visual culture. Women must be emancipated from the margins of graphic design history, while design history itself must recognise and embrace cultural difference, and question stereotypes and the oppression of other voices. Steps towards this have been taken (for example, by WD+RU) but there is still a long way to go. It is only by challenging historical conventions, that we are able to resurrect what graphic design history has thus far forgotten.

Notes

1. Sheila de Bretteville, 'Some Aspects of Design', p. 4.
2. Barbara Kruger in Heller, 'Smashing the Myths', p. 274.
3. Griselda Pollock, *Vision and Difference*, p. 24.
4. At the 1997 biennial conference of the American Institute of Graphic Arts (AIGA), only thirty-seven of the 102 speakers were women, with four as part of a design partnership. This number was a dramatic increase on the previous conference when a group of Yale design students, Class Action, fly-posted the host city Miami in order to highlight the appalling lack of female speakers that year. The AIGA recently elected its first female president since its founding in 1914.
5. IPA, *Agency Census 1997*, p. 7.
6. Patricia Allen Dreyfus wrote about the state of women working in design in 'Women's Lib and Women Designers'. She argues that despite Women's Liberation, women in design still encountered low salaries, lack of promotion and stereotyping.
7. Cullen, 'Beyond Politics and Gender', p. 24.
8. Ibid. p. 26.
9. Ibid. p. 26.
10. Rock and Sellers, 'This is Not a Cigar', p. 45.
11. Wilkins, 'No More Heroes', p. 4.
12. Triggs, 'The Endless Library', p. 43.
13. Scotford, 'Messy History vs. Neat History', p. 370.
14. Scotford, 'The Tenth Pioneer', p. 54. Scotford's recent critical biography of Cipe Pineles (New York: W. W. Norton, 1999) is a significant contribution to the literature on mid-twentieth-century graphic design.
15. Salomon, 'The Art Historical Canon', p. 229.
16. Waaldijk, 'Of Stories and Sources', p. 24.
17. Buchanan and Margolin, *The Ideas of Design*, p. xiv.
18. Lacey, 'The Name of the Game', p. 65.
19. Vienne, 'Designers and Visibility', p. 35.
20. Lacey, 'The Name of the Game', p. 65.
21. Baker, 'A Poetics of Graphic Design', p. 252.
22. Carroll Smith-Rosenberg in Zinsser, *History and Feminism*, p. 45.
23. Waaldijk, 'Of Stories and Sources', p. 14.
24. Wilkins, 'No More Heroes', p. 4.
25. Buckley, 'Made in Patriarchy', p. 252.
26. Pollock, *Vision and Difference*, p. 1.
27. Nochlin's article 'Why Have There Been No Great Women Artists?' has been discussed at length and applied to the

areas of art history by Griselda Pollock, design history by
Cheryl Buckley, and graphic design history by Martha Scotford.

28. Nochlin, 'Why Have There Been No Great Women Artists?',
    p. 2.
29. Pollock, *Vision and Difference*, p. 1.
30. Attfield, 'FORM/Female', p. 200.
31. Buckley, 'Made in Patriarchy', p. 253.
32. Buckley, 'Designed by Women', p. 400.
33. Buckley, 'Made in Patriarchy', p. 254.
34. Scotford, 'Messy History vs. Neat History', pp. 372–3.
    Scotford suggests that this is one reason why women were
    kept away from 'business or vocational training' during the
    early days of typesetting and printing.
35. Scotford, 'Messy History vs. Neat History', p. 371.
36. Walker, *Design History*, p. 118.
37. Scher, 'The Boat', p. 57.
38. Makela and Lupton, 'Underground Matriarchy', p. 42.
39. Fairbairn, 'The Gendered Self', p. 237.
40. de Bretteville, 'Some Aspects of Design', p. 5.
41. de Bretteville, 'The Women's Design Program'.
42. Lippard, *The Pink Glass Swan*, p. 172.
43. Pollock, *Vision and Difference*, p. 14.
44. Farrelly, 'Mysterious Absence', p. 7.
45. Roux, 'Mags Out', pp. 46–55.
46. Three years later, FUSE '98 organisers had only addressed
    the issue in part, with three females out of twenty-eight
    speakers (excluding mixed collaborations such as Anti-
    Rom) on stage in San Francisco.
47. For the first few years WD+RU members included Siân
    Cook, Karen Mahoney, Liz McQuiston, and Teal Triggs.
    Since 1997 membership has shifted, losing Karen and Liz to
    work commitments while some projects have expanded to
    include new participants.
48. Lippard, *The Pink Glass Swan*, p. 178.
49. Jackson and Jones, *Contemporary Feminist Theories*, p. 8.
50. Triggs, 'Women's Political Posters', p. 27.
51. This project was generously funded by the Royal Female
    School of Art Foundation, London for the academic year
    1997–8.
52. Lippard, *The Pink Glass Swan*, p. 179.
53. de Bretteville in Nikitas, *And She Told Two Friends*, p. 11.
54. The poster was displayed again during an exhibition of
    women graphic designers, called 'And She Told Two Friends'
    held in Chicago in 1996, in order to establish how far, if at

all, women had been 'informed by what has been learned since 1973' (Nikitas, *And She Told Two Friends*, p. 11).

55. de Bretteville, 'Some Aspects of Design', p. 4.
56. Makela and Lupton, 'Underground Matriarchy', p. 47.
57. Tyler in Margolin and Buchanan, *The Ideas of Design*, p. 106.
58. Margolin and Buchanan, *The Ideas of Design*, p. 10.
59. Adkins in Jackson and Jones, *Contemporary Feminist Theories*, p. 37.
60. Pollock, *Vision and Difference*, p. 7.
61. The formal components of graphic design may also be described in gendered terms. For example, 'words' themselves may be associated with the male sphere while 'images' have been closely aligned with the feminine sphere. Or, the typographic profession has been male-dominated with the field of illustration female-dominated. Steve Baker observes in 'A Poetics of Graphic Design' that 'words, somehow, continue to be regarded as having a masculine orientation, and images a feminine one'. With this in mind, Baker questions the relative power structures found between word and image in the construction of graphic design writing (p. 251). His conclusion, which parallels the findings of the feminist literary writer Luce Irigaray, is that the 'generation of messages is not neutral, but sexuate' (p. 252). Whereas 'design' has been addressed primarily as a male activity, the spaces occupied by the decorative including the 'craft-making' of pottery, calligraphy, and textiles, have been deemed as feminine. In a patriarchal structure these areas are given an 'inferior status' (Whiteley, *Design for Society*, pp. 136–7). Some critics have warned that there is also a danger that creativity is located as 'an exclusive masculine prerogative' (Pollock, *Vision and Difference*, p. 21).
62. Lippard, *The Pink Glass Swan*, p. 172.

Bibliography

Adkins, L., 'Feminist Theory and Economics Change', in S. Jackson and J. Jones (eds), *Contemporary Feminist Theories* (Edinburgh: Edinburgh University Press, 1998).

Anscombe, I., *A Woman's Touch: Women in Design from 1860 to Present Day* (London: Virago Press, 1984).

Attfield, J., 'FORM/female FOLLOWS FUNCTION/male: Feminist Critiques of Design', in J. Walker, *Design History and the History of Design* (London: Pluto Press, 1989).

Baker, S., 'A Poetics of Graphic Design', in A. Blauvelt (ed.) *New Perspectives: Critical Histories of Graphic Design*, a special issue of *Visible Language* (1994) 28.3 pp. 245–59.

Bishop, L., 'Where are the Women?', *Creative Review* (1998) 18(9) pp. 53–4.

Buchanan, R., 'Wicked Problems in Design Thinking' in V. Margolin and R. Buchanan (eds), *The Idea of Design* (Cambridge, MA: The MIT Press, 1995).

Buchanan, R. and V. Margolin, 'Introduction' in V. Margolin and R. Buchanan (eds), *The Idea of Design* (Cambridge, MA: The MIT Press, 1995).

Buckley, C., 'Designed by Women', *Art History* (1986) 9(3) pp. 400–3.

Buckley, C., 'Made in Patriarchy: Toward a Feminist Analysis of Women and Design', in V. Margolin (ed.), *Design Discourses* (Chicago: The University of Chicago Press, 1989).

Cullen, M., 'Beyond Politics and Gender – The Hillary Factor', *Communication Arts* (1993) May/June pp. 24–30.

de Bretteville, S., 'Some Aspects of Design From the Perspective of a Woman Designer', *Icographic* 6 (1973) pp. 4–6.

de Bretteville, S., 'The Women's Design Program', *Icographic* 6 (1973) pp. 8–11.

Dreyfus, P., 'Women's Lib and Women Designers', *Print* (1970) May/June, pp. 29–34, 74, 76.

Fairbairn, J., 'The Gendered Self', in S. Heller and M. Finamore (eds), *Design Culture: An Anthology of Writing from the AIGA Journal of Graphic Design* (New York: Allworth Press, 1997).

Farrelly, L., 'Mysterious Absence at the Cutting Edge', *Eye* (1995) 19 (5) pp. 6–7.

Heller, S., 'Barbara Kruger: Smashing the Myths', *Design Culture: An Anthology of Writing from the AIGA Journal of Graphic Design* (New York: Allworth Press, 1997).

Institute of Practitioners in Advertising, *Agency Census 1997* (London: IPA, 1998).

Jackson, S., and J. Jones, 'Thinking For Ourselves: An Introduction to Feminist Theorising', in S. Jackson and J. Jones (eds), *Contemporary Feminist Theories* (Edinburgh: Edinburgh University Press, 1998).

Kirkham, P., *Charles and Ray Eames: Designers of the Twentieth Century* (Cambridge, MA: The MIT Press, 1995).

Lacey, S., 'The Name of the Game' *Art Journal* (1991) 50 (2) pp. 64–8.

Lippard, L., 'Sweeping Exchanges: The Contribution of Feminism to the Art of the 1970s', in L. Lippard (ed.), *The Pink Glass Swan: Selected Essays on Art* (New York: The New Press, 1995).

McQuiston, L., *Women in Design: A Contemporary View* (New York: Rizzoli, 1988).

McQuiston, L., *Suffragettes to She Devils: Women's Liberation and Beyond* (London: Phaidon, 1997).

Makela, L. and E. Lupton, 'Underground Matriarchy', *Eye* (1994) 14 (4) pp. 42–7.

Nikitas, K., *And She Told Two Friends* (Chicago: Michael Mendelson, 1996).

Nochlin, L., 'Why Have There Been No Great Women Artists?', in T. Hess and E. Baker (eds), *Art and Sexual Politics: Women's Liberation, Women Artists and Art History* (New York: Collier Books, 1971).

Pollock, G., *Vision and Difference: Femininity, Feminism and Histories of Art* (London: Routledge, 1988).

Rock, M., and S. Sellers, 'This is Not a Cigar', *Eye* (1993) 8 (2) pp. 40–5.

Roux, C., 'Mags Out For the Lads', *Eye* (1997) 24(6) pp. 46–55.

Scher, P., 'The Boat', in R. Marsack, *Essays on Design 1: AGI's Designers of Influence* (London: Booth-Clibborn Editions, 1997).

Scotford, M., 'Messy History vs. Neat History: Toward an Expended View of Women in Graphic Design', in A. Blauvelt (ed.), *New Perspectives: Critical Histories of Graphic Design*, a special issue of *Visible Language* (1994) 28.4 pp. 367–87.

Scotford, M., 'The Tenth Pioneer', *Eye* (1995) 18 (5) pp. 54–63.

Salomon, N., 'The Art Historical Canon: Sins of Omission' in J. Hartman and E. Messer-Davidow (eds), *(En)Gendering Knowledge: Feminist in Academie* (Knoxville: University of Tennessee Press, 1991).

Thomson, E., *The Origins of Graphic Design in America 1870–1920* (New Haven: Yale University Press, 1997).

Triggs, T., 'The Endless Library at the End of Print', *Eye* (1998) 7 (27) pp. 38–47.

Triggs, T., 'Women's Political Posters', *Graphics International* (1998) 58 pp. 24–7.

Tyler, A., 'Shaping Belief: The Role of Audience in Visual Communication' in V. Margolin and R. Buchanan (eds), *The Idea of Design* (Cambridge, MA: The MIT Press, 1995).

Vienne, V., 'Designers and Visibility: Design – Not Biology – Is Destiny', *Communication Arts* (1994) Sept/Oct pp. 30–6.

Waaldijk, B., 'Of Stories and Sources: Feminist History', in R.

Buikema and A. Smelik (eds), *Women's Studies and Culture: A Feminist Introduction* (London: Zed Books, 1993).

Walker, J., *Design History and the History of Design* (London: Pluto Press, 1989).

Whiteley, N., *Design For Society* (London: Reaktion Books, 1993).

Wilkins, B., 'No More Heroes', *Eye* (1992) 6(2) pp. 4–7.

Zinsser, J., *History and Feminism: A Glass Half Full* (New York: Twayne Publishers, 1993).

Chapter 8

Ceramics

Cheryl Buckley

WOMEN HAVE BEEN ACTIVELY involved in the production
and consumption of ceramics in most societies. Historically the
production of pottery, as both a craft and an industrial process,
has involved them as workers and designers, while women have
also been consumers of domestic tablewares and decorative
wares, patrons and entrepreneurs in ceramic manufacture, marketing and retailing. The cultural, economic and political history
of women's engagement with ceramics is a complex one, drawing
on traditions from non-Western cultures as well as being fundamentally affected by the development of capitalism and patriarchy in the West from the eighteenth century. In Britain, the
focus of this study – both women's relationship to ceramics and
the description of this in the history of ceramics – has been
essentially patriarchal. However, the critiques of history and
knowledge – particularly in relation to visual culture – which
have emerged within the context of feminism offer alternative
theoretical frameworks for analysing ceramics. These acknowledge the ideological nature of existing accounts and provide a
new critical vocabulary for discussing and evaluating the aspects
of ceramics with which women have engaged.

Focusing on a number of key debates alongside an examination
of the work of three women designers – Hannah Barlow (1851–
1916), Clarice Cliff (1899–1972) and Susie Cooper (1902–95) – I
will address a number of important theoretical and historiographical themes. First, I will assess the position of women in
histories of ceramic design, production and consumption; secondly, I will examine the ways in which definitions of gender and
feminine identities have shaped and have, in turn, been shaped by
the nature of ceramic design and production and thirdly, I will

discuss the question of how gender conditions evaluations and interpretations of both women designers' roles and their ceramic designs.

Moulding a history: accounting for women and ceramics

Historically, women have had a complex relationship with ceramics. This relationship has been shaped by diverse factors, but particularly important from the late eighteenth century in Britain were the inter-related issues of economics, class, and labour divisions based on sex. Working-class, middle-class and some aristocratic women engaged with ceramics as skilled artist/designers, as semi-skilled and unskilled industrial workers, and as consumers, while a few women were involved with design theory and education.[1] An examination of the majority of the literature on the subject would lead one to conclude otherwise – that women were largely absent from all stages of ceramics – except at strategic historical points when they provided a counterpoint to men's activities.[2]

Gender-blind historiographical methods are evident in the writings of highly influential design historians such as Nikolaus Pevsner in his seminal design history text *Pioneers of Modern Design* and, particularly important in relation to ceramics, Gordon Forsyth's *20th Century Ceramics*.[3] In both, the writers are anxious to establish the validity of the modern movement in design and, in so doing, examined only those few individuals who designed in a modernist idiom. Only rarely did the work of women designers surface in these accounts, usually if it provided useful evidence in support of a particular point as it did in Pevsner's modernist account of 1930s British design *An Enquiry Into Industrial Arts in England*. In this, the work of the ceramic designer Susie Cooper was deemed to be essential evidence of modernist design practice in Britain.[4]

For the feminist historian, this emphasis on modernism has its problems as most modernist histories of design have been essentially masculinist, prompted by the desire to lionise men and enshrine their values. In Pevsner's meta-narrative of modernism, the 'pioneers' are all men and there is little space for women in the triumphant march of modernism. Unlike architects, and furniture and graphic designers, ceramic designers were not at the forefront of modernist innovation in Europe in the 1920s.[5] Furthermore, in Britain, pottery manufacturers adopted new technologies un-evenly and depended on handcrafted methods of production until well after World War Two. As a result, the history of ceramics has been largely neglected by those writers, critics and historians whose writings proved critical in the establishment of modernist theories and practice, and there are few accounts of ceramic design and designers in modernist histories of British and European design.[6]

The collecting of fine china, porcelain and earthenware by museums, antique collectors and wealthy individuals has gener-ated different types of ceramic histories, for example those on individual companies such as Doulton and Wedgwood; those on different types of ware; and those on individual designers – most of which are written by collectors or museum curators and are often financed by specialist dealers.[7] Most of these histories share certain qualities: first, they tend to be specialist, emphasising pottery type, manufacturer or designer; secondly, they are con-cerned mainly with quality (aesthetic and/or technical), authen-ticity, uniqueness, and distinctiveness; thirdly, they are primarily object-based focusing on individual pots; and fourthly, they aim to provide data for identifying and dating pottery stamps and basemarks. Although useful in their own way, these books constitute only a part of a history of design, as they usually underplay social, economic and technological factors in their eagerness to stress the artistic input of individual designers and the aesthetic standing of certain factories.

The publication of books on individual women ceramic de-signers is a relatively recent phenomenon, occurring primarily because of collectors' interest in their work.[8] Most provide detailed information about the women designers' lives, careers, and designs including chronologies and lists of pottery patterns, shapes, backstamps, and numbers.

Shaping the 'feminine': ceramics and gender identities

Within ceramic production and consumption, appropriate roles for women have been articulated within an essentially patriarchal framework. In order to understand these, it is particularly important firstly to examine the specific manifestation of patriarchal power relations in labour divisions in the pottery industry and within craft workshops, and secondly to map out the articulation of gender difference in relation to design skills and roles. Labour divisions based on sex were pervasive throughout the organisation of ceramic design and manufacture in the pottery industry from the eighteenth century onwards, thus enshrining "men's control over women's labor power".[9] Underpinning this sexual division of labour were ideas and beliefs that constructed a 'feminine' identity in design and led to the articulation of a 'separate sphere' for women designers and decorators. Taken together, this contributed to and reinforced the internalising and 'naturalising' of patriarchal norms of femininity throughout the pottery industry. The role and work of the nineteenth-century designer/decorator Hannah Bolton Barlow perfectly exemplifies this.

Women from the aristocracy, the upper-middle and middle classes had designed pottery decoration from the eighteenth century, for example Lady Diana Beauclerk (1734–1808) and Lady Elizabeth Templetown (1747–1823) had provided designs for surface decoration for Josiah Wedgwood and Sons Ltd, and several women designers in the continental factories of Sèvres and Meissen had specialised in pattern design.[10] However, in the latter part of the nineteenth century opportunities for the employment of women as pottery designers and decorators were substantially enhanced for a variety of reasons – in particular, the plight of untrained women who were widowed or had little hope of marriage and had no facility to earn a living was of growing social concern.[11] At the same time, nineteenth-century writers and commentators were increasingly convinced of women's suitability for only certain types of work. The journals of the day were filled with discussions regarding the abilities of women and their appropriateness to particular aspects of art and design practice.[12]

Former aristocratic connections and the perception that certain aspects of pottery design and decoration required skills peculiar to the female sex ensured that by the 1880s pottery design and decoration were considered appropriate artistic occupations for middle-class women. The *Art Journal* commented in 1872, there is perhaps no branch of Art-work more perfectly womanly and in every way desirable than painting on china. The character of the designs brings them within the reach of even moderate powers, and it must be admitted that painting flowers and birds and pretty landscapes, or children's heads, is work in itself more suitable for women than men.[13]

The connection between middle-class women and pottery was reinforced at Henry Doulton's Lambeth Art Pottery, a commercial enterprise established in 1870 and based on the design and decorating skills of women. In addition, the Doulton Art Pottery provided a model and prototype for the way that middle-class women could be gainfully employed in the 'lesser arts'. Numerous women designers and decorators worked at Doulton's including Hannah Barlow, and her work is typical of that produced at the Doulton Art Pottery in that it was elaborate and decorative, combining incised or *sgraffito* figurative designs of animals, birds, flowers and children with borders of scrolls, beads and dots (Figure 8.1). It was clearly 'artistic' in the terms of the period, in that it was hand-decorated and illustrated by an artist and importantly, each piece was a 'one-off'. Although Barlow could throw pots, like the other Doulton women designers, her work was mainly confined to the design of surface pattern. In fact, most of the designs by women at Doulton's were dependent on recognised 'feminine' skills: they were small-scale, ornamental, elaborate and based on aspects of nature.

Although earning their living in manufacturing industry, the Doulton women designers and decorators designed highly ornate ware, and they worked in good clothes in comfortable, private studios away from the taint of commercialism and the glare of male eyes. Crucial to Doulton's enterprise was the renovation of separate studios for the women designers and paintresses in order to provide them with clean and private facilities. Henry Doulton's experiences in Stoke-on-Trent had initially turned him against employing women:

I have seen women in the most coarse and degrading labour, such as turning the wheels, wedging the clay, etc. I always declined to employ female labour in the ordinary work of the factory, and it was not until Mr Rix placed before me a well-organised scheme that I agreed to employ girls and women in our art department.[14]

Doulton's ideal of middle-class women's artistic work was represented in the decorated, signed pages of the commemorative volumes presented to him by the women in 1882.[15] In these books, numerous idealised images of wholesome, healthy women in elegant, 'aesthetic' gowns captured perfectly Henry Doulton's intention in establishing the Doulton Art Pottery: to provide a private space in a public sphere.[16]

Women's concentration in the decoration of ceramics, rather than the forming of ceramic shapes, linked not only to the perception that pottery decoration was thought to require 'feminine' skills such as a facility for detail, decorativeness and patience, whereas the design of shape required abstract, conceptual, 'masculine' abilities, it was also indicative of the relative status of each aspect of design in business. The design of pottery shapes was probably the most important job in the pottery factory because a successful product shape formed the basis for a profitable business. In contrast, a range of decorations could be added to a viable shape and these could be adapted according to market changes. It was no accident then, that within the sexual division in design in the pottery factory, the job of designing shape – with its central role in the success or failure of a pottery business – should be controlled by men. At this point, men assumed the highest status in pottery design as a result of the combination of patriarchal and capitalist interests.[17]

Figure 8.1 Hannah Barlow, Doulton saltware lemonade jug with relief modelled, carved and beaded decoration with sgraffito drawing from nature, c. 1870s. Photograph courtesy of Royal Doulton.

Sexual divisions were found throughout all work organisation in the pottery industry, not just in design, although these divisions could be changed. Overlying this sexual division was a demarcation of jobs based on craft, which distinguished skilled from unskilled work. Men monopolised most skilled jobs and controlled access to these through the apprenticeship system, and, in general terms, the net result of these labour divisions was a hierarchical industrial structure with skilled men at the top and unskilled women at the bottom. Men and their unions had traditionally controlled definitions of craft skill and access to most craft jobs, although as the pottery industry was increasingly technologised, they tried to dominate and control the new

processes. However, at specific historical moments such as the first half of the twentieth century, redefinitions of skill took place which worked to women's advantage. As a result of conflicting patriarchal and capitalist interests, women held onto traditional craft skills such as decorating, while at the same time developing new technological skills in, for example, forming, decorating, and marketing ceramics. A number of women contributed to this, but two women stand out: Susie Cooper and Clarice Cliff. They pioneered the introduction and development of new decorating technology, and developed new ceramic shapes, as well as new marketing and retailing techniques.[18]

Modernity and ceramics: value, interpretation and women designers

The parallel career paths of Susie Cooper and Clarice Cliff and the designs which they produced during the 1930s highlight the complexities of interpretation of both design and designer at a particular historical point. Both were relatively young women in 1930 – Susie Cooper was twenty-eight years old and Clarice Cliff was thirty-one – and both were established within the pottery industry as designers: Cooper in her own company (the Susie Cooper Pottery established the year before), and Cliff with the pottery manufacturer, A. J. Wilkinson. Throughout the 1930s, both women gained good reputations for their designs, although what is interesting is the way that class, gender and competing ideas of value and significance in design shaped the contemporary and subsequent reception of their work and roles.

Both women were born, brought up and educated in the 'Potteries' of north Staffordshire, albeit with different class backgrounds. Clarice Cliff was one of the few working-class women to become a designer. She trained as a decorator at two companies before joining A. J. Wilkinson in 1916 as a trainee lithographer, and at the same time she attended art school for two evenings a week.[19] In contrast and more typically, Susie Cooper was brought up in a moderately wealthy family. In 1919, she gained a three-year scholarship to study at Burslem School of Art, after which she started as a trainee designer at A. E. Gray and Co. Ltd, a company specialising in handpainted pottery decorated with *moderne* and Art Deco motifs.[20] After two years acquiring hand-decorating skills, she was promoted to designer, and, to coincide with this, a special named backstamp 'Gray's Pottery Designed by Susie Cooper' was produced for all ware which she designed.

Despite lacking the educational advantages of Cooper, Cliff worked her way up to the position of designer at A. J. Wilkinson's. After four years learning lithography, her ability came to the attention of Colley Shorter, the managing director, who agreed to give her the space and opportunity to develop her talents. From 1926, with Shorter's encouragement, she developed a range of decorative patterns which became known as 'Bizarre Wares'. At the same time, she too was given her own backstamp 'Hand Painted Bizarre by Clarice Cliff'. Bizarre wares were geometric, boldly patterned designs, which were mainly based on abstracted forms. Colours were vibrant and striking, with blues, oranges, yellows, reds, turquoises, greens and purples handpainted on a cream earthenware body. Stylistically, these designs were influenced by Art Deco.

From 1929 Cliff designed new shapes which suited the angularity of her patterns, and these included 'Conical', then 'Stamford' in 1930, and then 'Biarritz' and 'Le Bon Jour' in 1933 (Figure 8.2) Most of Clarice Cliff's new shapes were geometric, with triangular handles, circular sides and conical bodies which posed some difficulties for mass-production because of their unsuitability for the established methods of pottery manufacture. However, although these shapes relied on manual skills in their production, they functioned as powerful and effective symbols of modernity for the middle-class consumer. (Indeed, the use of handicraft techniques was not uncommon in the production of those 'pioneering' designs – including Mies van der Rohe's Barcelona Chair – which were to become exemplary modernist products.) Significantly, Cliff recognised the essential unity between shape and pattern and the importance of these shapes for the success of the highly modern patterns. And cleverly responding to the burgeoning interest in popular representations of modernity, she also designed a range of fancies which included teddy-bear bookends and cat-shaped pencil holders as well as the hugely popular wall masks and figures of dancing couples, banjo players and trumpeters which perfectly epitomised the 'Jazz Age' 1920s.

In a similar fashion, the Susie Cooper Pottery was noted from the outset for modernity. Like Cliff, Cooper began by designing patterns which were handpainted and based on dots and dashes combined with shaded and washed bands of colour in subtle shades of green, blue, mauve, and terracotta. By 1932, Cooper, like Cliff, had designed her own pottery shapes – Kestrel and Curlew – to be produced in an ivory-bodied earthenware. These shapes represented a different response to modernity: whereas Cliff was influenced by Art Deco, Cooper's work revealed an interest in European and Scandinavian modernism. Both designers were undoubtedly innovative, although in significantly different ways. Shapes such as Cooper's Kestrel and Curlew related to the smooth, undecorated forms found in modernist-inspired architecture and design of the 1930s, in which form was emphasised in preference to applied decoration.

Both women were modern in other ways, particularly in relation to marketing and retailing. Cliff, for example, promoted and advertised the new Bizarre wares with great imagination. In August 1928, along with the Bizarre paintresses, she staged a demonstration of hand-painting at Waring and Gillow's furniture store, which subsequently toured the country.[21] As well as opening a new showroom in London, Cooper designed display stands which were described as 'totally unlike anything else.'[22] Both were responsive to the changing demands of the middle-class consumer who, with smaller houses, fewer children and no servants, required smaller sets of pottery.

In many ways, both women challenged the stereotypes which had hitherto governed women's roles in the pottery industry. They designed shapes and decoration, and in so doing they challenged the sexual divisions within the pottery industry which assigned women to the design of decoration and men to the design of pottery shape. They combined professional and personal lives, and once established, their careers ran in parallel. Cliff stayed at Wilkinson throughout her professional life, whereas Cooper set up her own company with the aid of family money in 1929. Whereas Cooper rigidly separated her professional and private lives, only marrying in 1938 after her company was well established, Cliff's personal life was increasingly unconventional. From the late 1920s, she had an affair with Colley Shorter, generating a great deal of gossip and disapproval as he was married with two daughters. She also behaved quite differently to other single

Figure 8.2 Clarice Cliff, earthenware sugar sifter in enamel colours with 'Fantasque' pattern, 1929-1934. Copyright: The Potteries Museum and Art Gallery.

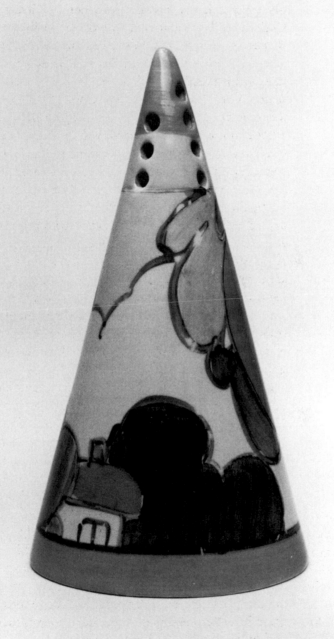

women with the same class background, moving into her own flat in 1925 and driving a motor-car, thus projecting an image as a modern young woman.

The critical reception and subsequent evaluation of Cooper and Cliff's work could hardly contrast more strongly. Critical support for Cliff's modern designs was not forthcoming from the promoters of modernism in Britain in the 1930s who thought her work superficial. In a context of almost religious fervour, certain theorists extolled and promoted the virtues of modernism to the detriment of all other approaches to design, and Cliff's work was certainly a casualty of this. In *An Enquiry into Industrial Arts in England*, Nikolaus Pevsner criticised Cliff's 'jagged handles, square or polygonal shapes',[23] while Gordon Forsyth believed that her geometric patterns revealed a lack of real understanding of the principles of modern design and that the triangular-handled cups and teapots were impractical and unsuited to regular use.[24] In fact, as I suggested earlier, Cliff's new shapes represented a redefinition of modernism in that they were neither determined solely by function nor production processes. Adherence to the narrow dictates of European modernism was not Cliff's objective; rather she was seeking to respond to and evoke the conditions of modernity by using imaginative colour, form and decoration in her design. As a designer, she displayed sensitivity and skill in utilising a variety of design forms to symbolise modernity. For contemporary consumers and for many subsequent writers on design, Cliff's designs represented the essence of modern design in the 1930s. However, for theorists such as Pevsner and Forsyth, instilled with Bauhaus principles about form and function, and the rational use of modern materials and mass-production techniques, the aptly-named Bizarre shapes remained anathema and ultimately, anachronistic.[25]

Cooper's work represents a different paradox with regard to interpretation.[26] Two conflicting accounts of her work coexisted in the 1930s: one, evident in the pottery trade press, discerned in her designs a 'feminine' style.[27] At a time when Cooper was challenging the dominant stereotype by working as a business-woman, independent designer and manufacturer, her designs were being analysed within a framework of conventional gender attributes which linked her work to the biologically-determined 'feminine'; a category shared, theoretically, with all other women artists and designers, but not with those male pottery designers with whom she had most in common. The 'feminine' analysis of Cooper's products, which was mainly the invention of the trade journals, was superseded by a modernist analysis. In the work of those writers who had castigated Cliff, the modernist qualities in Cooper's work were emphasised: Pevsner and Forsyth, anxious to establish the viability and credibility of modernism, made much of the technical innovation of her lithographic designs.[28] Emphasis was placed on the simplicity of her shapes and patterns, and the formal agenda shifted from delicate and feminine to rational and modern. As with the 'feminine' analysis, the modernist one led critics to evaluate her designs in a partial manner. Little was said of factors which fell outside the modernist agenda, but as a result of the attention of this small powerful group of writers, Cooper's designs were highly regarded whereas Cliff's were dismissed. It is significant, however, that the tableware designs of both invoked the domestic and the decorative at a precarious moment in the emergence of British modernism. The domestic 'perpetually invoked in order to be denied remains throughout the course of modernism a crucial site of anxiety and subversion', and decoration functioned as modernism's 'other'.[29] It is not surprising, therefore, that within this context, interpretations of the work of these two highly influential designers were contradictory.

For feminists, Cooper and Cliff demonstrate the ways in which women ceramic designers of the 1930s in Britain challenged the patriarchal boundaries of the pottery industry, helping to change the nature of women's engagement with ceramics. Their legacy as designers has been considerable, and this is due in no small part to the fact that they signed their own wares, designed shapes as well as decoration, and in the case of Cooper, owned the company.

In conclusion, this study has demonstrated that feminist critiques of culture and history provide a range of critical tools that enable those approaching specific aspects of women's design history, such as ceramics, to unpick the complexities of key patriarchal structures which relate to women and ceramics. The relationships between ceramics and feminism are fruitful avenues for further investigation, not least because of the longevity, pervasiveness and complexity of women's engagement with this area of cultural activity.

Notes

1. See Buckley, *Potters and Paintresses,* and Buckley, 'Women Designers in the North Staffordshire Pottery Industry, 1914–1940', PhD thesis, University of East Anglia, 1992.
2. For more discussion of the theoretical ideas highlighted by this, see Buckley, 'Made in Patriarchy', and Attfield, 'FORM/ Female'.
3. N. Pevsner, *Pioneers of Modern Design. From William Morris to Walter Gropius* (London: Penguin, 1936), and Forsyth, *20th Century Ceramics.*
4. N. Pevsner, *An Enquiry into Industrial Art in England* (Cambridge: Cambridge University Press, 1937).
5. In his introductory essay, Paul Greenhalgh discusses the importance of architects, furniture and graphic designers to the development of what he describes as the 'pioneer' phase of modernism. See P. Greenhalgh, *Modernism in Design* (London: Reaktion Press, 1990).
6. An excellent example to emphasise this point can be seen at the Bauhaus in the 1920s. Although Gillian Naylor in her book *The Bauhaus Reassessed* (London: The Herbert Press, 1985) makes the point that the pottery workshop at the Bauhaus demonstrated the potential of the Bauhaus system, she tells us little about it. Instead, in a manner shared by other Bauhaus historians, she emphasises the foundation course, the wood and metal workshop and the theories of the Bauhaus.
7. See, for example, M. Batkin, *Wedgwood Ceramics 1846–1959* (London: Richard Dennis, 1982); D. Eyles, *The Doulton Lambeth Wares* (London: Hutchinson, 1975); R. Reilly, *Wedgwood Jasper* (London: Charles Letts, 1972); M. Haslam, *English Art Pottery 1865–1915* (London: Antiques Collectors' Club, 1975). Eyles was co-sponsored by Royal Doulton.
8. Eatwell, *Susie Cooper Productions*; Casey, *Susie Cooper Ceramics*; Woodhouse, *Susie Cooper*; Griffin et al., *Clarice Cliff*; Bumpus, *Charlotte Rhead*; Rose, *Hannah Barlow.*
9. Quoted in L. Sargent (ed.), *The Unhappy Marriage of Marxism and Feminism. A Debate on Class and Patriarchy* (London: Pluto Press, 1981), p.15. In her essay in this book, Heidi Hartmann analyses the relationship between patriarchy and capitalism, and the sexual division of labour, from the viewpoint of a feminist with an interest in Marxist theories and methods. Fundamentally, Hartmann insists on an interactive, dependent relationship between capitalism and patriarchy.
10. See Buckley, *Potters and Paintresses,* pp. 70–95.

11. In 1872, women outnumbered men by nearly one million, and three million of the six million adult women in Britain had to support themselves and their dependent relatives. See 'Art-Work for Women II. Why the Work is Not Done', *Art Journal*, 1872, vol. XI, p. 103.

12. L. Scott, 'Women at Work: Their Functions in Art', *Magazine of Art,* 1872, vol. VII, p. 98.

13. 'Art-Work for Women I. The Work to be Done', *Art Journal*, 1872, vol. XI, p. 66.

14. E. Gosse, *Sir Henry Doulton. The Man of Business as a Man of Imagination* (London: Hutchinson, 1970), p. 209.

15. *Commemorative Volumes (2) presented to Henry Doulton, dated from 1871–1881*, at the Minet Library, Lambeth, London.

16. See Buckley, 'A Private Space in a Public Place'.

17. See Buckley, 'Craft Hierarchies'.

18. For more detailed discussion of this, see Buckley, 'Women Designers in the North Staffordshire Pottery Industry, 1914–1940', PhD thesis, University of East Anglia, 1992, and Buckley, 'Design, Femininity and Modernism'.

19. Lithography was one of the most widespread methods of decorating wares in the industry, and it was particularly popular in the 1930s as it allowed a complex, multicoloured design to be transferred onto pottery relatively cheaply and without intensive hand-finishing. As a technique, it was regarded as inferior to hand-painting until it was revolutionised in the early-to-mid 1930s by Susie Cooper and later in the 1930s by the design team at Josiah Wedgwood and Sons Ltd, who brought to the process a delicacy and subtlety of colour and design to rival the best hand-decorating.

20. Cheryl Buckley, interview with Susie Cooper, March 1983.

21. For example, the 'British Industrial Art in relation to the Home' exhibition held at Dorland Hall in 1933, and the 'British Art in Industry' exhibition at the Royal Academy in 1935.

22. 'Report on the British Industries Fair', *Pottery Gazette and Glass Trade Review*, 1 April 1932, p. 489.

23. N. Pevsner, *An Enquiry into Industrial Art in England* (Cambridge: Cambridge University Press, 1937), p. 81.

24. Cheryl Buckley, interview with Moira Forsyth (daughter of G. Forsyth), July 1987

25. To some extent, Cliff has been ill-served by her subsequent, erstwhile supporters. Len Griffin's book (*Clarice Cliff. The Bizarre Affair)* is naively titled, drawing attention to her

notorious affair with Colley Shorter which damaged her reputation (see my review of this book in *Woman's Art Journal,* Spring/Summer 1989, vol. 10, no. 1, p. 49). Cliff's dismissal by serious critics at the time, although ostensibly about modernism, was also framed by class and sex. Cliff did not conform to the tasteful, polite middle-class values of her critics – she was full of life and keen to take advantage of the opportunities which she had fought for. Perhaps most disappointing are the comments on Cliff by Isabelle Anscombe in *A Woman's Touch. Women in Design From 1860 to the Present Day* (London: Virago, 1984) which replicate the patriarchal and modernist values of Pevsner and his ilk.

26. See Buckley, 'Design, Femininity and Modernism'.
27. 'Buyer's Notes', *Pottery Gazette and Glass Trade Review*, 1 October 1932, p. 1249, and 'Buyer's Notes' 1 August 1935, p. 975.
28. See, for example, Forsyth, *20th Century Ceramics,* and Pevsner, *An Enquiry into Industrial Art in England* (Cambridge: Cambridge University Press, 1937).
29. See Christopher Reed, *Not At Home. The Suppression of Domesticity in Modern Art and Architecture* (London: Thames & Hudson, 1996), p. 16; Tag Gronberg, 'Décoration: Modernism's Other', in *Art History*, vol. 15, no. 4, December 1992, pp. 547–53.

Bibliography

Attfield, Judy, 'FORM/female FOLLOWS FUNCTION/male: Feminist Critiques of Design' in J. A. Walker, *Design History and the History of Design* (London: Pluto Press, 1989).

Attfield, Judy and Pat Kirkham (eds), *A View From the Interior: Feminism, Women and Design* (London: The Women's Press, 1989).

Buckley, Cheryl, *Potters and Paintresses. Women Designers in the Pottery Industry 1870–1955* (London: The Women's Press, 1990).

Buckley, Cheryl, 'Made in Patriarchy: Towards a Feminist Analysis of Women and Design' in *Design Issues*, vol. 3, no. 2, Fall 1986, reprinted in V. Margolin (ed.), *Design Discourses* (Chicago: University of Chicago Press, 1989).

Buckley, Cheryl, 'A Private Space in a Public Place', in *Royal Doulton International Collectors' Club Journal*, vol. 10, no. 1, 1990.

Buckley, Cheryl, 'Craft Hierarchies, Gender Divisions and the Roles of Women Paintresses and Designers in the British Pottery Industry, 1890–1939' in *Journal of Design History*, vol. 2, no. 4, 1989.

Buckley, Cheryl, 'Design, Femininity and Modernism: Interpreting the work of Susie Cooper', in *Journal of Design History*, vol. 7, no. 4, 1994.

Bumpus, Bernard, *Charlotte Rhead. Potter and Designer* (London: Kevin Francis Publishing, 1987).

Casey, Andrew, *Susie Cooper Ceramics. A Collectors Guide* (Stratford-upon-Avon: Jazz Publications, 1992).

Eatwell, Ann, *Susie Cooper Productions* (London: Victoria and Albert Museum, 1987).

Forsyth, Gordon, *20th Century Ceramics. An International Survey of the Best Work Produced by Modern Craftsmen, Artists and Manufacturers* (London: Studio, 1936).

Griffin, Len, Louis K. Meisel, and Susan P. Meisel, *Clarice Cliff. The Bizarre Affair* (New York: Abrams, 1988).

Hannah, Fran, *Ceramics* (London: Bell & Hyman, 1986).

Niblett, Kathy, *Dynamic Design. The British Pottery Industry 1940–1990* (Hanley: Stoke-on-Trent City Museum & Art Gallery, 1990).

Rose, Peter, *Hannah Barlow, A Pioneer Doulton Artist* (London: Richard Dennis, 1985).

Sarsby, Jackie, *Missuses and Mouldrunners. An Oral History of Women Pottery Workers at Work and at Home* (Milton Keynes: Open University Press, 1988).

Shaw, Christopher, *When I Was a Child. By an Old Potter* (London: David and Charles Reprint, 1969; first published London: Methuen, 1903).

Vincentelli, Moira, *Women and Ceramics. Gendered Vessels* (Manchester: Manchester University Press, 2000).

Woodhouse, Adrian, *Susie Cooper* (Shirland, Derbyshire: Trilby Books, 1992).

Chapter 9

Textiles

Janis Jefferies

What can she Know?

As a young woman and a painting student in the early 1970s, there were many arguments and anxieties with art about art. The desire to retrieve women's work from neglect and the 'female' category to which it was usually assigned profoundly affected my thinking and making for the next two decades. Armed with my copy of *Art and Sexual Politics: Why Have There Been No Great Women Artists?* and a subscription to *Spare Rib*, I resolved to make change.[1]

In her 1987 essay 'Feminism and Modernism', the British feminist art historian Griselda Pollock mapped out some of the discourses that informed much of the cultural work produced by women in the USA and Britain during the past thirty years. During the 1960s and the 1970s, she argued, modernism was the dominant paradigm for all artistic practices.[2] This was contested by the many different groups that constituted the political movements of the 1960s, and new alliances, concepts and rhetorics were formed. The Women's Liberation movement, and I, emerged and grew during those halcyon days and formative decades of renewal and regeneration, as I have just described.

The writings of Linda Nochlin and Norma Broude introduced me to the 'femmages' of the American feminist artist Miriam Schapiro, whose strategy to create a deliberate continuity between her own work – her 'femmages' – and women's traditional arts in quilting and sewing, gave permission for the dismantling of the binary opposition between textiles, decoration and the 'fine art' hegemony of abstract painting.[3] The realisation that bits and pieces of fabric could close the gap between pure studio and the everyday reality of her home, allowed Schapiro to say that, 'the story of my evolution is typical of what happens when fabrics become a metaphor for quiet revolution'.[4]

A not-so-quiet fabric revolution and an icon of 1970s feminist art is Judy Chicago's *The Dinner Party*.[5] In this piece, a banquet table was laid out for thirty-nine luminaries of women's history, each represented by vaginal folds. These folds were fixed in porcelain plates and ceremoniously placed on lavishly embroidered and quilted runners. The names of 999 less famous women were inscribed into a 'heritage' floor and banners floated in the exhibition entrance hall to celebrate what had previously been hidden from history. The resonances set up between craft, textile and female genitalia struck a positive cord for many women, but *The Dinner Party* also became open to all kinds of appropriation in a cultural context which already positioned women as closer to the body via the tactile and the sensual. Such positions seemingly celebrated the specificity of women's identity as being defined through their bodies, and sexuality as an essential basis for a female aesthetic. However, according to the critic Lucy Lippard,

> Feminist methods and theories have instead offered a socially concerned alternative to the increasingly mechanical evolution of art about art. The 1970s might not have been pluralist art at all if women had not emerged during the decade to introduce the multicoloured threads of female experience into the male fabric of modern art.[6]

Lippard's metaphor for the impact of feminism on contemporary art practice, with its strong textile references to 'weaving' and 'fabric', underscores a particular relationship between female experience, textiles and feminism. Lippard privileged the quilt as a 'prime visual metaphor for women's lives, for women's culture', whether sewn by many hands (as a seminal sign for collective, shared endeavour) or by one pair of hands with many memories. For Lippard, the quilt embodied a collective sign of political networking and a material diary of women's interrupted lives, as well as establishing a framework in which 'high' and 'low' arts were to be interpreted.[7]

Rozsika Parker and Griselda Pollock also started to write about quilts as a distinctive form of art that was potentially richer than the relationship of making, using and reception usual in 'high' art. As a consequence, quilts were accorded a new and particular value in the battle of the 'crafty arts'.[8] Parker had explored the relationship between ideas of femininity, work and stitch as early as 1975,[9] while Lisa Tickner wrote a definitive study on the imagery of the women's suffrage movement, and

Elaine Showalter researched the relationship between American women's quilts and women's writing.[10]

Such research, constructed by these historians and theorists, began to articulate the rich complexity of historical and cultural data encoded within forms once thought of as ideologically bereft and politically benign. It became generally acknowledged that many women were inscribing in quilts and stitch, banners and samplers, the stories of their lives as a source of pleasure and painful recollection, using this as a weapon against the constraints of femininity, and as a potential means of, radically challenging masculine meanings and dominance in the visual arts and society.

This potentially radical yet problematic promotion of women's 'traditional' arts in textiles enabled not only a distancing from an aesthetics of the 'purely' visual but also provided a strategy for mobilising textiles as a weapon of resistance against a inculcated 'feminine' ideal. This double strategy had clear implications for future, feminist textile-based practices that desired public recognition, via exhibitions and writing. On the one hand, collage or montage, in the form of piecing and patching (for example, quilts), and on the other, scriptovisual, mixed-media techniques could be adapted and combined to present the conditions and causes of women's oppression instead of simply reproducing its appearances. In my view, textiles were transformed into a feminist *coup de grace*, in this brave new world of defying worn-out dichotomies and hierarchies. However, there were some dissonant voices, like Michele Barrett, who argued that the recovery and elevation of a collective gathering of women's 'traditional' arts around Chicago to the status of art objects hung in a gallery, was not necessarily feminist art. Feminism, as espoused by Rosalind Coward, was an alignment of political interests and not a shared female experience. Feminist art, in their view, was not the same as any art that emphasised women's experience.[11] Even if these cautionary tales voiced a political unease at conflating the retrieval of women's 'traditional' arts with feminist politics, textiles, within an expanded field of practices and methodologies, provided an unusually productive and critical space for a post-1960s generation of art school graduates. Textiles, both as a material set of practices and as a fluid set of mobile signs, became available for use in many different ways. Whether as an art of personal negotiation (as in Schapiro's 'femmages') as a critique of patriarchal society (problematically in Chicago's *The Dinner Party*), or as an examination of domesticity and the sexual division of labour (the 'Feministo' and 'Womanhouse' exhibitions), textiles were used to explore the personal and the political, craft and class, piecework and global industrialisation.

The sexual division of labour, craft and class were just some of the aspects of women's work in the late 1970s. In 1980 Lucy Lippard curated 'Issues: Social Strategies by Women Artists', an exhibition at the Institute of Contemporary Arts (ICA) in London. 'Fenix Arising' was a cooperative travelling installation made by Su Richardson, Monica Ross and Kate Walker, and all of these artists had been part of 'Feministo', the postal event exhibited as 'Portrait of the Artist as a Young Housewife'. In 1974 Kate Walker and Sally Gollop began exchanging art works through the post. In 'Issues', these artists explored a 'nurturant' kitchen in *The Other Side of the Blanket*. Walker's pink and blue knitted mat contained the stitched apology: 'Heart not Art, Homemade I'm Afraid'. Fenix's combinations of fried egg/breast motifs, crochet breakfasts, and 'pregnant' cushions seemed clichéd but were also wickedly funny. These themes were directly inspired by 'Womanhouse', an exhibition created by Judy Chicago, Miriam Schapiro and students from the Feminist Art Programme at the California Institute of the Arts in 1972. Lippard had already written about 'Household Images in Art' and the phenomenon she describes best sums up the impact of the Women's Movement on art-making processes that deployed textiles: ' "Female techniques" like sewing, weaving, knitting . . . were avoided by women. They knew they could not afford to be called "feminine artists" . . . Some of this has been changed, or at least modified by the Women's Movement.'[12]

A second work had an even greater impact on my own studio practice throughout the 1980s. Margaret Harrison's collage paintings and documentation pieces focused on women and work, craft and class. The visual core of *Craftwork* consisted of three versions of each craftwork: the actual lace doily, a painting of it and a photograph. The items belonged to her mother-in-law, and the work traced the 'deskilling process' of working-class women since industrialisation by moving from a handmade patchwork to a cheap doily made in the factory by working women and sold back to them. Both Harrison's *Craftwork* and *Homeworkers* (Figure 9.1) were, for me, seminal works of the period.[13]

Figure 9.1 Margaret Harrison, Homeworkers in 'Women and Work: a Document on the Division of Labour in Industry', an exhibition organised by Kay Hunt, Mary Kelly and Margaret Harrison for the South London Art Gallery, 1975. Photograph by Janis Jefferies.

I should stress at this point that these textile-based investigations into women's experience, within the home and at work, are echoed in feminist writing interested in textile production as a source of literary and critical metaphor and in critiques of philosophy and science. Both discourses revolve around the re-evaluation of experience and its relation to constructed knowledge.[14]

In another register, the feminist philosopher Lorraine Code discusses the exclusion of women and their 'traditional' skills from those who count as knowers and that which counts as the known.[15] She suggests there has been a withholding of authoritative epistemic status from the knowledge women have rationally constructed out of designated areas of experience. It is an area in which the politics of gender finds itself allegedly illustrated through 'gossip', 'old wives' tales', 'women's lore' and 'witchcraft', and yet which is illuminated via another text 'Art or Women's Work? News from the Knitting Circle'.[16] Both the subjugation and trivialisation of women's 'traditional' skills can only be meaningfully explained in terms of structures of power and differential authority encoded in the purity demanded by an ideal objectivity. Code concludes that women's knowledge cannot attain this ideal standard because it would appear to grow out of experiences, and out of continued contact with particularities of material which are strongly shaped by the subjectivity of its knowers: women.

It was within this framework, that I, Marysia Lewandowska, Sara Bowman, Gillian Elinor and Pauline Barrie from the Women Artists Slide Library, organised 'Women and Textiles: Their Lives and Their Work' at Battersea Arts Centre in London in 1983, without any public funding.[17] The preface of the exhibition catalogue outlined our intentions and the issues we wanted to raise. Through the exhibition, together with a number of seminars, discussions, performances, films and conference addresses, we sought to provoke a debate on the problems of form and function, the values of use and exchange, the definitions of art and craft, and the meanings of the personal and the political. We showed collective work, organised manufacture, commissioned work, and work drawn from personal and political motivation.

The exhibition was devised on the basis of an open submission and had been advertised in many textile and regional art/craft newsletters, as well as in magazines and non-art journals. There was an overwhelming response, with the largest number of submissions coming via *Spare Rib*. Since the exhibition was called 'Women and Textiles: Their Lives and Their Work', we devised a questionnaire for prospective exhibitors to complete, and the questionnaire and exhibitors' responses to it formed the basis of the catalogue. This gave an opportunity not only for exhibitors to theorise their practice, but for the different publics to have a sense of why textiles had been chosen by them as a particular medium of personal expression. We concluded our introduction by asserting that like all artefacts, textiles were the products of complex social relations.

Most exhibitors and their statements commented on the possibility of using textiles as a way of articulating a diverse and multifaceted range of experiences. As it transpired, and as I myself would testify, even the simplest form of observational knowledge depends on corroboration and acknowledgement in either word or deed. When someone is in doubt about what she knows or hears or sees, she is likely to call on someone else to confirm her experience, and 'Women and Textiles' provided just such an opportunity.

Of course the 'she' is also the 'I', and as with any autobiographical utterance, the status of the self is problematised even at the moment when the very programme of much current feminist theory is concerned with reclaiming the female subject. I am not suggesting that privileged access through appeals to the first person are more elaborately 'natural' to women, but that autobiographical speaking and writing and making can become an exercise, at one and the same time, of critical tellings and critical readings.

The statements in 'Women and Textiles' spoke with a subjectivity that was specially located, yet open to interpretation, dialogue and analysis, on the very basis of the positions that were occupied and also refused. 'Women and Textiles', as an exhibition, was not confined to the hallowed space of the gallery. To emphasise the point that textiles have long been woven into history as sites of resistance, we showed several women's suffrage banners lent by the Fawcett Library in London. Chilean *arpilleras* (patchwork pictures) made by collectives of women who defied, defined and described the brutalities of General Pinochet's Chilean government of the 1960s, were hung alongside patchworks made by women in the black townships of South Africa. Mobile exhibitions of women's textile work in London were lent by the Inner London Education Authority, at the same time as Dutch and Indian self-help groups illustrated the issues of women homeworkers in relation to the global textile industries. Children fell into Teana Gould's *Womb Cube*, squealed at Su Richardson's crocheted bodies, and hung over the fence of the Blackie Group's communally-made garden. Angela Williams reworked *The Dinner Party* into a humorous and pun-like sewing machine table, which still brings a wry smile, while Francesca Souza's shimmering silks branded with political texts were firmly located in feminist art practice. In *Dying for the Cause* (Figure 9.2), she used the printed image of mother and child on silk, but instead of communicating a sense of glorious visitation, she cited the words of Department of Health and Social Security handbooks, and those who tell you what is normal.[18] Marysia Lewandowska and I made a photographic document (Figure 9.3) dedicated to women at Greenham Common – women who had literally woven themselves into the site of their protest (against nuclear armaments and American missiles on English soil) and had also encircled the fence one day in June with an assortment of banners and quilts as in the manner of a textile dragon. We exhibited the photographic panels with an accompanying text to signify textiles as a critical language, and photography as a questionable means of representing visual truth.

A decade later, and in revisiting these pieces and my own work on Greenham Common and Chernobyl, my questions trouble the once confident readings of how meanings might be made out of a subversive stitch. 'The Subversive Stitch: Women and Textiles Today' (Figure 9.4) opened in Manchester in 1988 and was a major examination of textiles informed by feminist theory.[19] My contribution to the exhibition consisted of Greenham scriptovisual collages like *Home of the Brave?*, *Lest We Forget*, and the tapestry *Closed Circuit/Open Book- A Greenham Reader 1981–198?*. The Chernobyl series was stitched, or montaged using photo-emulsion processes, as dedications to my father in the manner of a family album, a social document, some ten years on. Do they solicit or frustrate? Are they nostalgic or melancholic or do they lay claim to what was culturally and politically significant? Are they directly transparent to this signification?

Figure 9.2 Francesca Souza, Dying for the Cause, *1983, print on silk, 1 × 1m, shown in 'Women and Textiles: Their Lives and Work'. Photograph by Janis Jefferies.*

Do they seem strangely incomplete? Are they just fragments to be deciphered?

Paradoxically, while a model of critical practice had been crucial in establishing the visibility of feminist discourses and practices, it also became increasingly narrowly employed to promote a prescriptive and proscriptive conception of 'proper' feminist art practice, which seemed to admonish sensual or visual pleasure.[20] Could there also be

Figure 9.3 Marysia Lewansdowska and Janis Jefferies, Greenham *document for 'Women and Textiles: Their Lives and Work',* 1983. *Three photographic panels, each 25 × 140cm, installation of a textile dragon by women at Greenham Common, 1983. Photograph by Janis Jefferies.*

Figure 9.4 Janis Jefferies, installation shot of work for 'The Subversive Stitch: Women and Textiles Today'. Photograph by Mark Sanderson at Waterman's Art Centre, London, 1989.

prescriptive and prospective conception of 'proper' feminist textile practice? Both the 1983 and the 1988 exhibition on women and textiles included mixed-media, scriptovisual and textile-based work. As women-only shows, which predominantly promoted a feminist position and analysis, they were not free from controversy.[21]

As feminism expanded throughout the late 1980s and early 1990s, material practices were diversified and expanded into broader cultural discourses. The boundaries of feminist art theory were opened up and renegotiated within psychoanalytic, anthropological, postcolonial and queer studies. Dangerous, vulnerable, angry, chaotic and multifariously defined desires were conjured by textile metaphors, processes and materials. As represented by Christine, Irene and Heidemarie Hohenbuchler, textiles became a guiding metaphor to their ideas and working practices. In the exhibition 'We Knitted Braids for Her', language, texts and textiles were interwoven to explore the conditions of female subjectivity caught in a complex web of chain-knitting, dream diaries, woven bundles of cloth, and sexually charged motifs of pomegranates in homely rugs.[22] More recently, Tracey Emin's colourful blankets, quilts and embroidered tents often elicit emotional responses from women (and men), possibly because she dwells on a traumatised, living autobiography of self-abuse, abortion, suicide, debt and lust.[23] As in 'We Knitted Braids for Her', there is a wilful, rather than worthy, disregard of artistic boundaries as the gaps between high and low, fine art and textiles, private and public, professional worlds are elided in a whirl of frenetic transgression and confessional anecdotes.

Hybrid practices and heterogeneous forms of production have transformed mainstream 'art' making and 'high' art institutions (public and commercial galleries) to an extent inconceivable in the 1970s. In the late 1980s and 1990s, the processes and languages of fibre and thread, stitch and weave finally unravelled the hierarchies of my youth. For example, Bonnie Lucas and Colette

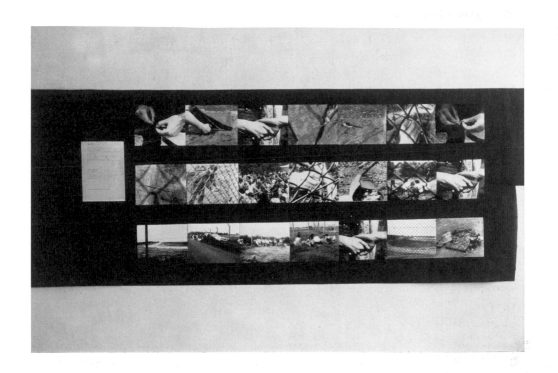

explore the worlds of girlhood and feminine sexuality through material and decorative excess; Polly Appelbaum makes fabric constructions; Ann Wilson explores the sensuality of hair with the cultural associations of domestic linens; Beverly Semmes produces overscaled clothing structures; Ann Hamilton produces material installations around the condition of blue-collar workers; and Joyce Scott marks political events in a fury of crocheted mayhem. In a rare interview, Rosemarie Trockel, as early as 1985, re-dramatised the cultural production of gendered consciousness, thus: 'What is most painful, what is most tragic, about (women's art) is that women have intensified this alleged inferiority of the "typically female" '.[24]

Trockel's textile masquerades and her semiotics of play may yet become icons for the 1990s, as the work of some women artists continues to 'destabilise' the hierarchies of gender and categories of cultural production. All the above mentioned examples of feminist-inspired art, using textile processes and materials, are more likely to address differences among women in terms of race and ethnicity, gender and individual networking than the universalising tendencies of 1970s Western feminism in all its experimental diversity. Although there is little infrastructure in terms of a collective network of magazines like *Spare Rib* and *FAN* or the American journals such as *Heresies* and *MS* (to devour and communicate the latest feminist thoughts and political actions), the Women's Art Library in London continues to publish the independent journal *make*. *N. paradoxa* also flourishes in both printed and Internet form. Debates about women, textiles and feminism in a new political and cultural era can still be found in the pages of these magazines. Equally, there are exciting new and unresolved questions around textiles, touch and new technologies. Textiles, textile production and textile metaphors have become a renewed area of focus and debate through contemporary feminist discourses, for example in *Zeros + Ones: Digital Women + The New Technoculture*, Sadie Plant insists that textiles are literally the software linings of all technology.[25] In the USA, exhibitions like 'The Presence of Touch' (1996) examined the relationships between the immaterial and the material, via *Hermes' Mistresses* and *The Glass Bead Game*.[26]

But as anyone may have noticed over the last few years, 'female-associated' craft-like processes, and most notably textiles, have had something of a resurgence in work made by men, in what I call 'the boys that sew club', and there has been an unprecedented amount of material fabrication and stitch manipulation in the 1990s. One of the ways, it could be argued, in which textile-based work made by men gets its charge is role play; it participates in a critique of an essential masculinity (and femininity) that began to be articulated after the 1970s. Identity is destabilised, and plays off, often acknowledges, and frequently disguises quite serious attempts to weave together, the legacies of feminism and textiles. I would argue that Oliver Herring's transparent knitted eulogies to Ethyl Eichelberger, Michael Raedecker's and Roy Voss' deceptively 'nostalgic' threads of domestic solitude, Yinka Shonibare's 'mimicry' of Victorian crinoline dresses, Neil McGinnis's celebration of gay culture through computer-generated rococo silks, and Mayer Vaisman's parody of tapestry in Disneyesque prints all have their antecedents in early feminist art of the 1970s – witness the obsession with domestic interrogations, the phenomenon of empty garments, a labour-intensive aesthetic, and the assumptions that the personal and the political can be meaningfully bound together. Such work may not demonstrate the 'authentic' agitation of a 'Sisterhood is powerful' slogan, nor subscribe to a consciousness-raising collective, but paradoxically it might just conform to a feminist model of rendering the personal within the political; a site where traditional, gendered biographies and identities are loosened by fragments of cloth and fragile bits of sewing.

Notes

1. Linda Nochlin: 'Why Have There Been No Great Women Artists' in Thomas B. Hess and Elizabeth C. Baker (eds), in *Art and Sexual Politics* (New York: Collier Books, 1971), pp. 1–39.
2. Griselda Pollock, 'Feminism and Modernism' in Rozsika Parker and Griselda Pollock (eds), *Framing Feminism: Art and the Women's Movement 1970– 1985* (London: Pandora Press, 1987) pp. 81–96.
3. Linda Nochlin, 'Miriam Schapiro: Recent Work', *Arts Magazine*, November 1973, pp. 38–41, and Norma Broude, 'Miriam Schapiro and "Femmage": Reflections on the Conflict between Decoration and Abstraction in Twentieth Century Art', *Arts Magazine*, February 1980, pp. 83–7.

4. Miriam Schapiro quoted in Charlotte Robinson, *The Artist and the Quilt* (Kent: Quarto/Columbus books, 1983), p. 29.

5. Judy Chicago, *The Dinner Party, A Symbol of Our Heritage* (New York: Doubleday/Anchor, 1979), and *Embroidering our Heritage* (New York: Doubleday/Anchor, 1980). *The Dinner Party* was first shown in London in 1984.

6. Lucy Lippard, 'Sweeping Exchange: The Contribution of Feminism to the Art of the Seventies', *Art Journal*, 1980, vol. 4, no. 1/2, p. 362.

7. Lucy Lippard, 'Up, Down and Across: A New Frame for Quilts', in Charlotte Robinson, *The Artist and the Quilt* (Kent: Quarto/Columbus books, 1983), p. 32.

8. Rozsika Parker and Griselda Pollock, 'Crafty Women and the Hierarchy of the Art' in *Old Mistresses: Women Art and Ideology* (London: Routledge, Kegan and Paul, 1981), pp. 50–82.

9. Rozsika Parker, 'The Word for Embroidery was WORK', *Spare Rib*, 1975, no. 37, pp. 41–5, and *The Subversive Stitch: Embroidery and the Making of the Feminine* (London: Women's Press, 1984).

10. Lisa Tickner, *The Spectacle of Women: Imagery of the Suffrage Campaign 1907–14* (London: Chatto & Windus, 1987), and Elaine Showalter, 'Piecing and Writing' in Nancy Miller (ed.), *The Poetics of Gender* (New York: Columbia University Press, 1986), pp. 222–47.

11. Michele Barrett, 'Feminism and the Definition of Cultural Politics' in Rosalind Brunt and Caroline Rowan (eds), *Feminism, Culture and Politics* (London: Lawrence and Wishart, 1982), pp. 37–59.

12. Lucy Lippard, 'Household Images in Art', was first published in *MS* magazine 1, no. 9, in March 1973, and reprinted in Lippard, *From the Center: Feminist Essays on Women's Art* (New York: Dutton, 1976), p. 57.

13. 'Women and Work: A Document on the Division of Labour in Industry' was organised by Kay Hunt, Mary Kelly and Margaret Harrison at the South London Gallery in 1975.

14. Anne Brennan, 'Running Stitch and Running Writing: Thinking About Process', and Dorothy Jones, 'The Floating Web' in Sue Rowley (ed.), *Craft and Contemporary Theory* (Australia: Allen & Unwin, 1997), pp. 85–98 and pp. 98–112.

15. Lorraine Code, *What Can She Know? Feminist Theory and the Construction of Knowledge* (Ithaca and London: Cornell University Press, 1991). I have made extended use of Code's ideas for discussing feminism and textiles as an interrelated set of experiences and signs from the 1970s.

16. Pamela Johnson, 'Art or Women's Work? News from the Knitting Circle' in *Oral History, Special Issue on the Crafts*, 1990, pp. 50–3, in which Anne Lydiatt, Lyn Malcolm, and Kate Russell and myself were interviewed as contributors to 'The Subversive Stitch' exhibition. The 'knitting circle' was how one of Kate's male colleagues described her textile department.

17. The exhibition 'Women and Textiles: Their Lives and Their Work' was presented by the Women Artists Slide Library at Battersea Arts Centre, London in November 1983. The exhibition included the work of twenty-eight contemporary women artists using textiles. As part of the ongoing series of events around the exhibition, films like Judy Chicago's *The Dinner Party* and *Awake from Mourning* (on black women's struggle in South Africa) were shown. During the two-day conference, Cas Holmes spoke on how the sex of the artist mattered in respect of her own practice and Swasti Mitter analysed the effects of new technology on home-workers. The second day of the conference focused on education, with a slide seminar by Pennina Barnett, based around 'Domestic Hiss' (an article for *Crafts* in 1982 on women working in textiles), Hilary Sleiman on why the evolution of knitting had led to it being a predominately female occupation, and Audrey Walker, then Head of Textiles at Goldsmiths College, discussing textile education in art schools, alongside performances by Barbara Harrow, and June Freeman's 'Sewing as Women's Art' lecture based on her highly influential exhibition of 1982.

18. Janis Jefferies, 'Banners of the Future,' *FAN* 1986, vol. 2, no. 4, pp. 34–5, and Theresa Whitten's review in *Spare Rib*, 1985, no. 44 of 'Textiles Making and Meaning', Brixton Art Gallery, London, January-February 1985. This exhibition was organised by Terri Bullen, a graduate of the textiles programmes at Goldsmiths College's Department of Visual Arts. Many of the exhibitors had been involved with the 'Women and Textiles: Their Lives and Work' exhibition.

19. 'The Subversive Stitch: Women and Textiles Today' was selected by Pennina Barnett and organised with Bev Bytheway for Cornerhouse, Manchester in 1988. This exhibition, which predominately featured the work of textile graduates from Goldsmiths College, was based on Rozsika Parker's book, *The Subversive Stitch: Embroidery and the Making of the Feminine* (London: Women's Press, 1984).

20. Angela Partington, 'Conditions of a Feminist Art Practice,' and Katy Deepwell, 'In Defence of the Indefensible: Femin-

ism, Painting and Post- Modernism,' *FAN*, 1988, vol. 2, no. 4, pp. 13–15 and 9–12 respectively.
21. Pennina Barnett, 'Afterthoughts on Curating "The Subversive Stitch"', in Katy Deepwell (ed.) *New Feminist Art Criticism* (Manchester: Manchester University Press, 1995), pp. 76–86.
22. 'We Knitted Braids for Her', September-November 1995 at the Institute of Contemporary Arts, London. See my review 'Text, Textiles, Sex and Sexuality' in *Women's Art*, 1996, January/February, no. 68, pp. 5–10.
23. Tracey Emin, 'I Need Art Like I Need God', South London Gallery, 1997.
24. Jutta Koether, 'Interview with Rosemarie Trockel, *Flash Art*, May 1987, no. 134, p. 42.
25. Sadie Plant, *Zeros + Ones: Digital Women + The New Technoculture* (London: Fourth Estate, 1997), p. 61.
26. 'The Presence of Touch' exhibition was organised by Joan Livingstone and Anne Wilson for the Art Institute of Chicago in 1996 and featured *Hermes' Mistress* by Regina Frank. Frank's *The Glass Bead Game* (after the novel by Hermann Hesse) combined bead collecting, woven paper texts (in the form of a Japanese kimono), performance and a 'virtual' mantle of textile sentences, via her Web site. The work was first shown in England in the 'Loose Threads' exhibition at the Serpentine Gallery, 1998.

Bibliography

Agosin, M., *Scraps of Life: Chilean Arpilleras* (London: Zed Press, 1987).
Barrett, M., and A. Phillips (eds), *Destabilising Theory: Contemporary Feminist Debates* (Cambridge: Polity Press, 1992).
Broude, N., and M. Garrard, *The Power of Feminist Art* (New York: Harry Abrams, 1994).
Chapkis, W., and C. Rose, *Of Common Cloth: Women in the Global Textile Industry* (Amsterdam and Washington: Transnational Institute, 1983).
Elinor, G., S. Richardson, S. Scott, A. Thomas, K. Walker (eds), *Women and Craft* (London: Virago, 1987).
Felshin, N., *Embedded Metaphor* (New York: Independent Curators Inc, 1996).
Felshin, N., *Empty Dress: Clothing as Surrogate in Recent Art* (New York: Independent Curators Inc, 1994).

Freeman, J., and L. Edwards (eds), *The Quilters' Review*, Autumn 1997, no. 24; Winter 1995, no. 29; and Summer 1998, no. 25.

Jefferies, J., 'Autobiographical Patterns', *Surface Design Journal*, Summer 1997, vol. 21, no. 4.

Lippard, L., *Get the Message? A Decade of Art for Social Change* (New York: Dutton, 1984).

Studio International, Women's Art, special issue, 1977, vol. 193, no. 987.

Yee, L., *Division of Labor: Women's Work* (New York: Bronx Museum of the Arts, 1995), pp. 9–47.

Chapter 10

Fashion

Rebecca Arnold

OVER THE PAST THIRTY years, fashion has reflected the fragmentation of postmodern culture through the blurring of its previously hierarchical structure, and the cross-fertilisation of subcultural styles with high fashion. While this break-up may have diminished the power of *couture* to dictate a single fashionable silhouette, reliant upon a newly reshaped vision of femininity each season, it has not erased the unease many feminists feel about the power and influence fashion wields over women's minds and bodies. The myriad of styles that congregate in glossy magazine pages and shop windows present a complex and contradictory insight into the ways in which late twentieth-century culture has been interpreted and represented in fashion's field of vision. The possibility of a reconciliation between feminist thought and fashion theory may be closer than it was in the 1970s, when the careful adornment and assimilation of feminine ideals required by fashion appeared anathema to the liberation of women from oppressive patriarchal constructs, but the varied strands of contemporary feminist thought remain wary of fashion's glittering embrace.

Significantly, despite the friction and mutual suspicion that distinguishes feminism's relationship with fashion, the latter – as the most instant visual means of signalling shifting definitions of self – has been a major arena in which the deconstruction and reconstruction of notions of sexuality, gender and desire have been played out. The shifting discourses of femininity, of seeking to express or subvert ideals of femaleness, are constantly being explored in both garment design and styling. The potentially transgressive construction of the self through clothing has led some feminist writers to embrace fashion as a means to reclaim the masquerade of femininity and consumption for the pleasure of women themselves. However, the poor conditions that many fashion workers experience, and the fears surrounding fashion's perceived desire for conformity, have meant that debates continue to reflect ambiguity and ambivalence rather than consensus.

In this chapter, I examine contemporary thought on the emotive nature of feminism's reading of fashion, and set it within the context of earlier discussion of the subject. The issues this analysis raises will be explored further in a case study of female fashion designer Miuccia Prada, whose work highlights the complexity of the debate which typifies this as a period of transition, when patriarchal definitions of femininity and representation have been challenged, but remain unresolved.

Natasha Walter's book *The New Feminism* (1998) sought to project a positive vision of women's relationship to fashion, stating, 'the traditional feminist desire to desexualise women's bodies looks unnecessary and miserable. Many feminists today feel that the battle over appearance is an old one, and not worth the anger it once engendered.'[1] She is referring to the work of writers like Susan Brownmiller, whose abandonment of any trace of traditionally feminine dress during the 1970s, was because she felt it induced 'the body to strut about in small, restrained yet show-offy ways', preventing women from being taken seriously.[2] Her decision to adopt more masculine attire was a means to challenge dominant ideals of femininity, promoting utilitarian dress, although she did admit that this denied the pleasure in the sensual.

Walter seeks to assert the idea that women should enjoy, without feeling guilty, the pleasures that clothing can bestow upon the wearer, the power to be had from being well-dressed, and confident in your appearance. Men are also included in this rejection of 'puritan feminist' ideals, encouraged to 'play with the dressing up box'[3] and rethink masculinity through fashion. Her words reflect the alienation many young women feel from the whole notion of feminism, which still bears the mark of stereotypes, formed thirty years ago, of the feminist as man-hater and apocryphal bra-burner.

However, while advocating that feminists should focus upon more deep-seated problems of a social, economic and political nature, Walter tends to gloss over the problems inherent in a

complete acceptance of fashion as an aid to women's advance-
ment, for example, the fact that many women feel excluded from
mainstream fashion because they 'lack' the current body ideal or
the financial ability to consume such goods. There has undoubtedly been a shift towards women using fashion and its dress codes
in a self-conscious and empowering way, but it is too soon to
claim victory over the debates it raises. As Sheila Rowbotham has
pointed out, although there is now less sense of being judged by
your clothing as either 'good' or 'bad', fashion can impose new
pressures. 'The problem now is it seems [women] have to be a
Madonna *and* a whore'.[4]

The discussion of fashion as part of a wider debate on attitudes
to consumption within feminist theory has reiterated the contradictions set up by fashion's ability to enable the construction of
new subjectivities (something which most theorists agree upon),
yet to simultaneously raise questions as to just how individual
these new 'selves' can be. Celia Lury has written of the increased
power available to the consumer as the huge choice of products
on offer enables the construction of a variety of group identities.[5]
Mica Nava, while stating that consumption historically offered
new outlets for women and opened up the opportunity to claim
greater powers, via new types of work and awareness of consumer rights, also recognises that these choices lead to a complex
set of meanings and responses. She writes, 'Consumerism is far
more than just economic activity: it is also about dreams and
consolation, communication and confrontation, image and identity. Like sexuality, it consists of a multiplicity of fragmented and
contradictory discourses.'[6]

Consumption is therefore viewed as a method of producing as
well as consuming meaning, of signalling desires and aspirations
yet to be achieved. Jane Gaines, in her discussion of the relationship between film costume, fashion and feminism, took her cue
from Walter Benjamin's notion of commodities as 'dream forms'
when she said, 'Can we also see a premonition of what revolution
might "feel like" prefigured in the fresh consciousness proposed
by the strikingly new season in styles, even the taste of victory in
the culmination of a purchase?'[7] The idea that fashion's seasonal
tread might produce a sense of the potential for change and
renewal in a positive way, providing an environment in which to
dream of revolution, radically rewrites second-wave feminists'

opinions of the pressures asserted on women to constantly alter their appearance in line with fashion's biennial collections while remaining simultaneously representative of the 'eternal feminine'.

It was Betty Friedan who crystallised fears about the pernicious nature of consumption in 1963. Her trailblazing book, *The Feminine Mystique*, drew upon the ideas of Herbert Marcuse to formulate an attack upon consumer culture as the creator of false desires that trapped the consumer into the role of victim, anaesthetised by advertising's enticing images. This then forced women to learn 'to "adjust" to their biological role. They have become dependent, passive, childlike; they have given up their adult frame of reference to live at the lower human level of food and things'.[8] Indeed, there has been suspicion since the early part of the century that women lose sight of feminist goals once they are drawn into the realm of consumption.

The later revision of attitudes about fashion's potential is in part a response to the postmodernist breakdown of overarching theories, which enabled previously marginalised (and often female-dominated) areas like fashion to be re-evaluated as having equal significance in reflecting, and indeed constructing, cultural ideas and identities. Elizabeth Wilson has written convincingly on fashion's ability to represent the self and the body as a cultural product, allowing for a more fluid approach to identity which enables both resistance to pervasive 'norms' and the construction of counterdiscourse. Wilson comments on the possibility of consciously using fashion as a means of adapting to, and aestheticising, the confusion of postmodern existence: 'dress could play a part, for example, either to glue the false identity together on the surface, or to lend a theatrical and play-acting aspect to the hallucinatory experience of the contemporary world'.[9] In this light, dress becomes a channel for experimenting with the body, masking and transforming it, creating a web of different meanings according to the fashionable disguise adopted.

For Naomi Wolf, however, this playful use of fashion remains problematic, constantly drawing women back into patriarchal definitions that trap the body into ideal forms, even if the clothing itself is less physically repressive than in the past. She wrote, in 1990, that a 'lighthearted' approach to dressing will only become possible when women are in control of their own sexuality, and are 'granted rock solid identities',[10] an idea which conflicts with the very notion of playful, postmodern fluidity of image and identity.

Wolf's concerns about the transferral of restraints upon women from the clothes they wear, to their bodies has, however, been articulated elsewhere. Susan Bordo has written of fashion's involvement in homogenising ideals of the body, adding to a fear of difference, rather than providing a platform to display and explore diversity. 'The general tyranny of fashion – perpetual, elusive, and instructing the female body in a pedagogy of personal inadequacy and lack – is a powerful discipline for the normalization of *all* women in this culture.'[11] Certainly, there has long been an idea that 'one thing fashion is quite categorically *not* is an expression of individuality'.[12] Fashion's construction of lifestyle categories to many feminists prohibits the creation of unique subjectivities, a view at odds with the postmodern appropriation of the 'surface' of appearance as a liberating submersion in the world of costume and disguise.

In contrast once more to the theories of writers like Walter, who feel attacks on fashionable dress hinder women's empowerment, is the feeling among some feminists, that consumption of fashion via the shining magazine photograph is fraught with contradictions. Myra Macdonald articulates the perceived problems when she says, 'however extravagant the fashion images, the urging to participate, to indulge in fashion as a wacky form of self-expression denies the simplicity of the passive gazing invited by the high fashion magazines.'[13]

Angela McRobbie wrote in the early 1990s of women's (in particular teenage girls') readings of the fashion spread as more subversive, allowing for the adaptation rather than the adoption of the images and advice such magazines contain.[14] While recognising, as others have, that fashion has the potential for both pleasurable and transgressive appropriation by women, she has called for a wider reading of the subject. She feels that there is a need for a complete overhaul of the entire fashion system, from product design, manufacture, and retail, to the education of fashion designers, and the creation of images and consumption of fashion. Only by taking all these elements together, and addressing the problems of, for example, the continued use of sweatshop labour, can fashion be reconciled with feminist thought and ideals.

McRobbie acknowledges the importance of analysis of image and representation, which has dominated feminist discussion of fashion since the mid 1980s, but says that the 'exclusive focus on the fashion spectacle reinforces the wider cultural emphasis on the image. The sexual politics of the page produce a kind of sociological amnesia as if nobody was employed to produce the pages or to create the clothes.'[15]

It was Elizabeth Wilson's ground-breaking book, *Adorned in Dreams*, first published in 1985, which opened up the field of debate on fashion, focusing mainly upon the way it represented women. She seized upon feminists' rejection of fashion as a conflict between the 'authentic' and the 'modern', a false search for the 'real' woman beneath the imposed feminine ideals – which ultimately created another style of dress closely related to fashion – rather than the dreamed of 'genderless space' that would speak of true equality. For Wilson, the spectacle of fashion was all-important, 'a performance art', which reflects 'the ambivalence of the flawed culture of modernity'.[16] By recognising fashion itself as an ambivalent phenomenon of visual culture, she pinpointed the reason for the contradictory responses it provokes: 'that is why we remain endlessly troubled by fashion – drawn to it, yet repelled by a fear of what we might find hidden within its purposes, masked by the enigma of its Mona Lisa smile'.[17]

This approach was further expanded upon by Caroline Evans and Minna Thornton, who advocated an interdisciplinary approach to the study of fashion, drawing in particular upon psychoanalytical theory to examine the means by which the contemporary 'multiplicity of feminisms', could be discussed in relation to the multiplicity of fashionable femininities.[18] Their close analysis of specific images and designers, along with subcultural dress, sought to reclaim voyeuristic pleasure for women, who could renegotiate gender definitions by embracing the masquerade of fashion, and a new, positive vision of female narcissism. They wrote, 'when women identify with fashion, they are celebrating experimentation'.[19]

While such positivity enabled the study of fashion in a new light, as has been seen, feminists in the 1990s continue to be concerned about its multiple, and often blurred meanings. If 1960s feminists sought to reject fashion altogether, and 1970s writers focused on the evils of advertising and pornography, then the 1980s and 1990s saw attempts to employ a variety of methodologies in recognising both the real pleasures to be gained from the visual and literal consumption of fashion and its surrounding representations of women, and to push for a rigorous approach to all aspects of fashion's creation and consumption. Ambiguity and ambivalence may be the defining features of fashion and the debates it provokes, but, as Wilson has pointed out, these are also the defining features of the culture they are rooted in.

Fashion in the 1990s has been marked by a sense of confusion, as designers have sought to recognise shifting attitudes to gender, sexuality, status and wealth in their work. Fred Davis has said, 'no designer of stature nowadays can pretend indifference to the antifashion sentiments emanating from feminist quarters'.[20] Although feminist attitudes to fashion are clearly more complex than being merely 'anti', it is true to say that an awareness of issues raised concerning the representation of women in fashion has entered the mainstream. While few designers will admit to being feminist themselves, afraid of the unfashionable connotations such an appellation might imply, there has been an adoption of the use of postmodern irony as a distancing device in many designers' work. Attempts have been made to address negative ideas about overtly sexy clothing by emphasising that this can empower women, and stressing the play element involved in reclaiming traditionally feminine garments and accessories. While doubts remain about just how deep the changes have been in the fashion industry's portrayal of women, discussion of the fashion system, and related issues of gender and sexuality, the debate in the popular media has increased awareness of the previously unspoken dress codes which influence the way people wear clothes and respond to the multiplicity of meanings they can produce.

There are also a growing number of female designers who have gained influence and status since the 1980s, bringing a greater awareness of the way women feel about their bodies and the clothes that adorn them. While some, like Donna Karan, have chosen to construct identities of independence and control via softly tailored, functional designs, which draw on menswear as a means to bestow connotations of power upon the wearer, others have been driven by a desire to question the basis of fashionable dress itself. Anne Demeulemeester has sought to draw attention to the artificial nature of fashion and traditional gender definitions, deconstructing the process of design in her reworked fabrics and the deliberate dishevelment of her styling.

As with theories of fashion, diversity and shifting interpretations remain. Miuccia Prada's work has been hugely influential, inspiring imitations at all levels of the fashion spectrum. Her work is interesting from a feminist perspective, as it offers renegotiations of femininity which recognise, and draw attention to, the complex identities created by fashion and fashion advertising, instead of trying to smooth over the contradictions and normalise them for the consumer. She has also endeavoured to keep control of all aspects of the production of her designs, preferring small Italian manufacturers, and in some cases investing in factories with particular production skills, thus maintaining contact with all stages of the product development process. Her label specialises in high fashion and accessories that combine minimalist style with an interesting use of colour and textiles, and are subtly subversive.

Prada's family company originally specialised in accessories, and she has revived the 'proper' handbag and the high-heeled shoe as necessary elements of female dress. While this could be seen as retrogressive, forcing women back into defining themselves via the groomed management of details, her designs have been more subversive. The feminine connotations of the handbag have been contradicted, their simple forms rendered in tough industrial nylon, a fabric normally used by the Italian military. This cheap and utilitarian material lends the swagger of 'masculine' authenticity to an object previously reviled by many women as a symbol of oppressive ideas of 'ladylike' femininity. The confusion of signifiers encapsulated within the Prada bag, its triangular silver nameplate adding a layer of fashion and financial status to the already loaded mix of meaning, emphasises Caroline Evans and Minna Thornton's suggestion that 'fashion has always existed as a challenge to meaning where meaning is understood to involve some notion of coherence, a demonstrable consistency'.[21]

Meaning has become more complex, more unstable as categories of identity have been questioned and blurred. Fashion in the late twentieth century has been able to reflect, and in some cases prefigure, the flickering connotations of femininity, masculinity and status that have been experimented with by designers responding to and anticipating cultural shifts.

For Prada, a primary site for this experimentation has been challenging notions of taste. Her bags, also made up in clear plastic or sequins for her second line Miu Miu, were a direct assault on the traditional sedate leathers of the status-symbol handbag. The fashion press has deified her accessories collections, at first as the secret treasure of the fashion *afficionado*, aware of the subtle messages of cultural value they gave off, and then, as her work gained confidence, for her subversion of bourgeois taste in the fabrics and retro styles she uses. Her assertion that 'looking at bad taste is more interesting'[22] may infer feminist ideals of breaking up the tyranny of a repressive, defined, bourgeois taste that stifles anything categorised as low-class or non-conformist, but the high prices of her designs exclude many from buying genuine Prada. For them, the only options are the copies of Prada's bags, sold in markets across the globe, but lacking the refinement of detail and quality of the original. Once more, the 'authenticity' of the original carries cultural value for those who can afford it. It may be possible to argue that there is a different kind of pleasure for women consuming cheaper *simulacra* of high fashion – the appeal of the 'bargain', perhaps a subversive delight in defying the exclusivity and alienation of the world of designer boutiques – but the clearly illegal nature of such merchandise and the lack of any control over its manufacturing conditions calls this into question.

In her clothing lines, Prada's designs have been equally successful and equally contradictory, and here again she has explored issues of taste and 'acceptability' in high fashion. In her spring/summer 1996 collection, she continued her fetishisation of the *accoutrements* of femininity that was apparent in her accessories: in Figure 10.1, the model wears a light, empire-line slip dress, its dainty white background an echo of early nineteenth-century fashions. However, its abbreviated hemline, cut just above the knee, short-circuits so innocent a reading, calling to mind the Lolita-style babydoll dresses of the 1960s. This dissonance is reinforced in the 'off-tones' of creeping foliage print that cling to the silhouette of the dress, breaking up its surface, and preventing the eye from focusing on any one area of the garment. Over this is worn a narrow three-quarter length coat; once again, the ground of the fabric is bright white, but a conflicting pattern in the same olive greens adds an edge to the sweetly girlish overview. Double squares are printed across the fabric, producing a check that echoes the design of 1970s floor tiling. The retro theme continues in the stark, black Mary Jane shoes, their childish connotations made sinister by the seeming over-attention to the details of their design: the toes appear too rounded, the thick heels too high, the stitching on the T-bar over- emphasised. As a whole, the collection epitomises Prada's style. It contains subtle elements and simple forms, with dissonant details that are at once feminine and distancing, drawing attention to their constructed, artificial nature. As ever, darts are made visible, and the construction of the garments remains apparent, forcing an acceptance of their embodiment of a fashionable ideal, instead of smoothing over their artificiality, their 'corrections' of the body beneath.

The retro style and eclectic styling of Prada's designs has encouraged a trend towards thrift shop dressing. Women have drawn inspiration from her work, adapting the tenets of her style to their own ideas, and creating eclectic mixes of old and new clothes which whisper re-evaluations of existing notions of femininity and integrate them into contemporary ideals. This has reiterated the more sophisticated responses to fashion that women have now: fashion is interpreted more freely, with consumers taking a less passive view of the products and images set before them.

Some fashion commentators have welcomed this questioning of ideas of taste and beauty, in Prada's mix of synthetic fabrics and unusual colours and patterns. Richard Martin spoke of her retro/thrift shop references as enabling women to buy 'souvenirs of their collective past', a comment which suggests fashion's ability to assuage the confusion of contemporary life, as well as to celebrate it.[23] Others have rejected Prada as producing 'ugly' visions of awkward girl-women. Robin Givhan wrote that, 'for some the embrace of ugly signifies an underlying desire to shed the accoutrements of wealth and to connect with those less privileged. For others it is yet another chapter in the book of slumming.'[24]

Prada's work is an embodiment of both the complex and

Figure 10.1 Miuccia Prada, Spring/summer 1996 collection. Photograph courtesy of Niall McInerney.

contradictory nature of the fashion system in terms of both representation and consumption. The varied responses to her work echo the conflicting theoretical standpoints adopted by feminists to fashion, which can prompt simultaneous feelings of pleasure and desire, alienation and anxiety. Miuccia Prada herself campaigned for women's liberation during the 1970s, and the ambivalent relationship with the fashion world into which she was drawn is embodied in her designs, which are deliberately difficult and complex in the messages they emanate. In an interview in 1997, she articulated the conflicting emotions inherent in feminist discussion of fashion, saying, 'even in my political phase I loved fashion, but people made me feel ashamed of it . . . I don't see a contradiction between beauty and politics: politics is man trying to live better; aesthetics is man trying to improve the quality of his life.'[25]

For feminists, the dilemma of how fashion can be reconciled with ideals of equality and liberation, is yet to be solved. Prada's designs, like those of many 1990s designers, push us to view fashion's contradictions as a complex of representations that visualise and create femininities, enabling us to explore and assess the fragmentary identities of postmodern culture.

Notes

1. Walter, *The New Feminism*, p. 95.
2. Brownmiller, *Femininity*, p. 79.
3. Walter, *The New Feminism*, p. 104.
4. Sheila Rowbotham, quoted in Decca Aitkenhead, 'Fern *and* Us', *The Guardian*, 13 May 1997.
5. See Celia Lury, *Consumer Culture* (New Jersey: Rutgers University Press, 1996).
6. Nava, *Changing Cultures*, p. 167.
7. Gaines, Jane, 'Introduction: Fabricating the Female Body', Gaines and Herzog, *Fabrications, Costume and the Female Mystique*, p. 13.
8. Friedan, *The Feminine Mystique*, p. 266.
9. Elizabeth Wilson, 'Fashion and the Postmodern Body', in Ash and Wilson, *Chic Thrills, A Fashion Reader*, p. 8.
10. Wolf, *The Beauty Myth*, p. 273.
11. Bordo, *Unbearable Weight*, p. 254.

12. Coward, *Female Desire*, p. 29.
13. Myra Macdonald, *Representing Women, Myths of Femininity in the Popular Media* (London: Edward Arnold, 1995), p. 110.
14. See McRobbie, *Feminism and Youth Cultures*.
15. McRobbie, *British Fashion, Rag Trade or Image Industry?*, p. 166.
16. Wilson, *Adorned in Dreams*, p. 246.
17. Ibid. p. 247.
18. Evans and Thornton, *Women and Fashion*, p. xiii.
19. Ibid. p. 15.
20. Davis, Fred, *Fashion, Culture and Identity* (Chicago and London: University of Chicago Press, 1994), p. 178.
21. Caroline Evans and Minna Thornton, 'Fashion, Representation, Femininity', in *Feminist Review*, no. 38, Summer 1991, p. 48.
22. Miuccia Prada, quoted in Lesley White, 'Visible Party Line', *Frank*, December 1997, p. 116.
23. Richard Martin, quoted in Vanessa Friedman, 'What Makes Gucci and Prada Great?', *Financial Times Weekend*, 12/13 April 1997, p. xi.
24. Robin Givhan, 'The Problem with Ugly Chic', in Ross, *No Sweat*, p. 273.
25. Miuccia Prada, quoted in Lesley White, 'Visible Party Line', *Frank*, December 1997, p. 116.

Bibliography

Ash, Juliet, and Elizabeth Wilson (eds), *Chic Thrills, A Fashion Reader* (London: Pandora, 1992).
Bordo, Susan, *Unbearable Weight, Feminism, Western Culture and the Body* (Berkeley and London: University of California Press, 1995).
Brownmiller, Susan, *Femininity* (London: Hamish Hamilton, 1984).
Coward, Rosalind, *Female Desire: Women's Sexuality Today* (London: Paladin, 1984).
Evans, Caroline and Minna Thornton, *Women and Fashion, A New Look* (London and New York: Quartet Books, 1989).
Friedan, Betty, *The Feminine Mystique* (London: Penguin, 1983).
Gaines, Jane, and Charlotte Herzog, *Fabrications, Costume and the Female Body* (New York and London: Routledge, 1991).

Hanson, Karen, 'Dressing Down, Dressing Up, The Philosopher's Fear of Fashion', in Hein, Korsmeyer, Hilde and Carolyn Korsmeyer (eds), *Aesthetics in Feminist Perspective* (Bloomington and Indianapolis: Indiana University Press, 1993), pp. 229–41.

McRobbie, Angela, *Feminism and Youth Cultures, from Jackie to Just Seventeen* (London: Macmillan, 1991).

McRobbie, Angela, *British Fashion, Rag Trade or Image Industry?* (London and New York: Routledge, 1998).

Nava, Mica, *Changing Cultures, Feminism, Youth and Consumerism* (London: Sage, 1992).

Ross, Andrew (ed.), *No Sweat, Fashion, Free Trade, and the Rights of the Garment Worker* (New York and London: Verso, 1997).

Silverman, Kaja, 'Fragments for a Fashionable Discourse', in Modleski, Tania (ed.), *Studies in Entertainment, Critical Approaches to Mass Culture* (Bloomington and Indianapolis: Indiana University Press, 1986), pp. 139–52.

Walter, Natasha, *The New Feminism* (London: Little, Brown & Company, 1998).

Wilson, Elizabeth, *Adorned in Dreams, Fashion and Modernity* (London: Virago, 1987).

Wilson, Elizabeth, 'Fashion and the Postmodern Body', in Ash, Juliet, and Elizabeth Wilson (eds), *Chic Thrills, A Fashion Reader* (London: Pandora, 1992).

Wolf, Naomi, *The Beauty Myth* (London: Vintage, 1990).

Part III

Mass media

"Custom-Corner" TV, Malvern. Gives room-wide viewing, 262 square inch viewable picture. In walnut grained finish with blond face (21T847) $289.95.

Trim table TV, Holme Deluxe. Bigger picture in a smaller cabinet, 262 square inch viewable picture. In ebony finish (21D828) $219.95.

Table TV that swivels, Blaine Deluxe. Touch-turn convenience, 156 square inch viewable picture. In limed oak grained finish (17D818) $189.95.

Fits close to wall—saves up to 9½ inches. Longport. Dramatically slender, clean-lined console, 262 square inch viewable picture. In mahogany grained finish (21T842) $299.95.

Lean, clean lowboy, Fairhaven Deluxe. Luxurious modern cabinetry, 262 square inch viewable picture. In limed oak grained finish (21D856) $349.50.

See how new RCA Victor TV fits anywhere—
it's lean, clean, mirror-sharp, from $129.95!

Here RCA Victor shows you slender, clean-lined TV at its best.

The cabinets save up to 36% floor space, *fit in beautifully where other TV couldn't go at all*—close up to walls, on narrow tables and shelves, even in corners! There's no space-wasting bulge in back, no needless knobs or gadgetry anywhere. Here are new table models, consoles and lowboys that really help you decorate; and more than that—

They give you the sharpest picture in black-and-white TV. "Mirror-Sharp!" You get the blackest blacks, the whitest whites, the clearest, cleanest contrasts possible. You also get Balanced Fidelity FM Sound, "One-Touch" on-off control and other exciting advances—all at easy-to-take prices. Be sure to see new "Lean, Clean, Mirror-Sharp" TV from $129.95—at your RCA Victor dealer's—now!

RCA VICTOR FACTORY SERVICE CONTRACT

Fine service for the finest in television! Only RCA Victor TV owners can buy on RCA Victor Factory Service Contract for expert service and installation by RCA's own technicians. Branches in most TV areas.

BE SURE TO SEE the Perry Como show on Saturday evenings—and the George Gobel-Eddie Fisher shows on Tuesday evenings. Also "Tic Tac Dough" on Thursday evenings and "The Price Is Right" on Monday evenings. All on NBC-TV

RCA VICTOR
RADIO CORPORATION OF AMERICA

Mfr's nat'ly advertised VHF list prices shown. UHF opt., ext. Slightly higher far West, South, Canada. Prices, specifications subject to change.

Issues in feminist mass media

Claire Pajaczkowska

THE RAPID ACCELERATION IN the growth and development of the mass media over the past fifty years is the most significant of the factors that have led to the redefinition of contemporary culture as a visual culture. The growth of television especially has produced sociocultural changes that could barely have been imagined at its inception. Television production and broadcasting have changed as the technologies become less cumbersome and less costly, and the changes wrought by digital technologies are likely to multiply the rate and the breadth of the changes of the past decades. But the continuous transformations of both hardware and software make it difficult to establish any definitive analyses of the current impact of these media on cultural forms.

Probably the most significant effect of the past decade has been the spread of audiences on a global scale, bringing irreversible transformations of the definition of culture and changes in the relationship of culture to literacy. The potential for democratisation integral to mass media initiated with printing technology during the Renaissance, and developed through the rise of the publishing industries, and now newspapers, radio and film technologies have transformed the class distinctions that used to determine access to the production and reception of culture. The political struggle for a system of mass education, which began to take effect in the late nineteenth century in Britain, has changed the distribution of literacy that used to be the only means to access anything broader than a local culture. However, changes in the textual structures of the mass media over the twentieth century have altered the balance of power in the relation between word and image, making the newly accessed power of literacy seem of questionable value to those who perceive a mass culture that is becoming increasingly televisual.

It is difficult to establish the extent to which the new technologies of mass media and cyberculture are producing new textual forms. In many respects, the textual forms through which the webs and the Internet currently work are hybrid forms of existing cultural practices. The network infrastructure enables a form of growth and development that is 'rhizomatic' (a term adapted from the biological description of organic forms that grow outwards from roots, rather than spreading from a central stem or trunk, implying an organic metaphor for a growing network), quite different from the hierarchical organisation of industries or from the 'centre-out' model of other forms of publishing and broadcasting. However, the effect of this difference is not yet discernible within the textual systems that characterise the current presentation of information, entertainment, merchandising or games through the Internet. The textual forms owe something to the cinematic, diegetic structures of the classic realist text, some of the informal and familiar modes of address of popular culture, and many of the visual structures of television and advertising, and these are welded together through the interactivity put into place by telephone technology. If cyberculture's predominant narrative forms are more exegetic than diegetic, this marks its current textual structures as intertextual rather than self- referential, a cultural characteristic it shares with a number of other modern and postmodern cultural forms. The claims to being a qualitatively different, and revolutionary, development rest largely on the idea that cyberculture enables the once 'passive' spectators of television to become active users of an intersubjective relation. It remains to be seen how the public space of the Internet will differ from other conventional public spaces of broadcasting, publishing or urban geographies. The extent to which cyberculture requires a different conceptualisation of gender and spatial culture is under current debate, and the terms of this debate as it exists within visual culture are discussed by Sarah Chaplin in Chapter 13.

It may be the perspective of hindsight that enables the older media to have generated the most developed discourses of feminist analysis. Feminist film theory, as Sally Stafford explains in Chapter 11, began in the 1960s and has integrated many different methods and theories over the past three decades. The first terms of critical analysis were those of 'representation', and the central issue was that of cinematic realism: feminist criticism was expected to judge the plausibility of the 'role models' offered by popular cinema. From this, developed a more sophisticated paradigm, in which the deconstructive methods of structuralism changed the terms of reference to those of 'signification', and the encoding of gender was understood as being more integral to forms such as narrative structure, rather than being an issue of the acting styles and roles of actresses. Further feminist analysis focused on genre studies, so that new objects of study were identified and named. *Film noir* began to be seen as being more than merely of interest as a neo-gangster genre, and was recognised as having a wealth of representations of contradictions of sexual difference, such as the iconography of the *femme fatale*, the Oedipal structure of the narratives of detection, the relative authorities of masculine voiceover narration on soundtrack, and the significance of *mise-en-scène* and image track. As a result, there is now a substantial literature on *film noir* which raises issues of relevance to feminist research. Other popular genres noted, described and analysed include the melodrama (and its many subgenres), horror film, and science fiction. It is in feminist film theory that psychoanalytic theory has been most thoroughly explored, discussed and applied to textual analysis, to the study of cinema spectatorship, to the process of identification, and to other aspects of sexual difference and visual culture. Having introduced feminist film theory, and described its history, Sally Stafford analyses the hybrid genre of neo-*noir* and action film in *The Long Kiss Goodnight*, looking at the changes that three decades of feminism have brought to the iconography of the Hollywood *femme fatale*.

Independent and avant-garde filmmaking has been chosen as an alternative to working within mainstream film industry by many women who are unable or unwilling to assimilate into the mainstream. There is a history of filmmaking with textual strategies that diverge widely from the classic realism and the production values of industrial film, and there is also a substantial literature of criticism and analysis of independent and avant-garde film practice. One of the questions raised by independent filmmakers is that of access to technology, and women working outside the industry have usually opted to use non-industrial forms of film recording such as 16mm or super-8 film, video or digital technology. In Chapter 12, Julia Knight explores the interface between the history of independent film workshops in Britain over the past twenty years and the extent to which the textual strategies developed here have influenced the more recent emergence of independent video production. She also relates the textual analysis to the organisational forms of independent production and discusses the division of labour in the production process. The alternative forms of film distribution and exhibition that are necessary and possible in video practice also raise issues that impinge on the question of access to the dissemination of films through cyberculture.

Feminist film theory has an interface with media studies and its many sociological, anthropological, historical and analytical methods. Anne Hole describes in Chapter 14 the debates in the feminist study of television, then presents a Bakhtinian analysis of Jo Brand's humour. Anne Hole identifies the anxiogenic themes of the audience's ambivalent relation to the body of a female stand-up comic who is unusually big and who transgresses the conventions of what can be said, by a woman, in a public space. The themes of sex, violence, aggression and food are combined in a potentially explosive way, echoing the use of similar themes in a fine-art context by artists such as Meret Oppenheim, Louise Bourgeois, Judy Chicago, Sarah Lucas, and Tracey Emin. Because television comedy combines popularity, demographically significant audiences, and anarchic themes, it is a genre rich in possibilities for textual analysis: *Smack the Pony*, *The Fast Show*, *Goodness Gracious Me*, *Dinner Ladies* and *The Royle Family* are all popular comedy programmes that hyperbolise sexual and gender contradictions and relate them in complex and sophisticated ways to the linked issues of class and ethnicity. Other television genres discussed by feminist media studies include soap operas, game shows, 'confessional' audience participation shows, and children's programmes as well as the analysis of the gender coding of news values, and the analysis of television advertising.

Advertising was one of the cultural forms produced by the mass media that first came to the attention of feminist scholars. A number of studies of gender in advertising have appeared over the past three decades which locate it in woman's magazines, in television and in the national press. Bridging the disciplines of media sociology and cultural studies, Sarah Niblock analyses in Chapter 15 the way in which magazine advertising addresses women as mothers, exploiting the contradictions that motherhood generates in a patrilineal culture. She explores the way in which advertising interposes images of commodities between a mother and her anxiety, an anxiety that issues from the contradictory place of motherhood within a patrilineal culture, and which is especially strongly experienced by first-time mothers. If the enigma and fear of femininity is due, in some part, to the invisibility of the vagina, as birth canal, as organ of reception, as organ of pleasure and erotogenic zone, the anxiety surrounding the role of motherhood can be at least partly understood as a cultural category that defies definition. The image in advertising, as it is analysed here, is an image used in its capacity to alienate.

Chapter 11

Film theory

Sally Stafford

THIS CHAPTER TRACES SOME of the most influential developments in feminist film theory over the past thirty years with the
aim of giving the reader an outline of theoretical perspectives and
a guide for further reading (particularly through the footnotes), as
well as providing a commentary on a recent Hollywood film, *The
Long Kiss Goodnight*. In researching this chapter, I have felt an
overriding sense of pride that there is such a rich history to write
about. Beyond the evolution of a body of critical work are the
events – particularly in the 1970s – which played key roles in the
development of feminist film theory in Britain and the USA. The
well documented retrospective of women's films in Edinburgh in
1972, for example, and the 'Women and *Film Noir*' BFI Summer
School in 1978 have informed subsequent schools of thought,
publications and further events, while providing an historical
perspective of an emerging women's movement with its energy,
idealism and new ideas.[1] Reviewing the emergence and development of theory over the past thirty years can usefully inform
contemporary perspectives on film.

This chapter is divided into five sections of 'theory' and one
film case study. The sections will highlight the key shifts in
theoretical emphasis while the case study of *The Long Kiss
Goodnight* (Harlin, 1996) serves to reflect the diversity of critical
approaches adopted by feminist film theories and to reveal the
ways in which several layers of meaning can be determined
through one film text. Thus, the theoretical perspectives can be
viewed, in part, as tools with which to read the film discussed.

Two major methodological strands have been identified in feminist film criticism as having informed the perspectives of the 1970s
and subsequent work in the 1980s. These have been variously

described as the sociological and the psychoanalytic (or semiolo-gical),[2] or in terms of 'images of women' criticism (representation), and 'reading against the grain' (deconstruction).[3] The second ca-tegory, which is necessarily more lengthy and complex, describes psychoanalysis and deconstruction under the umbrella term of signification. As such, semiotics underpins a number of complex theoretical approaches in diverse discussions of the relationship between women and film. Both positions, as always, should be considered in the contexts from which they emerge, as they represent important developments in cultural theory and feminist criticism. It should also be acknowledged that the methodologies themselves have evolved and are both still employed in discussions of women and film inside and outside academia.

Representation

How women were represented in films dominated much feminist debate on Hollywood cinema in the 1970s. An analysis of 'images of women' raised many questions for feminist film critics: were the roles 'believable' or products of (generally male) fantasy? Were the representations positive or patronising? How did they embrace the diversity and complexity of women in a period of such political and social change? A desire for self-recognition through the screen representation of real women's complex lives was combined with a desire for roles that would be inspirational to female audiences. Critics sought to distinguish representations of complex, credible, three-dimensional female characters from the classic gendered stereotypes of Hollywood.[4]

Molly Haskell's book *From Reverence to Rape: The Treatment of Women in the Movies* takes the reader through each decade of Hollywood filmmaking from the 1920s to the 1970s (and 1980s in the second edition), scrutinising the representation of women in a diverse selection of film narratives. It is a text that embodies the spirit of the age in which it was written, as she writes in her preface to the second edition: 'In 1972–3 the rhetoric of the women's movement, then peaking, was at its most romantically utopian'. She claims the major message of the book to have been 'down with sexism, up with women!'[5]

Haskell's book was one of the first to offer critical studies of the representation of women in popular film which were informed by political debate and social comment. The possibility for equality and liberation is understood to lie in the representation of 'real' women (a project thought to be the aim and responsibility of women directors in particular). Subsequent theorists and critics have outlined the limitations of this perspective. First, it implies a monolithic view of the structuring forces of (male) society: patriarchy uniformly constrains all aspects of representations of femininity and this is merely replicated on film, where men control all aspects of production. Film, then, 'acts largely as a social mirror';[6] and there is an 'unmediated relationship between cinema and society'.[7]

Secondly, and as a consequence of this blanket acceptance of patriarchal power, there is no analysis of how social meanings are put in place; no account of the development of social codes and of forms of resistance to them, nor of the complex issue of identification. It is assumed implicitly that all women take up the same position in relation to the female characters at all times. In short then, the issue of representation and 'images of women' is limited by its lack of engagement with the ideologies surrounding the production and consumption of such images.

Politics, practice and pleasure

An important project of early 1970s feminism was to reclaim and re-establish the reputation of many women connected to the film industry who were hidden from its history, particularly that of Hollywood.[8] Thus, festivals of women's films (such as the Edinburgh festival already mentioned), and retrospectives of female stars became focal points in a refigured cultural landscape.

Such work successfully brought to light, and to mass exposure, the work of talented women poorly served by their culture. However, through its attention to the status of individual artists and to notions of equality (equal representation), other issues were perceived as marginalised, such as the question of who defines the terms of inclusion and exclusion, and how the notion of genius is defined? Debates within feminism developed to reflect the concern for an emerging essentialism implied by an uncritical celebration of women's work.

For film, the influence of feminism was felt not just in terms of retrospective work but through the burgeoning area of new directors and collective filmmaking activity. The relationship between theory and practice had a new edge through the political agenda of the women's movement. An increased interest and involvement in the production of feminist documentary or doc-udrama films evolved in the search for real representations of women.[9] As Laura Mulvey notes: 'These films sought to transform the nature of film through a transformation of its mode of production and consumption, making films, for the first time, "by, for and about women"'.[10] 'Counter cinema' (a term developed by Peter Wollen to describe alternative cinematic practices which deliberately countered some of the codes of classical Hollywood cinema such as narrative closure and processes of identification)[11] had particular significance for women through the backdrop of an active women's movement and led to a desire for an alternative cinematic discourse and dialogue between women.

A rejection of patriarchal systems of signification (necessitating at least a partial rejection of Hollywood) in favour of films that unsettled rather than reconfirmed oppressive ideologies, grew in the belief that liberatory pleasure was to be found in such disruptive texts. Independent, counter-cinema productions are seen as part of this strategy.[12]

Turning away from Hollywood was seen, by some, as both possible and politically necessary, but it proved problematic in subsequent debates concerning the effects of foregrounding politics over pleasure. Some critics were quick to defend the move, as Claire Johnston wrote in 1973, 'at this point in time a strategy should be developed which embraces both the notion of film as a political tool and film as entertainment. For too long these have been regarded as two opposing poles with little common ground.'[13]

The appearance of correct but decidedly unpleasurable films fuelled debates which questioned priorities for women's cinema. An example of a film which successfully bridged this gap might be *Born In Flames* (Borden, 1983) with its challenge to classic Hollywood structure combined with a political agenda and personal vision, and an energetic and imaginative narrative which still affords pleasure for the spectator.

Signification

Semiotic theorists such as Claire Johnston and Pam Cook reflected a shift from the quest for positive images reflecting gender
equality (or strong women) to an analysis of sexual *difference*
through gender and how that difference is signified cinematically.
They argued for an analysis of ideology as central to discussions
of representation and as a way of moving the debate forward,
recognising, as Maggie Humm puts it, that 'Images were not
simply mirrors of real life but ideological signifiers.'[14]

An increased interest in semiotics since the 1960s informed
discussions of how meaning is created. In film studies, there was a
move away in the 1970s from debates around realism and
authenticity to an analysis of the production of meaning through
the process of signification.[15]

Semiologists assert that there is no intrinsic meaning to what
we know, only what is generally understood and connoted by
particular words and images operating through systems of difference. Through semiotics, we understand how meanings in a
patriarchal system are not neutral but informed by the imbalances
of power inherent within that system. Meaning is not fixed but
mobile and often contradictory, or at least inconsistent. It follows
that mixed and complex messages will be manifest in the cultural
products of that system and that audiences will have some leeway
in decoding them. In terms of cinema and women, rather than
film offering a clear reflection of a defined social order and
hierarchical structures, what we see is more like a distorted
fairground mirror, in which we recognise what we see but it
does not necessarily correspond to how we perceive ourselves,
and the parts that we see do not always make a whole. The
relationship between female star, film text and female audience is
particularly contradictory and fragmented, and it is what feminist
film criticism has engaged with consistently since the mid-1970s.

Looking behind and beyond, as well as at the process of
representation enables the viewer to understand the multi-layered
meanings within narrative structure. To recap on the distinctions
between the two methodologies, Judith Mayne writes that:
'"Images of women" suggests a relatively simple manipulative
system of social control, while "reading against the grain" suggests
a system full of contradictions, gaps and slips of the tongue.'[16]

Mildred Pierce (Curtiz, 1945) is often discussed in the context of feminism and film theory for its eponymous female protagonist (Joan Crawford), its perspective on women's careers and motherhood, its negotiation between the gendered generic boundaries of melodrama and *film noir*, and its continued popularity with female audiences. A representational reading of this film would draw on sociological and historical arguments looking at the context of the film's production – World War Two – to make links between its treatment of the heroine, Mildred, and publicity campaigns to induce women back into the home at the end of the war. The film can be read as a vehicle for reinstating traditional gender roles for its 1945 audience and portraying the potential disaster for women who attempt to move beyond those roles.[17]

A semiotic reading of the film, as critics from Judith Mayne to Pam Cook have argued, draws on what is signified by the structure of the narrative rather than what happens to its female protagonist in the plot. *Mildred Pierce* is structured around two contrasting visual styles signified by a flashback. In the film, the past is evenly lit, often with light musical accompaniment, and the domestic setting denotes a family melodrama, while sequences in the present are harshly lit, dark and shadowy, crossing a generic boundary into *film noir*. Mildred's voiceover and character leads us between the film's fluctuating styles but her forays into the 'innocent' past are interrupted by the interrogation of the detective in the present. The notion of gender-inflected genres associated with melodrama (female) and *film noir* (male) are thus supported by the characters, with the male authority figure located firmly in the noirish present. Cook has pointed to how the fluctuating framework informs the perception of Mildred's character; for the majority of the film we are led to believe that she is guilty of the murder of her second husband.[18]

Psychoanalysis

In *Notes on Women's Cinema* (1973), Claire Johnston examines what is signified by 'woman' in Hollywood film. Johnston draws on psychoanalytic discourses and semiotic theory to argue that woman exists only as a coded convention and ultimately woman 'as woman' is absent from classic Hollywood narrative film.[19]

She asserts that under a system which privileges the male as the maker of meaning, woman can only be defined as 'non male'; as she writes elsewhere: 'In the asymmetry of patriarchal culture, woman is defined as other, as *that which is not male*.'[20] Furthermore, she asserts that Hollywood actually covers its tracks, disguising the absence of women's subjectivity through its display of constructed femininity as natural and belonging: 'In its turn, non-male is conflated with the stereotype of femininity in patriarchal culture: woman as locus of lack and castration fears or woman as image of lost maternal plenitude.'[21]

Johnston's argument here can be linked to Laura Mulvey's article on 'Visual Pleasure and Narrative Cinema',[22] both in terms of its use of the critical tools of psychoanalysis, and in the ambivalent response to Hollywood that results. Mulvey's essay, written in 1975, has been one of the most influential in the history of feminist film criticism and, more generally, of film theory. It uses key concepts from Freudian and Lacanian psychoanalysis as a basis for a discussion of cinema and sexual difference; scopophilia – the desire to look – and its centrality to cinema is at the heart of the essay. Mulvey explores how Freud used the term to explain how the desire to look, a sign of curiosity and learning in the development of children, may become an active and controlling gaze in adulthood and in extreme cases: 'it can become fixated, producing excessive voyeurs and peeping Toms, whose only sexual satisfaction can come from watching, in an active controlling sense, an objectified other'.[23]

Mulvey explains how in cinema this desire is manipulated and naturalised by the combined use of three aspects of the gaze: that of the camera, the spectator, and the gaze between the characters. The narrative of the film, the editing and the 'triple gaze' combine to endorse the active male perspective as owner of the gaze and (as Johnston also argued) as maker of meaning within the narrative. Women are contrasted as narratively passive and, 'The determining male gaze projects its phantasy onto the female figure which is styled accordingly. In their traditional exhibitionist role women are simultaneously looked at and displayed, with their appearance coded for strong visual and erotic impact so that they can be said to connote to-be-looked-at-ness'.[24] She argues that film narratives which incorporate backstage musicals (a show within a show) legitimise and naturalise the right to look, through the explicit use of woman as spectacle, a frequently quoted example of this is *Gilda* (Vidor, 1946).

The female spectator has few identificatory options. Mulvey argues that the female viewer initially evokes a memory of her past pre-Oedipal possibilities through identifying with the male, and thus experiences pleasure but she must shift her perspective to recognise that such pleasure is misplaced, she must repress her active phallic phase and recognise her 'lack' in order to take up a position of correct femininity. This is inevitably a masochistic process, as she writes: 'woman's desire is subjugated to her image as bearer of the bleeding wound'.[25] She outlines a 'restless transvestism' which women must adopt. It is deemed an unsatisfactory, oscillating position, sufficient for us to look forward to the demise of classical film form with only a sense of 'sentimental regret'.[26]

Mulvey's complex and rewarding text has been praised and challenged for its analysis of gendered cinema spectatorship and its polarised view of active male and passive female subject positions. There has been much debate concerning the fixity of such positions and criticism of the seemingly essentialist perspective offered by psychoanalytic interpretation. Mulvey revised the polemic in an article entitled 'Afterthoughts on Visual Pleasure and Narrative Cinema Inspired by *Duel in the Sun*'[27] (which can usefully be read in conjunction with 'Visual Pleasure') and in *Camera Obscura* she admits to a lack of emphasis on her part in her commitment to Freud: she was 'not referring to male in the sense of men in the audience but to the active element in the ambivalent sexuality of any individual'.[28] In the light of more contemporary theories, this ambivalence has been frequently returned to; her 'restless transvestism' could be seen to predate many ideas on the fluidity of gender positioning and identification and has sparked much debate in this area.

After Mulvey

The explosion of writing on feminism and film drawing on the discourse of psychoanalysis occurred during the late 1970s and all through the 1980s,[29] and Mulvey's article was seen as 'the inaugural moment of feminist psychoanalytic theories of specta-

torship'.[30] The British journal *Screen*, in which her article appeared, was at forefront of this arena, as Judith Mayne acknowledges, 'Throughout the 70s *Screen* was the most important testing
ground for the methodologies that have shaped contemporary
film theory: semiotics, Marxism and psychoanalysis'.[31]

Questions raised in, and beyond, the journal concerned identification and desire, with an analysis of the ownership of the gaze
playing a key part in the debates.[32] Concern over the possibility of
a distinct and autonomous female gaze (and hence the question of
pleasure for the female spectator) dominated much feminist
thought. Often theorists would offer negative perspectives: the
female spectator could only over-identify with the passive female
subject who was destined to have her desire denied by the
narrative.[33] An article by Lorraine Gamman and Caroline Evans
entitled 'The Gaze Revisited or Reviewing Queer Viewing' provides a summary of the different perspectives and further outlines
the potential limitations of psychoanalytically informed debates
of spectatorship, identification and desire. They argue against the
rigidity of a framework which cannot recognise and account for
the shifting multiplicity of subject positions and negotiations with
any given text.[34] Their arguments are echoed elsewhere, as
Maggie Humm notes, 'debates about spectatorship and identity
were theory's radiant centre but such debates seemed to occlude
other feminist perspectives, particularly those of Black and lesbian critics, as well as Black and lesbian creativity and theoretical
entitlement'.[35]

The Female Gaze, edited by Lorraine Gamman and Margaret
Marchment, and *Female Spectators* edited by E. Deidre Pribram,
provide useful and accessible collections of essays from the late
1980s that consider the diverse subject positions apparently
uncatered for by the psychoanalytic paradigm alone.[36] Both
books recognise a lack of engagement with perspectives on race
and sexuality. Jacqueline Bobo's essay '*The Colour Purple*: Black
Women as Cultural Readers' (in Pribram's book) explores the
responses of actual rather than imagined spectators of the Spiel-
berg film, and she notes that, 'Black women's responses confront
and challenge a prevalent method of media audience analysis
which insists that viewers of mainstream works have no control
or influence over a cultural product',[37] thus asserting the negotiated and discursive pleasures afforded by mainstream texts.

The need to recognise a broader conception of difference to include racial difference is further outlined in an article by Jane Gaines which examines the effects of a marginalised black women's presence under a coded system of looking and representation which privileges the white male gaze. For Gaines, such a system cannot incorporate the unknown, and therefore feared, arena of black women's sexuality, while such exclusion also recalls the historical taboo of the black male gaze.[38]

In Gamman and Marchment's book, Jackie Stacey attempts to explore the complexity of female relationships beyond the strait-jacket of sexual difference, and she writes, 'the rigid distinction between *either* desire or identification so characteristic of psycho-analytic film theory, fails to address the construction of desires which involve a specific interplay of both processes'.[39] Stacey is interested in issues beyond sexual difference – in differences (including potential desire) between women.[40] Both Bobo and Stacey are concerned to locate the historic and cultural specificity of the female spectator and stress the processes of negotiation of subjectivity necessary to engage with a mainstream text. (This is not to conflate the specific and distinct discourses of black and lesbian subjectivity but to illustrate how they have been histori-cally marginalised by psychoanalytic texts.)

Genderblending

More recently, a re-examination of the pleasures afforded by classical Hollywood film has developed through a lens of irony and appropriation, with a clear acknowledgement that there is always more than one way to read a text. Perhaps the most influential factor for feminist film theory in recent years (and for film theory in general) has been the rapid growth of cultural studies and its enthusiastic support for and engagement with popular culture. In conjunction with this (and perhaps partly because of it) has been the increased interest in the study of gender as a critical category. Such a school of thought is also indebted to feminism -an assertion that femininity is a series of complex constructions leads to an understanding that masculinity might be equally defined and further, that gender itself becomes open to debate and unstable, even as a biological given.

Key to the progression of this debate in recent years is the work of Judith Butler and the theory of gender as performance. The roots for such ideas can be traced back at least to 1929 to an article by the psychoanalyst Joan Riviere which has informed many contemporary discussions of female subjectivity.[41] In 'Womanliness and the Masquerade', Riviere discusses the case of an academic woman whom she describes as intelligent, articulate and a competent mother but who, in her professional life, compromises and disguises her intelligence. Riviere argues that this disguise is adopted through guilt and fear at taking the place of the father and that she repeatedly seeks approval through a denial of her own abilities. Riviere makes the point that the mask of womanliness is adopted to disguise the fact that the woman has assumed phallic mastery, and the threat that this represents, and consequently seeks to divert the retribution she fears. What is interesting about the article is that through a psychoanalytic discussion (which acknowledges the power of the phallus) she raises the possibility that for women there is only a mask, that true femininity and the mask of womanliness are the same. Femininity signifies another constructed and adopted part of the self.

This is linked to more contemporary feminist ideas concerning the social construction of femininity and its lack of essential substance, and further to discourses on gender performativity. Butler argues for a 'radical rethinking of categories of identity'[42] as the category of gender itself is unstable. Discussions of blurring of gender identities and masquerade have featured across disciplines from cultural studies to queer theory while sexual disguise and ambiguity have been at the heart of many film narratives including *Some Like It Hot* (Wilder, 1959), *Victor/Victoria* (Edwards, 1982), *The Adventures of Priscilla, Queen of the Desert* (Elliott, 1994) and *The Ballad of Little Joe* (Greenwald, 1995).

The Long Kiss Goodnight (Harlin, 1996) is a recent example of gender/genre blurring film which I will discuss in some depth in order to explore some of the theoretical perspectives outlined above. It is located within the genre of action films and, although this is traditionally a male genre, it is one of a recent trend featuring active female protagonists. The list includes such films as *Terminator 2: Judgment Day* (Cameron, 1991), *Twister*

(Almereyda, 1990), *Deep Impact* (Leder, 1998) and *GI Jane* (Scott, 1997), and the heroines of each might be compared with what Carol Clover terms the 'final girl' in her book on horror films, *Men, Women and Chainsaws*.[43] This 'survivor' is identified by her androgyny, her intelligence and resourcefulness, her independence and her non-sexual behaviour (in horror films, she is frequently set apart from her sexually-charged teenage peers, with the suggestion that her survival is linked to her abstinence). She is freer to act than women in most films, having an active, interrogating gaze. She pushes the narrative forward through her actions, providing a challenge to the passive role historically defined for women. In psychoanalytic terms, she is defined as a phallic woman, one who most definitely denies her lack.[44]

Such narratives can be described as rites of passage films for women. In *The Long Kiss Goodnight*, an Oedipal trajectory is outlined: Charly is reborn, her former family (the CIA), have turned against her, she must defeat them and move away in order to continue her journey into adulthood, and for order to be restored.

For Clover, the identity of the final girl and the killer/monster are blurred: she argues against the idea of monster/victim polarities in this context. The final girl shares a masculinity with the monster, her active gaze affords her points-of-view shots (unusual for women in classical Hollywood cinema), and through the use of weapons she achieves phallic power. Clover points out that the blurred, complex identity of the monster means that masculinity is not privileged. The monster partly reflects the final girl herself, it is part of her family, and the heroine of such films therefore needs to identify with it in order to control it. Classic examples of this relationship might be that of Ripley and the monster in the *Alien* film series which develops into a complex (if perverse) story of mothers and daughters as the cycle evolves, or the refigured father/daughter relationship of Hannibal Lecter and Clarice Starling in *Silence of the Lambs* (Demme, 1990). In *The Long Kiss Goodnight*, the CIA is wholly defined as Charly's family, as they 'created' her as an assassin: the narrative reveals how she knew nothing else, her personal relations were defined by work, and even her fiancé proves to have been a target. It follows that what they have taught her is what she uses to defeat them.

Such a blurring of gendered perspectives and processes of

identification leads Clover to believe that the audience, whether male or female, identifies with the final girl rather than with victim or monster, and she concludes that 'Masculinity and femininity are more states of mind than body'.[45]

The Long Kiss Goodnight explores gender performativity through the character of Samantha/ Charly. Through her, we see echoes of Riviere's ideas: Samantha/Charly wholly embodies the notion of femininity as masquerade. In her adopted life, Samantha is a happy partner and mother: we witness her in an almost sugary, idealised domestic setting, and this is heightened by the fact that the beginning of the film takes place at Christmas, a traditional time for families to be together. The Elvis Presley soundtrack completes the sentiment evoked by the Christmas-card scene in which Samantha parades as Mrs Santa. She is made object of the male gaze, a spectacle which the narrative legitimises by the use of the parade. This is not only endorsed by the male characters looking at her but further by their comments on her appearance – thus she is idealised as beautiful and passive. However, the film challenges such passive norms through her transformation into a killing machine, and it highlights the constructed nature of her adopted femininity.

In a scene reminiscent of a medieval test for witches – the ducking stool – Samantha is reborn in the water as her former self. She later completes the change through her own visual transformation, in which she adopts new clothes and make-up, and cuts and bleaches her hair. As Yvonne Tasker remarks, 'This sense of cross dressing within and across genders reinforces the ambiguous gender identity of the female action hero, or rather points to the instability of a gendered system, and the production of an alternative space through that instability.'[46]

The Long Kiss Goodnight is a self-reflexive narrative, openly stealing scenes and ideas from a number of other films and film genres. Charly's transformation is in the spirit of Hitchcock's *Marnie* (1964), in which the eponymous heroine recreates her identity to begin her life (of crime) as someone else. Our first introduction to Charley's sidekick, Hennessy (Samuel L. Jackson), shows him bursting into a room to point a gun at a man in bed with a woman. It is heavily reminiscent of blaxploitation films in which black masculinity seems inescapably linked to sex, violence and crime. Hennessy's wisecracking speech triggers further recognition: it is Jackson in his earlier role of Jules in *Pulp Fiction* (Tarantino, 1994), a film full of parody and genre play.

To return to psychoanalysis, female action films create heroines who, by virtue of their active, aggressive roles, can be termed phallic women. It has been argued that, as such, women (like the *femme fatale*) represent fetishised images of femininity, that is to say their adopted masculinity functions to disguise their lack. The male spectator, in seeking to deny the threat of castration posed by women, creates an excessively feminine or, in this case, masculine image. Thus, the high heels, long legs, long hair and finger nails, which appear as traditional Hollywood signifiers of femininity, function as reassurance devices against the threat of castration that women represent. In women's action films, the excessive weaponry and androgynous appearance of the heroine (more specifically, the gun in Charly's suitcase and her skills with a kitchen knife in *The Long Kiss Goodnight*) function in a similar way as phallic imagery. A more overt example might be found in the opening sequence of *Blue Steel* (Bigelow, 1990) starring Jamie Lee Curtis: the languorous, lascivious close-up shots of the gun are juxtaposed with shots of Curtis's body as she dresses in her police uniform.

In *The Long Kiss Goodnight*, Samantha is presented as a devoted mother whose general love for children is expressed through her job as a schoolteacher. Subsequently, as Charly, she is ambivalent about the whole role of motherhood and having a child. Through the course of the narrative, Charly relocates her maternal feelings to the point where the safety of her child becomes a motivating force for her action. This is critical to female action films and is one of their distinguishing features from their male counterparts. While men act in order to save the world – *Independence Day* (Emmerich, 1996) and *Armageddon* (Bay, 1998) – women are primarily motivated by the fight for the survival of their offspring (obviously in the case of *Terminator 2*, the future of the world is also dependent on the safety of her son, in a situation riddled with biblical overtones). Films such as *Strange Days* (Bigelow, 1995) and *Aliens* (Cameron, 1986) explicitly support this view. In psychoanalytic terms, the child functions as a phallic substitute and could be viewed as part of the denial of castration.

The Long Kiss Goodnight presents a challenge to maternal

ideology in Charly's temporary renunciation of her daughter; however, the rose-tinted conclusion requires her to learn to combine her careers as assassin and mother, as a giver of life and one who has the clear capacity to take it away. The conclusion implies that Charly/Samantha does achieve it all, and unlike in earlier maternal narratives (such as *Mildred Pierce*), there is no sense of punishment for her active desires. However, this is an offshoot of the action film genre, and as such its fast pace and quickfire dialogue render the film fantastic, ironic and parodic – it must be recognised that Charly achieves a fantasy. If the opportunities for filmic mothers in Hollywood have changed little, this film suggests (at least) the career options are a little broader. As a contemporary heroine, Charly embodies debates concerning the ambiguity of gender and gender-based identification and desire; as a lesbian icon, she is an article waiting to be written; as a mother, she would have been very handy!

This chapter has broadly outlined some of the contributions made to feminist film theory over the past thirty years and has applied some of those perspectives to the analysis of a Hollywood film. Aspects of the often ambiguous but productive relationship between feminism and Hollywood have emerged as well as questions concerning the current status of feminist film theory. There is a sense that recent feminist theory generally can be perceived as less cohesive than earlier trajectories have suggested; particularly in a 'post-theory' era defined by its sense of parody and play, where appropriation can be seen as key to the construction of meaning. An analysis of the full multiplicity of difference was, and is, essential to opening up the potential for feminism to reflect the diversity of discourse and challenges to polarised thought. However, the subsequent fluidity of categorisation can trigger anxiety. The debate is familiar: feminisms have replaced feminism, but does this plurality weaken its central unity? Did such unity ever exist or was it merely an exclusive and illusory concept conceived by a privileged few? The challenges offered by a shift in perspective are reflected in the ways in which feminism has informed academic disciplines, including the study of film. If feminism is seen to be less clearly delineated recently in relation to film theory, it may be that it has become more integrated and central to debates. In a cultural climate of appropriation, revisiting the not-too-distant history of feminist film theory can inform contemporary investigations of the categories of gender through its persistent attention to perceptions and representations of reality and diversity.

Notes

1. See accounts of both in Laura Mulvey, 'British Feminist Film Theory's Female Spectators: Presence and Absence' in *Camera Obscura*, nos 20/21, 1989, and Maggie Humm, *Feminism and Film*.
2. E. Ann Kaplan, *Women and Film, Both Sides of the Camera* (London: Methuen, 1983), p. 23.
3. Judith Mayne, 'The Female Audience and the Feminist Critic' in Janet Todd (ed.), *Women and Film* (New York: Holmes and Meier, 1988), pp. 22–3.
4. Stereotypes such as the saintly wife versus the *femme fatale* came under scrutiny in genre-based discussions; see, for example, Kaplan (ed.), *Women and Film Noir*.
5. Haskell, *From Reverence to Rape*, p. vii.
6. Humm, *Feminism and Film*, p. 13.
7. Anneke Smelik in Rosemarie Buikema and Anneke Smelik (eds), *Women's Studies and Culture: A Feminist Introduction* (London and New Jersey: Zed Books, 1993), p. 67.
8. See, for example, Claire Johnston (ed.), *The Work of Dorothy Arzner: Towards a Feminist Cinema* (London: BFI, 1975).
9. Brunsdon (ed.), *Films For Women* has some useful articles on feminist film, particularly the sections on women's documentary film, and exhibition and distribution. Relevant films might include *Jeanne Dielman, 23 Quai du Commerce, 1080 Bruxelles* (Chantal Ackerman, 1975), *Daughter Rite* (Michelle Citron, 1978), and *Maeve* (Pat Murphy, 1981).
10. Laura Mulvey, 'British Feminist Film Theory's Female Spectators: Presence and Absence' in *Camera Obscura*, nos 20/21, 1989.
11. See Pam Cook (ed.), *The Cinema Book* (London: BFI, 1985), p. 220, for a brief breakdown of the aims of Peter Wollen.
12. See Claire Johnston, 'Towards a Feminist Film Practice: Some Theses' in Bill Nichols, (ed.), *Movies and Methods, Volume II* (Berkeley: University of California Press, 1985).
13. Johnston, *Notes on Women's Cinema*.
14. Humm, *Feminism and Film*, p. 13.
15. For a useful introduction to the subject see Robert Stam,

Robert Burgoyne, and Sandy Flitterman, *New Vocabularies in Film Semiotics: Structuralism, Poststructuralism and Beyond* (London: Routledge, 1992).
16. Judith Mayne, 'The Female Audience and the Feminist Critic' in Janet Todd (ed.), *Women and Film* (New York: Holmes and Meier, 1988), p. 24.
17. This film is quoted in a similar exercise by Judith Mayne in *Women and Film*, ibid. pp. 24–30.
18. See Pam Cook, 'Duplicity in Mildred Pierce' in Kaplan (ed.), *Women and Film Noir*, pp. 68–82.
19. Claire Johnston, 'Women's Cinema as Counter Cinema' in *Notes on Women's Cinema*; see also Teresa de Lauretis, *Alice Doesn't: Feminism, Semiotics, Cinema* (Basingstoke: Macmillan, 1984) for similarly informed arguments.
20. Johnston, Claire 'Towards a Feminist Film Practice: Some Theses' in Bill Nichols (ed.), *Movies and Methods: Volume II* (Berkeley: University of California Press, 1985), p. 322.
21. Ibid. p. 322.
22. Laura Mulvey, 'Visual Pleasure and Narrative Cinema', first published in *Screen*, Autumn 1975, vol. 16, no. 3, pp. 6–18, and reprinted in Mulvey, *Visual and Other Pleasures*.
23. Mulvey, *Visual and Other Pleasures*, p. 17
24. Ibid. p. 19.
25. Ibid. p.14.
26. Ibid. p. 26.
27. Laura Mulvey, 'Afterthoughts . . .' in Kaplan (ed.), *Psychoanalysis and Cinema*.
28. Laura Mulvey, 'British Feminist Film Theory's Female Spectators: Presence and Absence' in *Camera Obscura*, nos 20/21, 1989, p. 73.
29. See, for example, Doane, *Femme Fatales*; Screen, *The Sexual Subject*; and Kaplan (ed.), *Psychoanalysis and Cinema*.
30. Humm, *Feminism and Film*, p. 25.
31. Judith Mayne, 'Feminist Film Theory and Criticism' in Signs 11, no. 1 (1985) pp. 81–100, p. 85.
32. See, for example, 'Is the Gaze Male?' in Kaplan, *Women and Film: Both Sides of the Camera* (London and New York: Methuen, 1983).
33. As Mary Ann Doane writes, the female spectator 'exists nowhere but as an effect of discourse'; see Mary Ann Doane, *The Desire to Desire: The Woman's Film of the 1940s* (London: Macmillan, 1987), p. 9.
34. Caroline Evans and Lorraine Gamman, 'The Gaze Revisited or Reviewing Queer Viewing' in Burston and Richardson (eds), *A Queer Romance*.

35. Humm, *Feminism and Film*, p. 15.
36. Gamman and Marchment (eds), *The Female Gaze,* and Pribram (ed.), *Female Spectators.*
37. Jacqueline Bobo, in Pribram, *Female Spectators*, p. 95.
38. Jane Gaines, 'White Privilege and Looking Relations: Race and Gender in Feminist Film Theory', *Screen*, vol. 29, issue 4, pp. 12–27.
39. Jackie Stacey, 'Desperately Seeking Difference' in Gamman and Marchment (eds), *The Female Gaze,* p. 129.
40. For a more detailed and assertive proposition of an active lesbian subject, see Teresa de Lauretis, 'Film and the Visible' in Bad Object Choices (eds), *How Do I Look?* (Seattle: Bay Press, 1991); or Teresa de Lauretis, *The Practice of Love: Lesbian Sexuality and Perverse Desire* (Indiana: Indiana University Press, 1994), pp. 103–23.
41. Joan Riviere, 'Womanliness and the Masquerade', in Victor Burgin et al., *Formations of Fantasy* (London: Methuen, 1986).
42. Butler, *Gender Trouble*, p. 11.
43. Clover, *Men, Women and Chainsaws.*
44. For a full exploration of the term in relation to horror films, see Creed, *The Monstrous Feminine.*
45. Clover, *Men, Women and Chainsaws*, p. 22.
46. Tasker, *Working Girls*, p. 68.

Bibliography

Brunsdon, Charlotte (ed.), *Films For Women* (London: BFI, 1986).

Burston, Paul and Colin Richardson (eds), *A Queer Romance: Lesbians, Gay Men and Popular Culture* (London and New York: Routledge, 1995).

Butler, Judith, *Gender Trouble: Feminism and the Subversion of Identity* (New York: Routledge, 1990).

Clover, Carol, *Men, Women and Chainsaws: Gender in the Modern Horror Film* (London: BFI, 1992).

Creed, Barbara, *The Monstrous Feminine: Film Feminism, Psychoanalysis* (London and New York: Routledge, 1993).

Doane, Mary Ann, *Femme Fatales: Feminism, Film Theory and Psychoanalysis* (London and New York: Routledge, 1991).

Gamman, Lorraine and Marchment, Margaret (eds), *The Female Gaze: Women as Viewers of Popular Culture* (London: The Women's Press, 1988).

Gledhill, Christine (ed.), *Home is Where the Heart Is: Studies in Melodrama and the Woman's Film* (London: BFI, 1987).

Haskell, Molly, *From Reverence to Rape: The Treatment of Women in the Movies* (Chicago: University of Chicago Press, 1973).

Humm, Maggie, *Feminism and Film* (Edinburgh: Edinburgh University Press, 1997).

Johnston, Claire (ed.), *Notes on Women's Cinema* (London: Society for Education in Film and Television, 1973).

Kaplan, E. Ann (ed.), *Women and Film Noir* (London: BFI, 1978).

Kaplan, E. Ann, (ed.), *Psychoanalysis and Cinema* (London and New York: Routledge, 1990).

Mulvey, Laura, *Visual and Other Pleasures* (Basingstoke: Macmillan, 1989).

Pribram, E. Deidre (ed.), *Female Spectators: Looking at Film and Television* (London: Verso, 1988).

Screen, The Sexual Subject: A Screen Reader in Sexuality (London: Routledge, 1992).

Tasker, Yvonne, *Working Girls: Gender and Sexuality in Popular Cinema* (London and New York: Routledge, 1998).

Chapter 12

Video

Julia Knight

WOMEN WORKING CREATIVELY WITH video in Britain
have suffered from a lack of critical recognition on three levels.
First, at a general historical level, there has been 'the denigration
of women's art as second rate and innately inferior to that of
men'.[1] Secondly, video has been critically neglected as an art form
in Britain. And thirdly, women working with video in Britain
have been marginalised within the video sector itself, for example,
in 1983 London Video Arts (LVA) – a production workshop and
video art distributor – reported, 'Of over 250 tapes in the library
only twenty-five are by women and an even smaller minority
(about 7.5 per cent) of workshop members are women.'[2]

It is unsurprising therefore that there is a dearth of literature
addressing women working with video in Britain. Although
numerous publications have revealed the existence of women
artists both past and present, women working with video have
been noticeable by their virtual absence. There have been a
handful of articles in festival programmes, magazines and distribution catalogues, and the now defunct *Independent Media*
magazine (formerly *Independent Video*) also gave some coverage
to women's work, but such publications are highly ephemeral,
and any sense of a history of feminist engagement with video is
not immediately evident.

It is difficult to offer an overview of feminist engagement with
video in the UK because of its very diversity. Nevertheless, a
peculiarity of the British video scene makes it possible to identify
recurring trends and concerns. As elsewhere, video work in
Britain can be characterised by its broad split between artistic
practices and community/political activism, but in Britain there
was a concerted effort to construct an overarching and unified

'independent video sector'. This was partly because there were some real points of connection, and as a result, community-originated material would frequently be screened alongside video art. At the 1987 National Festival of Independent Video, for instance, the community-based *How Can I Ignore the Girl Next Door?* was screened alongside Pratibha Parmar's video art tape *Emergence* on the basis that both videos were 'made by women on issues particularly connected with women's lives'.[3] Made by Hammersmith and Fulham Young Lesbian Group in 1987, the former is a low-budget, technically shaky and poorly acted comedy drama about lesbian lifestyles, while *Emergence* (1986) is an imaginatively edited, well paced and experimental exploration of the lives of four black women artists.

This 'video sector' created a forum in which women could voice concerns, campaign for their interests, and find support for their work, and analysis of the sectoral concerns and initiatives reveals some broad characteristics of feminist work in video. Partly because of the existence of this all-encompassing video sector and partly because of genuinely shared concerns among women, it is also difficult to isolate one area of practice and see it as discrete. Thus, in considering feminism and video in Britain, it is necessary to address both artistic practices and community activism.

The independent video sector

Although video had been used as a creative medium since the mid-1960s, it was not until the 1980s, particularly with the launch of Channel Four, that a sense of an established video sector began to emerge. Channel Four's main significance for those working with video was its charter to encourage independent production and its commitment to offer programmes by and for a whole range of minority groups. The new channel drew up a Workshop Declaration with the (then) television technicians' union ACTT allowing the setting-up of franchised workshops to make film and video productions for broadcast outside usual union agreements. This opened up an avenue of funded production work for social groups who had traditionally been underrepresented, misrepresented or excluded by the mass media – such as people of colour, the disabled, gays and, of course, women. Channel Four's support for independent production, often in conjunction with co-funding from the Arts Council, regional arts organisations, the British Film Institute and local authorities, began to provide an institutional framework for the rapidly growing number of video organisations and initiatives. As David Critchley has observed, 'the whole thing went mad in the early 1980s. There were forty or fifty video organisations in London alone at one point. And the GLC were literally throwing money at groups to set up.'[4]

The sense of a 'sector' was reinforced by an increasing number of screening and discussion forums, and two regular outlets set up in the 1980s were particularly important. In 1980 Bracknell's Media Centre at South Hill Park Arts Centre staged the first National Festival of Independent Video, which became an annual event for video art and community-based video work and a lively focus for screenings and debate until its final year in 1988. In 1982 the Centre also launched *Independent Video* magazine. Produced monthly until its demise in 1991, it was Britain's only publication devoted to alternative forms of video production and gave coverage to both community video and video art.

Within this sector there were a number of feminist initiatives. Most notably, throughout the 1980s a number of women-only video groups and workshops were set up, including Women in Sync, Aphra Video, Cinestra Pictures, Seeing Red and Video Vera. Although the orientation of each group varied, they shared similar overall aims: the London-based Women in Sync were typical and described their aims as follows:

1. to set up women's video productions
2. to aim for (ultimately) a women's video resource/equipment/skill-sharing service
3. to inform ourselves of current debates in the medium, and to build up a feminist critique
4. to build up a directory/library/distribution network of women's videotapes
5. to campaign for exhibitions of women's video work.[5]

Most women's groups undertook production work, training, and screenings of work by women in a women-only environment. Publicising their work in 1983, Women in Sync reported that the previous year they had held screenings at the West London Media Workshop, the National Film Theatre and the London Film-makers Coop, and had run courses on the introduction and practical use of VHS, two-colour camera (KY2000) and mixer, the technical background to the video camera, lighting and studio production. Feminist initiatives were also mounted in other organisations as well: both LVA and Connections Community Video also ran women-only video production courses; in 1982 two women on LVA's organising committee set up a Women's Committee to ensure gender parity in the organisation; and in 1987 the Rio Cinema in London set up a new video exhibition facility for women.

By October 1987, it seemed as if these initiatives had paid off with the staging of the First National Women's Video Festival. Funded by Greater London Arts, the Arts Council, Channel Four, Thames Television, the BFI, Spare Rib, City Limits and Camden Playbox, it demonstrated the breadth of women's creative work with video by presenting screenings, practical workshops, and social events. The screenings covered topics as diverse as sexuality, institutional structures, sport, health, women's history, violence against women, Northern Ireland, media representation of women, narrative fiction, and work. Alongside the more predictable selections of documentary, experimental, fiction and campaigning tapes, there was also a selection of music videos by women presented at the Fridge nightclub in Brixton. The workshops were equally varied, including beginners courses and sessions on working with the community, black women and representation, women and media education, and grant aid. The festival was deemed an enormous success: not only did one reviewer comment on 'the evident enthusiasm of the women who attended the various festival events',[6] but the launch event attracted 400 women and the music videos at the Fridge attracted 600. At the same time, the range of work submitted represented, for one member of the selection committee, nothing less than 'a sophisticated women's video culture'.[7]

A critique of representation

Any existence of a women's video culture in Britain also has to be viewed in the context of the women's art movement. From the beginning of the 1970s, feminist artists in Britain (and elsewhere) set up a whole range of collective projects, organised all-women exhibitions, and intervened in many related cultural and political spheres, and this necessarily impacted on women's creative engagement with video.

In the late 1960s, women artists started to challenge modernism as the dominant paradigm in art, art criticism and art history for its privileging of both male artists and a particular kind of art practice. Contrary to the feminist slogan 'the personal is political', modernist art practice could be characterised by what Catherine Elwes has termed its 'impersonal formalism',[8] and the art world generally by its operation outside of and separate to the complex relations of everyday life. In rejecting modernism, feminist artists examined the selective processes by which modernist art had come to represent the tradition of twentieth-century culture in the West, and started to develop alternative forms of artistic production.

In order to produce their own discourses, a significant number of women artists turned to precisely that which had been marginalised within mainstream art practice: the personal. According to Elwes, video had a particular appeal in this project for several reasons. First, the technology is easy to operate and so artists could work alone without the intrusive presence of a film crew. Video is also relatively cheap to use which meant artists could retain a greater degree of independence. Both these factors allowed the artist to have more control over her work. But video also offered immediately accessible footage, either as a live image relayed to a monitor or via instant playback of recorded material:

> As a result it could act as a mirror in which the artist could enter into a dialogue with the self she encountered everyday, and the potential selves she was seeking to uncover. It was possible to commit personal testaments to tape in any environment, however intimate, and in complete privacy.[9]

This is particularly evident in Elwes' tape *With Child* (1985), in which she explores her pregnant self (Figure 12.1). The first half of the tape conveys her fascination and preoccupation with the prospect of having a child, as we see repeated images of children's toys and hear Elwes reacting with 'oohs' and 'aahs'. Indeed, she demonstrates a childlike innocence and pleasure, and has stated in interview that 'when I was pregnant . . . I spent a lot of time mentally reliving my childhood'.[10] A second series of images suggests the duration of pregnancy as the artist is seen collecting baby clothes, while external shots mark the passing of the seasons. Elwes then reminds us that her pregnant self is also a sexual self, by having two toy monkeys mimic sexual activity. This suggests pregnancy can be a joyous experience, something which she reinforces by writing 'CE LOVES JM' across her pregnant belly. But the final sequence contrasts this with images of the artist wielding a knife both towards herself and a doll. As Elwes has commented, 'You are supposed to feel fantastic and fulfilled as a pregnant woman. But there is an underside . . . You can feel murderous not only towards yourself but also towards the child.'[11]

Thus, *With Child* draws heavily upon the personal: it is her pregnancy she uses as subject matter, her experiences she represents, and herself she puts on camera. Furthermore, a close-up of the artist's eyes both opens the tape and recurs at regular intervals, forcing us to view Elwes' experience of pregnancy through her eyes: 'It is also important for me . . . to emphasise that it is me, I as a female, who is making the tape. It's through my eyes, my perceptions that people are momentarily experiencing the world.'[12] However, the experience of pregnancy is something which she shares with other women, and although we view it through her eyes, she also brings to the making of the tape her knowledge of how the female body operates as a site of meaning. Part of her rationale for making the tape was precisely to challenge both the dominant 'fantastic and fulfilled' image of pregnancy and the way a pregnant woman is seldom seen as sexual. Hence the personal becomes political. Traditionally represented as an object of male desire, the female body is reappropriated by Elwes to portray pregnancy 'from the perspective of the woman who inhabits the body'.[13]

As is evident, the rejection of modernism was not purely a question of aesthetics: in turning to the personal, women artists necessarily became involved in questions of representation. This engagement with the representation of women was a crucial point of connection with women working in the community sector. Within community video circles, there was an overriding concern

Figure 12.1
Catherine Elwes,
With Child,
video, 1985.

to demystify television by providing wider access to the means of production. This was highly significant for those social groups who had historically been under- or misrepresented by the mass media: it allowed them not only to see themselves represented in a medium that had largely excluded their concerns, but also to take some control of the process of representation.

Work within the community video sector was also informed by the developing discipline of media studies. A major research concern was to analyse the representational strategies employed by the mass media in order to examine how these function to marginalise the voices of certain social groups and exclude particular issues. In the case of women, an article by Laura Mulvey proved particularly influential.[14] Drawing on psycho-analytic theory, she argued that the textual strategies of Hollywood films position women as passive sexual spectacles and construct an implied male heterosexual spectator for those images. The image of woman therefore signifies nothing for herself: she is a signifier only of male desire. Although subsequent work on cinema spectatorship has challenged Mulvey's ideas, her analysis of the positioning of women was seen to hold true in other areas of the mass media and much community video work was concerned with putting on screen those issues and experiences that had previously been excluded. For women, this meant addressing areas such as childcare, lesbianism, ageing, rape, menstruation, childbirth, domestic violence, and differences between women on the basis of class, race and so on.

This is very apparent in Albany Video's tape *Mistaken Identity* (1985), which comprises a series of sketches and songs, written and performed by young, and mostly black, women and girls from London youth projects (Figure 12.2). The first section is a song performed by five young woman about sitting in the waiting-room of a family planning clinic, worrying about being pregnant, and the attendant feelings of nervousness, shame and guilt. This is followed by a short sketch about how embarrassing it can feel, as a young woman, to stand at a shop counter buying tampons. Other sketches deal with shopping in the West End, periods, finding out about sex, and being given a hideously old-fashioned pair of trousers by your mother for your sixteenth birthday. All the sketches are performed with enthusiasm, imagination and humour. Thus the tape not only shows aspects of the

Figure 12.2
Albany Video,
Mistaken
Identity, *video,*
1985.

lives of young black women that had been excluded by the mass media, but shows the young women having fun. As the girls involved in the tape observe, 'You hardly ever see black people enjoying themselves on television . . . if you see them they're shown rioting . . . as problems . . . or in other countries.'

Appearances can be deceptive I: it's a man's world

Although it is possible to assert the existence of 'a sophisticated women's video culture' in Britain, women's concerns and work were frequently marginalised within the video sector. This was evident both in *Independent Media* magazine and at the annual National Festival of Independent Video. When its editors launched *Independent Video*, they stressed, 'We are aiming to produce ultimately a publication on behalf of and for all independent workers. The greater the involvement, the more successful and comprehensive a service we will be able to provide.'[15]

Those editors, however, were two men and, although some work by women was featured, any involvement by women was not immediately apparent. Consequently, many women became unhappy with what they saw increasingly as a boy's magazine. Similarly, although the festival had screened work by women, it had not always provided a particularly conducive environment for women's concerns. In 1984, for instance, Tina Keane's *In Our Hands Greenham* (1984) was screened with the artist present. This highly impressionistic tape about the women's peace camp at Greenham Common met with bafflement and anger from some male members of the audience, which stifled any possibility of a constructive discussion. Things came to a head at the 1986 festival:

> Whispers of discontent grew into a loud chorus . . . at the predominantly (white) male selection of unrepresentative (at best) work on show. Programmes ended in rows, people stormed out . . . and the weekend deflated into pessimism . . . Women in particular were outraged by the crude marginalisation of their work and contribution to the sector.[16]

The Media Centre responded by appointing a woman as their education worker and employing a female contributing editor on *Independent Media* to encourage women contributors. They also invited more women to take part in the festival selection process the following year, resulting in a larger number of tapes by women being selected.

However, women's marginalisation and under-representation remained a persistent problem. In 1988, LVA found it necessary to advertise for women artists to submit work to their video library. The following year the Liverpool-based Video Positive festival asked a number of artists, technicians, critics and funders to write a paragraph on the future of video art for the festival catalogue. Of the eleven responses published, only two came from women, prompting the editor to note, 'Whither replies from more women, gay and black artists? Does this imply a continued and just as systematic exclusion of such groups from 'mainstream' video art circles?'[17] The marginalisation of women is obviously part of a wider issue, but it meant that the First National Women's Video Festival was viewed almost universally in positive terms, rather than as a form of continuing ghettoisation of women's creative work generally.

Appearances can be deceptive II: production values and skills

Any analysis of women's video work also reveals a prevalence of minimal production values. Although women did produce some accomplished work – such as *With Child*, *Mistaken Identity*, and *Emergence – How Can I Ignore the Girl Next Door?* suffers from a lack of production skills among its makers: '[it has] recognised technical faults (some scenes drag, or seek to include too many issues; why so few cutaways filmed?)'.[18] Nor was *How Can I Ignore* an isolated case: an indication of women's lack of production skills was the inclusion of a guide to video and audio leads in the First National Women's Video Festival catalogue.

Poor technical skills among women were the result of a number of factors. Within community video circles, workshops often undertook process work, that is video workers prioritised the processes used to produce a tape rather than the end product: 'It's about bringing groups together and getting them to communicate about shared interests . . . and that communication is important even if it doesn't end up on the tape; it's the fact that it has happened that's the point.'[19] As a result, those taking part were more involved in creating their own representations, but teaching technical skills was not the main aim.

In view of the paucity of audiovisual material addressing certain issues, there was also a tendency to be more tolerant of low production values in women's work. Thus the selection guidelines for the First National Women's Video Festival specified that, 'the Festival should not be over concerned with "QUALITY" or production values, but more with content.'[20] Hence, *How Can I Ignore* was screened at the festival, and also at the 1987 Bracknell festival, and was picked up for distribution because of the scarcity at the time of tapes addressing lesbian sexuality. However, the concomitant outcome is that women were viewed as incapable of producing more proficient work and denied the opportunities of improving their skills.

A major contributing factor to poor technical skills among women was inadequate training opportunities. Women tended to be disadvantaged in training situations through the sexist attitudes of teachers and male students and through a lack of consideration of their needs, such as creche facilities. Indeed, Al Garthwaite has argued that most video training courses were designed and taught by men for men, hence women were usually under-represented.[21] Women-only courses were set up in an attempt to counter this, but given women's lack of skills, most of these were pitched at a basic introductory level. In 1987 Bracknell's Media Centre sent out a 'Women and Training' questionnaire to all workshops in Britain to assess the specific training needs of women in the independent sector. Over 100 workshops responded and indicated that the majority of women were now interested in intermediate and advanced-level training. As the 1980s progressed, the argument for improving technical skills within the video sector both generally and for women in particular became more vocal:

> Tapes such as *How Can I Ignore the Girl Next Door?* . . .
> and *The English Estate* (Community Arts Workshop), both
> dealing with important issues, only reaffirmed for me the

need for basic production skills. It is difficult to really hear a voice that is muffled, or see a picture that is unstable or dark, or attend to a tape that is overlong and under-edited. An important, hitherto unheard, voice is not enough for effective video communication; it must be trained in the medium before it can be understood. This is not to encourage mainstream follies but to know the basic vocabulary of TV and film from which video is derived; a language unknown cannot be subverted.[22]

By the end of the decade, the need for training was so well recognised that it had become relatively easy to get funding for running courses, but this had an unwelcome side-effect:

A major dilemma facing many is that funding for training work is both easier to get and something [women] feel committed to doing so as to develop women's access to production. But at the same time this eats up their own time and energy and means precluding production work.[23]

Conclusion: forward into the past

As the 1980s came to a close, the notion of a 'video sector' was difficult to sustain. Funding structures had changed, giving way to the so-called 'enterprise culture', with less grant aid available for the kinds of work that had given rise to a women's video culture. At the same time, any distinctiveness video may have initially had as an art form had rapidly been eroded: in view of the encroaching camcorder culture, video artist Jon Dovey observed, 'We may use video, but then so does everyone else.'[24] Video aesthetics had 'established themselves within the mainstream of TV',[25] and now, with digital technology, video is being superseded by multimedia. Hence, the women's video culture that developed in the 1980s is arguably a thing of the past.

However, it is important to prevent the debates and work generated by women videomakers from sinking into oblivion. Not only have feminist initiatives improved the position of women in the audiovisual industries generally, but they remain relevant in the new digital era. Although numbers are increasing, any analysis of artists' work with computers shows women to be similarly in the minority. According to Julie Myers, this is partly due to women's attitudes: 'Men identify with the computer . . . Women, on the other hand, seem to view this new technology with suspicion'.[26] This means computer access and training for women are crucially important, just as they were with video. If women's engagement with older media technologies, such as video, is forgotten, we risk having to fight the same battles all over again.

Notes

1. Parker and Pollock, *Framing Feminism*, p. xiii.
2. 'Women's Media: Women's Video Group', *Independent Video*, no. 15, March 1983, p. 4.
3. *Independent Media*, no. 70, October 1987, p. 9.
4. Quoted in Knight, *Diverse Practices*, p. 227.
5. From an early, undated and unpaginated issue of *Independent Video*.
6. Lisa Haskel, 'Women's Video Takes London by Storm', *Independent Media*, no. 71, November 1987, p. 11.
7. Helen Doherty, 'Fun, Love and Scopophilia', *Independent Media*, no. 69, September 1987, p. 5.
8. Elwes, 'The Pursuit of the Personal in British Video Art', in Knight, *Diverse Practices*, p. 265.
9. Ibid. p. 266.
10. Ilppo Phojola, 'Winter Break', *Independent Media*, no. 77, August 1988, p. 3.
11. Ibid. p. 3.
12. Ibid. p. 3.
13. Elwes, 'The Pursuit of the Personal in British Video Art', in Knight, *Diverse Practices*, p. 265.
14. Laura Mulvey, 'Visual Pleasure and Narrative Cinema', *Screen*, vol. 6, no. 3, 1975, pp. 6–18.
15. 'How Independent Video Works . . .', *Independent Video*, no. 2, February 1982, p. 1.
16. Mary Downes, 'National Festival of Independent Video', *Independent Media*, no. 73, January 1988, p. 5.
17. Video Positive '89 catalogue (Liverpool: Merseyside Moviola, 1989), p. 58.
18. 'Festival Screenings: Spare Rib – selection by Marcel Farry and Al Garthwaite (Video Vera)', *Independent Media*, no. 70, October 1987, p. 9.

19. Peter Lawrence, 'Learning Through Collaboration', *Independent Media*, no. 82, October 1988, p. 10.
20. The First Women's Video Festival catalogue, p. 18.
21. 'Training: Paper by Al Garthwaite, Video Vera', *Independent Media*, no. 59, November 1986, pp. 33–4.
22. Mary Downes, 'National Festival of Independent Video', *Independent Media*, no. 73, January 1988, p. 6.
23. Eileen Phillips, 'Not Just the Icing – a Bigger Share of the Cake', *Independent Media*, no. 61, January 1987, p. 3.
24. Jon Dovey, 'Talking Television', *Independent Media*, no. 94, December 1989, p. 10.
25. Ibid. p. 11.
26. Julie Myers, 'Women and Computer Images', Video Positive 1991 catalogue (Liverpool: Moviola, 1991), p. 32.

Bibliography

Cubitt, Sean, *Time Shift: On Video Culture* (London: Routledge, 1991).

Cubitt, Sean, *Videography: Video Media as Art and Culture* (Basingstoke: Macmillan, 1993).

Elwes, Catherine, 'Behind the Pretty Face – British Women Artists Working with Video', *LVA 1984 Distribution Catalogue* (London: LVA, 1984), pp. 13–16.

Feminist Arts News, vol. 2, no. 7, film and video special issue, undated.

Independent Video/Independent Media

Knight, Julia (ed.), *Diverse Practices: A Critical Reader on British Video Art* (Luton: University of Luton Press, 1996).

Parker, Rozsika, and Griselda Pollock (eds), *Framing Feminism: Art and the Women's Movement 1970–1985* (London: Pandora, 1987).

Video Vera, *Careers Day for Girls in Film, Video & Television Report* (Leeds: Video Vera, 1986).

Chapter 13

Cyberfeminism

Sarah Chaplin

Feminism and technology

This chapter reviews the development and impact of feminist theory within the field of digital technology, particularly in relation to the social use of and meanings surrounding the growth of the Internet. This aspect of contemporary visual culture has offered a rich new area of study for feminist historians, scientists, and sociologists alike, who have generated new categories for critical analysis and posed new questions about the nature of identity and visuality in a computer-dominated era. The figure of the cyborg and the term 'cyberfeminism' have emerged as central to this new discourse; both have been interpreted, represented and appropriated in a number of different ways in academia and in mainstream media. This chapter will therefore examine the different visions/versions of cyberfeminism and their implications for the study of visual culture, and it will offer a visual analysis of some popular cyborg personae by way of a case study.

The question to be asked is whether 'cyber' is merely the prefix of the moment, bestowing the highest caché on any outmoded terminology, or whether its effect is to confirm a deeper restructuring of meaning and human consciousness. In other words, is cyberfeminism simply a rebranding exercise or is it a real shift in the way feminism tackles patriarchy and other given hierarchies embedded within contemporary society? And what is its effect on the evolving feminist project in terms of visual culture? Sadie Plant, one of the main proselytisers of cyberfeminism makes great claims for its potential: 'Cyberfeminism is an insurrection on the part of the goods and materials of the patriarchal world, a dispersed, distributed emergence composed of links between women, women and computers, computers and communication links, connections and connectionist nets.'[1] But Plant's apolitical vision makes feminist artist Catherine Elwes nervous and despairing of its potential to offer a way forward. She laments, 'Cyberfeminism means the death of feminism, and a post-political world.'[2] It is clear that cyberfeminism has engendered considerable debate and, as Barbara Kennedy observes in a section devoted to the subject in *The Cybercultures Reader*, 'Cyberfeminism has been crucial to the current elan of cross-cultural, theoretical and differential plateaux of contemporary feminisms.'[3]

Feminism's engagement with cyberculture and technoscience is something of a recent departure – as Carol Stabile puts it, 'feminists have been amongst the last to jump on the technological bandwagon'.[4] Compared with the prevailing tendency towards technomania, or what Gill Kirkup describes as 'a disease of 1990s culture studies',[5] feminist theory in the 1970s and 1980s was typically technophobic, proposing that 'a rejection of technology is functionally identical to a rejection of patriarchy'.[6] However, Stabile argues in her book *Feminism and the Technological Fix* that feminist interpretation of technology is no longer a strictly polarised field of enquiry, and she cites more recent work which mediates between two opposing voices apparent within the body of feminist literature on technology: 'Attempting to bridge the gap between technophobia and the new technomania, feminist theorists have now produced a body of work analysing how technoscience has inscribed itself on the bodies of female or feminised subjects.'[7] Similarly, Judy Wajcman in her book *Feminism Confronts Technology* shows how recent feminist thought has sought to engage with a revised notion of technology, and how new theoretical insights have therefore emerged which recast women's relationship to technology, overriding the essentialism, binarism and humanism which characterise most previous accounts.[8]

Cyborg or goddess?

In many accounts, feminist biologist Donna Haraway is seen as the primary instigator in the discourse on cyberfeminism, although Judith Squires claims that 'one of the most exciting visions of cyberfeminism to date is still to be found in a text from cyberculture's prehistory, Shulamith Firestone's *The Dialectic of Sex* (1972).'[9] In 1985, Haraway wrote a now-seminal essay, entitled 'A Manifesto for Cyborgs'. Her stated aim was to 'build an ironic political myth faithful to feminism, socialism and materialism'.[10] At the centre of this myth is the figure of the cyborg, a hybrid of machine and organism, 'a creature of the post-gender world', of social reality as well as science fiction.[11] In Haraway's schema, the cyborg is 'resolutely committed to parti-ality, irony, intimacy and perversity'.[12] 'It is oppositional, uto-pian, and completely without innocence', according to Haraway, and operates by breaking down three important boundaries: between humans and animals, animal-humans and machines, and between physical and non-physical states.[13] The Manifesto proposes a new logic that is not structured by polarities, that is wary of holism and paternalism, and fundamentally reworks the distinctions between nature and culture. She visualises the cyborg as 'a condensed image of both imagination and material reality, the two joined centres structuring any possibility of historical transformation',[14] and she indicates that as a 'kind of disas-sembled and reassembled, postmodern collective and personal self' the cyborg is 'the self feminists must code'.[15] Famously, she ended the essay by declaring, 'I would rather be a cyborg than a goddess', and it would seem that a whole spate of science fiction films have heeded this, replacing screen sirens with technologi-cally augmented and implanted cyberheroines.

While Haraway is now something of a heroine in her own right and has generated a committed and vocal following, she also has her detractors. Kathleen Woodward claims that 'A Manifesto for Cyborgs' is 'theoretical science fiction; she envisions a conver-gence of biotechnology and communications technology in the figure of the cyborg'.[16] Haraway remains unfazed: in her view the boundary between science fiction and social reality is an 'optical illusion'.[17]

Kirsten Notten is critical of the way in which Haraway mounts her critique of science: 'Haraway uses the heroic status of tech-noscientific practice to shift the meaning of heroism. She redraws the boundaries of high-tech to incorporate women into the heroic charisma of technology.'[18] Using a traditional feminist argument,

Notten writes, 'High tech is partly constructed precisely by excluding women. It is therefore necessary to rearrange the way high-tech gets its meaning,'[19] and she suggests that 'Haraway reinforces this hierarchy of values by using high-tech to make women into cyborgs and heroines. To give female activities a revaluation the boundaries between high and low tech along gender lines need to be dismantled.'[20] However, this is not the boundary condition which Haraway sought to dismantle: she has her sights set on other binaries, citing an example beloved of cyberculture: 'There is no fundamental, ontological separation in our formal knowledge of machine and organism, of technical and organic. The replicant Rachel in Ridley Scott's film *Bladerunner* stands as the image of a cyborg culture's fear, love and confusion.'[21]

The cyborg is not only a highly visible entity, it is big business: there is now a long list of box-office and CD-Rom hits featuring a variety of post-Frankenstein bodies that are represented as armoured, augmented, liquefied and cloned, while cyberpunk fiction features protagonists whose memories are implanted, downloaded, erased and exchanged. The cyborg tropes are well defined and we no longer need reminding of the extent to which we are all increasingly augmented by technology, that we are all in some senses already cyborgs, and are haunted, like Rachel, by our relationship to technology.

But what is perhaps less clear is the fact that, somewhat confusingly, there are least two kinds of cyborg currently in play: as Claudia Springer has noted, 'the idea of a feminist cyborg, like the idea of a militaristic cyborg, arises from dissatisfaction with current social and economic relations, but the two cyborg visions offer vastly different solutions to our social ills'.[22] While the militaristic cyborg treats technology as a given, the feminist cyborg calls technology into question and reworks it. In the introduction to *The Cyborg Handbook*, published in 1995, the editor loosely puts forward the concept of 'cyborgology', and asserts that 'even if many individuals in the industrial and post-industrial countries aren't full cyborgs, we certainly all live in a "cyborg society"'.[23] They define cyborg society as 'the full range of intimate organic-machine relations from the man-machine weapons systems of the postmodern military to . . . the genetically engineered mice of today to biocomputers, artificial life programmes, and any future extravaganzas'.[24] Somewhat evasively, they maintain 'cyborgology is not simple. For one thing there is no consensus on what a cyborg is.'[25] However, despite a foreword written by Donna Haraway, the consensus of the book seems to drift towards the militaristic end of the cyborg spectrum.

The military cyborg is the soldier engaged in high-tech forms of combat which afford a simulated and abstracted relationship to their 'targets' in order to safeguard their own sanity and preserve the illusion of war as accurate, efficient and effective. Vision is fetishised and enhanced, 'smart' functions are added to weapons which provide 'the ultimate voyeurism: to see the target hit from the vantage point of the weapon'.[26] Ken Robins and Les Levidow account for the mindset of the militaristic cyborg as follows: 'Through a paranoid rationality, expressed in the machine-like self, we combine an omnipresent fantasy of self-control with fear and aggression directed against the emotional and bodily limitations of mere mortals.'[27]

It is in fact this paranoid-aggressive version that dominates most recent Hollywood representations of cyborgs, in films such as *Terminator*, *Total Recall*, *Demolition Man*, and *Robocop*. To the cyberfeminist, however, these miss the point entirely, and are a product of the technologically determinist masculine rhetoric that dominates contemporary perceptions and visualisations of our changing bodies. Moreover, Haraway highlights the potentially damaging impact of a proliferation of military imagery upon contemporary consciousness:

> The culture of video games is heavily orientated to individual competition and extraterrestrial warfare. High-tech, gendered imaginations are produced here, imaginations that can contemplate destruction of the planet and a science fiction escape from its consequences. More than our imaginations is militarised.[28]

This is one of the underlying challenges for cyberfeminism to address, as Barbara Kennedy is at pains to point out: 'Cyberfeminism needs to move beyond the limitations of such representations; it has all been done before. What we need is creativity, an engagement with new modes of thinking and expression.'[29]

Cybervisuality

It becomes important, therefore, in terms of a feminist understanding of contemporary visual culture, to analyse an emergent
new scopic regime which we might term 'cybervisuality', as an
important aspect of the changing perceptual environment in
which we live. Just as cyberfeminism lays claim to being a radical
restructuring of feminism as a whole endeavour rather than just a
specialist branch of it, so too the notion of cybervisuality helps
reconceptualise existing scopic regimes, in such a way that the
work produced by so-called 'electronic artists' is no longer seen as
a specialist branch of fine art, but an integrated part of a new
continuum of cultural practice. In other words, as Margaret
Morse has emphasised, 'Art should not be ghettoised into the
electronic and/or virtual environment versus the rest, but thought
of as linked by metaphors across different degrees of materiality.'[30] Drawing on Luce Irigaray's work, Sadie Plant locates
artistic production in a broader context of the prevailing cultural
economy, in which she depicts it as being less and less potent in
terms of its impact or effect on society:

> As images migrate from canvas to film and finally on to the
> digital screen, what was once called art mutates into a
> matter of software engineering . . . and just as the image
> is reprocessed, so it finds itself embroiled in a new network
> of connections between words, music, and architectures
> which diminishes the governing role it once played in the
> specular economy.[31]

Elsewhere, Plant loads this concept more blatantly: 'At the end of
the twentieth century all notions of artistic genius, authorial
authority, originality and creativity become a matter of software
engineering.'[32]

One of the most active proponents of cyberfeminism, Rosi
Braidotti, in an online article called 'Cyberfeminism with a
Difference', makes a more positive case for the new possibilities
within visual culture which are brought into play by virtue of new
technologies for generating, manipulating and disseminating
images:

In all fields, but especially in information technology, the strict separation between the technical and the creative has in fact been made redundant by digital images and the skills required by computer-aided design. The new alliance between previously segregated domains of the technical and the artistic marks a contemporary version of the post-humanistic reconstruction of a techno-culture whose aesthetics is equal to its technological sophistication.[33]

While Braidotti is optimistic about the formation of new alliances, she is also extremely critical of virtual reality, which she claims 'belongs to the pornographic regime of representation'.[34] In her view, this is brought about by the fact that virtual reality is founded upon a contradictory premise: 'virtual reality images . . . titillate our imagination promising marvels and wonders of a gender-free world while simultaneously reproducing some of the most banal flat images of gender identity, class and race relations that you can think of.'[35] Haraway also draws attention to the sense of voyeurism which is accentuated by virtual reality: 'the technologies of visualisation recall the important cultural practice of hunting with the camera and the deeply predatory nature of a photographic consciousness.'[36]

Within the regime of cybervisuality gender certainly remains a key factor. As Springer has noted in her analysis of cyberpunk:

> gender, rather than disappearing, is often emphasised after cybernetic transformation. While Moravec asserts that gender will become obsolete once human minds have been transferred to software, cyberpunk points instead to a future in which gender and sex not only exist but have also become magnified.[37]

Rob Kitchin agrees that there is a significant gender dimension to cybervisuality:

> While some suggest that gender-swapping is opening the eyes of men to life as a woman and the oppression women face daily in negotiating their lives, others suggest that cyberspatial technologies are in fact reinforcing current representations of women through the prevalence of

pornography and the retention of stereotypical gender roles.[38]

According to Braidotti, the core problem to be addressed in order to transcend this tendency is our own stunted powers of imagination which have not kept pace with the kind of developments in new technology which in turn ought to have afforded new ways of thinking: 'The alleged triumph of high technologies is not matched by a leap in the human imagination to create new images and representations, . . . it just goes to prove that it takes more than machinery to really alter patterns of thought and mental habits.'[39] Haraway, too, intimates that it may be necessary to think outside a black and white mentality in order to make progress: 'Can cyborgs or binary oppositions or technological vision hint at ways that the things many feminists have feared most can and must be refigured and put back to work for life and not death?'[40]

Cybergrrl

Tackling this question head on in a paper called 'Where is the Feminism in Cyberfeminism?', Faith Wilding argues, 'if feminism is adequate to its cyberpotential then it must mutate to keep up with the shifting complexities of social realities and life conditions as they are changed by the profound impact of communications technologies and technoscience have on all our lives.'[41] She agrees that 'there is much to be said for considering cyberfeminism as a promising new wave of feminist practices that can contest technologically complex territories and chart new ground for women,'[42] but identifies the problem for cyberfeminism as being 'how to incorporate the lessons of history into an activist feminist politics which is adequate for addressing women's issues in technological culture'.[43] She concludes, 'it is a radical act to insert the word feminism into cyberspace and to attempt to interrupt the flow of masculine codes by boldly declaring the intention to mongrelise, hybridise, provoke and disrupt the male order of things in the Net environment.'[44] Offering evidence of a particular way forward for cyberfeminism, Wilding cites the movement known as 'cybergrrlism' as 'an important manifestation of new subjective and cultural feminine representations in cyberspace'.[45]

The cybergrrl phenomenon is a more proactive version of cyberfeminism, which situates the feminist project in the realms of cyberspace by invoking a plethora of Net-orientated tactics that are designed to disrupt and question the status quo. Braidotti sees herself as a proto-cybergrrl (RosieX), which she regards as a provocative linguistic phenomenon: a search for 'cybergirl' would yield many pornographic websites, whereas 'grrl' has something of a militant growl to it, enabling women to 'undertake the dance through cyberspace.'[46] As Nina Wakeford states, 'Grrls also appear to be ambivalent or even hostile to patterns of behaviour which they associate with an "older style feminist rhetoric", and in particular the idea of a prescriptive or homogenous women's movement.'[47] When set against a backdrop of computer games and other masculinist envisionings of cyberspace, the cybergrrl's radical political tactics are a positive reckoning force and belong to the regime of cybervisuality.

Many women regard the Internet as a misogynist zone to be confronted and challenged, and as Laura Miller contends, they see the typical envisioning of cyberspace as one which is fraught with the same territoriality as real space:

> If the romance of the frontier arises from the promise of vast stretches of unowned land, an escape from the restrictions of a society based on private property, then the introduction of women spoils that dream by reintroducing the imperative of property in their own persons . . . this set of unexamined assumptions follows us into the bodiless realm of cyber-space, not a desert landscape but a complex technological society where women are supposed to command equal status with men.[48]

As an alternative cyberfeminist visualisation, Nina Wakeford proposes that 'cyberspace is not a coherent global and unitary entity but a series of performances'.[49] She is concerned about the way in which the use of the Internet is depicted as trivial and asserts one of the performative aspects of cyberspace as a feminist act:

I resist the notion that working on the Web, whether surfing or creating the pages, is always or necessarily insignificant, marginal to women's lives and to cultures of feminism. I reclaim the activity known as surfing as serious play which can create and maintain relationships, be they between individuals, organisations or hypertext documents.'[50]

Her own contribution was the creation of the Octavia Project, a resource on the Net on gender and technology, which weaves together a dense and democratic texture of information.

Cyber-hype

One of the problems facing feminist Web activists such as Wakeford is the tendency to be cast into the category of hype and technomania to which Judith Squires alludes: 'Whilst there may be potential for an alliance between cyborg imagery and a materialist-feminism, this potential has been largely submerged beneath a sea of technophoric cyberdrool.'[51] Sadie Plant's version of cyberfeminism is often interpreted in this way, in that she extrapolates Haraway's premise but uses overly deterministic language to make universalising, essentialising claims: 'cyberfeminism is the acknowledgement that patriarchy is doomed and that no-one is making it happen, it manifests itself as an alien invasion, a program which is already running beyond the human.'[52] Or, more simply, 'cyberfeminism is the process by which [humanity's] history is racing to an end'.[53] Squires is particularly uncomfortable with the apolitical nature of Plant's predictions and with the fact that Plant and others like her largely misconstrue Haraway's irony and modesty in proposing a cyborgian consciousness: 'If the cyborg was, for Haraway, an ironic political myth which was created to symbolise a non-holistic, non-universalising vision for feminist strategies, it has been taken up within cyberfeminism as an icon for an essential female being.'[54]

Squires is ultimately disenfranchised with the project of cyberfeminism, arguing that:

Whilst cyberfeminism might offer a vision of fabulous, flexible, feminist futures, it has as yet largely failed to do so. Instead, cyberfeminism has become the distorted fantasy of those so cynical of political strategies, so bemused by the complexity of social materiality, and so bound up in the rhetoric of the space-flows of information technology, that they have forgotten both the exploitative and alienating potential of technology and retreated into the celebration of essential, though disembodied, women.[55]

Echoing these sentiments, Wilding charges all cyberfeminism's proselytisers with a clear imperative: 'If the goal is to create a feminist politics on the Net and to empower women then cyber-feminists must reinterpret and transpose feminist analysis, critique, strategies and experience to encounter and contest new conditions, new technologies and new formations.'[56]

Nevertheless, Squires is well disposed towards cyberculture as a whole in terms of its representational topicality:

> Cyberculture presents us with a particularly timely set of images which help us to think though the key theoretical agendas of the moment. Where multimedia provided a visual metaphor for the concerns of multiculturalism, virtual reality offers metaphors wonderfully resonant for the theoretical concerns of post-structuralism . . . Let us therefore note that for many, the developments of cybernetics and virtual reality are of interest primarily as a source of resonant images and icons with which to construct radical philosophical and political visions.[57]

Cyber-icons

To conclude, I will consider a few cyberfeminist cultural producers whose work is considered to occupy this category of resonant images. Rosi Braidotti has cited artists such as Laurie Anderson, Jenny Holzer, Cindy Sherman and Barbara Kruger as 'the ideal travel companions in postmodernity',[58] and she regards Catherine Richards and Nell Tenhaaf as artists who 'apply the technology to challenge the in-built assumption of visual superiority'.[59] She also offers three female icons or 'postmodern goddesses' whose posthuman body images have informed the 'socio-political representations of the cyber-body phenomenon from a feminist angle',[60] namely Dolly Parton, Elizabeth Taylor and Jane Fonda. All three are media stars and have artificially reconstructed, hyper-real bodies, subject not just to a compulsory heterosexual gaze, but to the commodification of sight *per se*.

If we were to update Braidotti's three icons for the cyber-age, we might look to a cyborg figure such as Lara Croft. As the buxom, fearless archaeologist heroine of the successful computer game *Tomb Raider*, Croft represents on one level all that is questionable about the synonymity between the masculinist hegemony of computer technology and the domination of women. Croft is a virtual computer-generated character designed to appeal to a male gaze, an object of scopophilia. However, she has also been upheld as an image of a strong woman, a more mainstream manifestation in many ways of the 'grrl' phenomenon, empowered and proactive. Croft has risen to pre-eminence within popular culture to epitomise in many ways the ironic feminist-materialist myth that Haraway defines. She is a myth, a creature of social reality, a product of human imagination and the representational capacity of the machine. Her image has now been recommodified in the service of the sports drink industry in recent advertisements for Lucozade. She is depicted in the TV commercial as a character who lives in cyberspace, engaged in adventurous pursuits at the mercy of the computer user's will, her actions dictated by the player while the game is in progress. But, as the advert implies with obvious irony, given a moment of 'free time' when the computer player takes a break, she relaxes with other characters in the game, sharing a virtual bottle of Lucozade, and demonstrates that like real 'actors' she too has an offscreen life and personality. The cultural impact of Lara Croft, part-cyborg, part-goddess of the small screen, has been immense: apart from ensuring the long-term popularity and household-name status for the *Tomb Raider* games, she has a dedicated on- and offline following, her own personal assistant, several human look-a-likes who do 'appearances' for her, and a real-life action film in production. In this respect, as a cyborg, Lara Croft manages to 'keep a foot in silicon and a foot in carbon . . . can run on blood and electricity,'[61] as 'an agent for fusing embodied, situated knowledge, and powerful fantasy'.[62]

Conclusion

As this chapter has shown, cyberfeminism faces several different choices and presents a multitude of guises, and it has
produced various effects within contemporary visual culture,
ranging from a new breed of women online; a feminist history
of computing that emphasises the likes of Ada Lovelace and
Grace Murray Hopper;[63] a new clutch of critical theories about
the creation and occupation of virtual reality and cyberspace in
relation to patriarchy and capitalism; and new terminology to
facilitate an intellectual grasp of a posthuman future, particularly in the form of the cyborg. If it steers a course through the
current hype, adopting a middle way that is about neither
technophobia nor technomania, cyberfeminist discourse can
offer a way for visual culture to engage with both technologies
of gender and the gendering of technology. It can be a way
forward not only in women's thinking about the meaning of
creativity and aesthetics in an electronic era, but also a means
to practise more critically and more insightfully. If so, cybervisuality would emerge in the long term as not just another
instance of technological determinism, but as a representation
of an actual shift towards a non-objectifying scopic regime,
which is democratic and empowering for all, and addresses
embodied as well as disembodied experience.

Notes

1. Sadie Plant, 'On the Matrix: Cyberfeminist Simulations' in
   Bell and Kennedy (eds), *The Cybercultures Reader*, p. 335.
2. Catherine Elwes, 'Is Technology Encoded in Gender-Specific
   Terms?', *Variant*, no. 14, Autumn 1993, p. 65.
3. Barbara M. Kennedy in Bell and Kennedy (eds), *The Cybercultures Reader*, p. 283.
4. Stabile, *Feminism and the Technological Fix*, p. 4.
5. Kirkup et al., *The Gendered Cyborg*, p. xiv.
6. Stabile, *Feminism and the Technological Fix*, p. 5.
7. Ibid. p. 5.
8. Wajcman, *Feminism Confronts Technology*.
9. Judith Squires, 'Fabulous Feminist Futures and the Lure of
   Cyberculture' in Bell and Kennedy (eds), *The Cybercultures
   Reader*, p. 366.

10. Donna Haraway, 'A Cyborg Manifesto: Science, Technology and Socialist-Feminism in the Late Twentieth Century' in Bell and Kennedy (eds), *The Cybercultures Reader*, p. 291.
11. Ibid. p. 292.
12. Ibid. p. 292.
13. Ibid. p. 292.
14. Ibid. p. 292.
15. Ibid. p. 302.
16. Kathleen Woodward, 'From Virtual Cyborgs to Biological Timebombs: Technocriticism and the Material Body' in Bender and Druckrey, *Culture on the Brink*, p. 55.
17. Donna Haraway, 'A Cyborg Manifesto' in Bell and Kennedy (eds), *The Cybercultures Reader*, p. 291.
18. Kirsten Notten, 'Keyboard Cowboys and Dial Cowgirls', *Soundings*, issue 3, Summer 1996, p. 188.
19. Ibid. p. 190.
20. Ibid. p. 190.
21. Donna Haraway, 'A Cyborg Manifesto' in Bell and Kennedy (eds), *The Cybercultures Reader*, p. 312.
22. Claudia Springer, 'Sex, Memories and Angry Women' in Dery (ed.), *Flame Wars*, p. 719.
23. Gray (ed.), *The Cyborg Handbook*.
24. Ibid.
25. Ibid.
26. Ken Robins and Les Levidow, 'Socialising the Cyborg Self: The Gulf War and Beyond', in Gray (ed.), *The Cyborg Handbook*, p. 121.
27. Ken Robins and Les Levidow, 'Soldier, Cyborg, Citizen' in Brook and Boal (eds), *Resisting the Virtual Life*, p. 105.
28. Donna Haraway, 'A Cyborg Manifesto' in Bell and Kennedy (eds), *The Cybercultures Reader*, p. 306.
29. Barbara M. Kennedy in Bell and Kennedy (eds), *The Cybercultures Reader*, p. 287.
30. Margaret Morse, 'Nature Morte' in Moser and MacLeod (eds), *Immersed in Technology*, p. 195.
31. Sadie Plant, 'On the Matrix: Cyberfeminist Simulations' in Bell and Kennedy (eds), *The Cybercultures Reader*, p. 332.
32. Plant, *Zeros and Ones*, p. 194.
33. Rosi Braidotti, 'Cyberfeminism with a Difference', http://www.let.ruu.nl/womens_studies/rosi/cyberfem.htm
34. Ibid.
35. Ibid.
36. Haraway, 'A Cyborg Manifesto' in Bell and Kennedy (eds), *The Cybercultures Reader*, p. 306.

37. Claudia Springer, 'Sex, Memories and Angry Women' in Dery (ed.), *Flame Wars*, p. 727.
38. Kitchin, *Cyberspace*, p. 69.
39. Rosi Braidotti, 'Cyberfeminism with a Difference', http://www.let.ruu.nl/womens_studies/rosi/cyberfem.htm
40. Haraway, *Simians, Cyborgs and Women*, p. 4.
41. Faith Wilding, 'Where is the Feminism in Cyberfeminism?', *n.paradoxa*, vol. 2, 1998, p. 10.
42. Ibid. p. 9.
43. Ibid. p. 7.
44. Ibid. p. 9.
45. Ibid. p. 8.
46. Rosi Braidotti, 'Cyberfeminism with a Difference', http://www.let.ruu.nl/womens_studies/rosi/cyberfem.htm
47. Nina Wakeford, 'Networking Women and Grrls with Information/Communication Technology: Surfing Tales of the World Wide Web' in Bell and Kennedy (eds), *The Cybercultures Reader*, p. 355.
48. Laura Miller, 'Women and Children First: Gender and Settling of the Electronic Frontier', in Brook and Boal (eds), *Resisting the Virtual Life*, p. 53.
49. Nina Wakeford, 'Networking Women and Grrls with Information/Communication Technology: Surfing Tales of the World Wide Web' in Bell and Kennedy (eds), *The Cybercultures Reader*, p. 351.
50. Ibid. p. 352.
51. Judith Squires, 'Fabulous Feminist Futures and the Lure of Cyberculture' in Bell and Kennedy (eds), *The Cybercultures Reader*, p. 360.
52. Sadie Plant, 'Beyond the Screen; Film, Cyberpunk and Cyberfeminism', *Variant*, no.14, Autumn 1993, p. 13.
53. Ibid. p. 17.
54. Judith Squires, 'Fabulous Feminist Futures and the Lure of Cyberculture' in Bell and Kennedy (eds), *The Cybercultures Reader*, p. 368.
55. Ibid. p. 369.
56. Faith Wilding, 'Where is the Feminism in Cyberfeminism?', *n.paradoxa*, vol. 2, 1998, p. 10.
57. Judith Squires, 'Fabulous Feminist Futures and the Lure of Cyberculture' in Bell and Kennedy (eds), *The Cybercultures Reader*, p. 365.
58. Rosi Braidotti, 'Cyberfeminism with a Difference', http://www.let.ruu.nl/womens_studies/rosi/cyberfem.htm
59. Ibid.
60. Ibid.

61. Fiona Hovenden, 'Introduction' to Part 4 of Kirkup et al., *The Gendered Cyborg*, p. 260.
62. Ibid. p. 260.
63. Plant, *Zeros and Ones*.

Bibliography

Bell, David, and Barbara M Kennedy (eds), *The Cybercultures Reader* (London: Routledge, 2000).

Bender, Gretchen, and Timothy Druckrey (eds), *Culture on the Brink: Ideologies of Technology* (Seattle: Bay Press, 1994).

Brook, James, and Iain A. Boal (eds), *Resisting the Virtual Life* (San Francisco: City Lights, 1995).

Dery, Mark (ed.), *Flame Wars* (Durham: Duke University Press, 1993).

Gray, Chris Hables (ed.), *The Cyborg Handbook* (London: Routledge, 1995).

Haraway, Donna, *Simians, Cyborgs and Women: the Reinvention of Nature* (London: Free Association Press, 1991).

Kirkup, Gill, Linda Janes, Kath Woodward and Fiona Hovenden (eds), *The Gendered Cyborg: A Reader* (London: Routledge, 2000).

Kitchin, Rob, *Cyberspace* (Chichester: John Wiley, 1998).

Moser, M.A., and D. MacLeod (eds), *Immersed in Technology* (Boston: MIT, 1996).

Plant, Sadie, *Zeros and Ones* (London: Fourth Estate, 1997).

Stabile, Carol, *Feminism and the Technological Fix* (Manchester: MUP 1994).

Wajcman, Judy, *Feminism Confronts Technology* (Cambridge: Polity Press, 1991).

Chapter 14

Television

Anne Hole

FEMINIST ANALYSIS OF TELEVISION has much in common
with other areas of feminist scholarship. Emerging in the 1970s, it
combined politics with academic study and embraced interdisci-
plinarity. This breadth of approach remains a crucial aspect of
feminist television criticism, which often applies a mixture of
methodological approaches to a range of issues, which are
themselves rarely discrete. The inter-relatedness of issues concerning women and television is evident, for example, in a piece
by Michèle Mattelart who demonstrates how the commercial
identification of the housewife as prime consumer (an economic
issue), the ways in which programmes are scheduled (an industrial matter) and the style and content of soap operas (a question
of genre) have at certain times combined to reinscribe the female
viewer into the domestic role.[1]

Feminist analyses of television are predominantly concerned
with issues around women and femininity. These can be broken
down as follows:

1. Women on television: images of women in television
   output, activism around 'positive' role models, discussion of stereotyping and representations of femininity,
   race and sexuality.
2. Women in television: women as producers of television
   texts (writers, performers, directors, and so on), questions about status, power and the division of labour
   within television production.
3. Television for women: 'feminine' genres such as soap
   opera.
4. Women watching television: female television spectator-

ship, women as consumers of television, and the operation of media technology in the home.
  5. Women, race and sexuality: all the above as they apply
     specifically to women of colour or non-heterosexual
     women.

Inevitably, these groups overlap: for example, study of genres
often involves asking questions about the audience and reception,
and a television phenomenon like Oprah Winfrey raises questions
both about women's status as producers and about the chat show
as 'feminine' genre.

Women on television

Much of the early work of feminist television critics (in the 1970s)
was linked to activism for 'women's liberation' and operated
from a conviction that representations of women in the mass
media had a real effect on the ways in which women were treated
by, and can operate in, society. The challenge was made on two
fronts: first, the under-representation of women on television,
which can be spoken of in terms of the 'symbolic annihilation of
women'[2] which left women largely invisible in the 'world' that
television claimed to bring into the home; secondly, when women
did appear on screen they were usually represented in traditional
domestic roles and frequently reduced to female 'types'; this was
particularly true of situation comedy which survived on a diet of
ditsy single women or new wives, muddled young mums, and
domineering middle-aged dragons.
  Much has changed since the 1970s, and women are now much
more visible on television, in a far wider range of roles. However,
this increased visibility is not without its problems, as Pat Holland
makes clear in her work on female newsreaders who, despite
being allowed into a traditionally male area, remain marked by
their femininity which both handicaps them and allows their
work to be trivialised.[3] Others argue that there has been not only
a quantitative, but also a qualitative shift: 'Contemporary popular television fiction offers an array of strong and independent
female heroines, who seem to defy *not without conflicts and
contradictions* stereotypical definitions of femininity.'[4] Such re-

presentations, and especially perhaps the 'conflicts and contra-dictions' which they address, offer new pleasures of identification for female viewers. Judith Mayne sounds another cautionary note, however, when she points out that 'increasingly, feminism is being appropriated by various mass cultural forms'.[5] Television is a business and if, in the 1980s and 1990s, female consumers can be attracted to programmes and thus advertisers' products by the addition of a dash of feminism, then that is as much a matter of economics as of politics.

Women in television

Feminist critics working on the issues surrounding women as producers of television content (as writers, performers, directors, and producers) may be better placed to offer an assessment of the extent to which television as an industry has really taken feminist principles on board.

Unfortunately, there are few examples of really powerful women in television, (with the notable exceptions of Oprah Winfrey and Roseanne Arnold in the USA, who have used their success as performers as the basis of a move into production), and there has not, as yet, been a great deal of analysis in this area. There has been work published on Lucille Ball,[6] Oprah Winfrey,[7] and Joan Collins,[8] but the female television 'star' has not received the attention of her sister in film or music. Much more work needs to be done in this area, and the 'invisible' women behind the scenes in 1990s television, like Jane Root, controller of BBC2, who wield significant influence over the programmes commis-sioned and made, must be incorporated into the analyses of women (or feminism) and television.

Television for women

Much more work has been done in the realm of genre, and particularly on those genres that have been perceived, and indeed constructed, as 'feminine'. The genre most researched is the 'soap opera',[9] which, from its inception in the earliest days of American television was intimately bound up with the idea of the housewife's dual role as homemaker and consumer. Nothing on television fitted so well into the day-to-day life of the housewife and addressed her so specifically as the soap opera, which combined family stories of tragedy and intrigue with advertisements for the products 'essential' to the 'proper' maintenance of a family (or the maintenance of a 'proper' family).

Central to the feminist discourse of soap opera is Annette Kuhn's question: '[d]o these "gynocentric" forms address, or construct, a female or a feminine spectator? If so, how?'[10] This question clarifies the need to consider, alongside the content of the programmes and the intent of the producers and sponsors, the whole question of reception, and the notion of female/feminine spectatorship. At this point, television criticism begins to overlap with film theory, which has taken the issue of spectatorship as central to an understanding of how screen texts work.

Women watching television

There are issues around women's reception of television which film theory cannot begin to address, because of the specifically domestic setting of television viewing. Women are addressed by television on their 'home ground', in the sphere that is supposedly especially theirs. This relationship has been complicated, however, by various other attributes of television: in its early days, again at the inception of video, and now with satellite, cable and digital services, television has been inscribed as a technology, and technology is often culturally categorised as masculine and thus belonging outside the home. The ways in which this technology relates to the domestic sphere have been discussed by, among others, Patricia Mellencamp[11] and Lynn Spigel.[12] Ann Gray addresses the early use of video cassette recorders (VCRs) in the home and the ways in which that use both reflects, and offers challenges to traditional understandings of television and female pleasure.[13] For a while, at least, the VCR recreated the social aspect of early television watching, but as taping of television programmes for watching at a later date has increased, the 'community' which television sought to create is breaking down. Over the years, familiarity, and the increasing number of hours of programming each day, has also led to a decentralising of TV.

Viewing is now, more than ever, likely to be 'background' to everyday life, rather than an attention-grabbing special event, and this renders it less amenable to ideas about reception borrowed from film theory, which focuses on the experience of cinema-going as its paradigm of spectatorship.

Women, race and sexuality

The same issues of invisibility and 'typing' that spurred main-stream feminist television criticism have also been raised by academics interested in representations of women of colour and non-heterosexual women. Much of the work on race is done within an American context and is part of a wider discourse of race and representation, just as analysis of representations of 'deviant' female sexuality has been taken up by queer theory, and informed by other theoretical positions than feminism. There is a considerable literature in both these areas and the issues have expanded to include studies of audience, genres, and institutional power.

Methods of analysis

Feminist television criticism is inherently interdisciplinary; in most of the literature I have mentioned, more than one metho-dology has been brought to bear on the problem, and there is a wide range of approaches available to researchers in this field. From literary theory comes 'textual analysis', the technique of close-reading which seeks to understand the ways in which a text creates meanings through the use of structure, imagery and style. This way of looking at television can be extended to consider context, using sociological insights into the ways in which the social setting produces, and is in turn produced by, television's modes of representation. At an institutional level, television can be scrutinised as an economic entity, an industry within a parti-cular economic system (capitalism). Such analysis integrates politics and economics and raises questions of ideology, which can also be addressed by textual analysis. The study of the audience for television draws on both sociological and anthropological methodology, as well as concepts used in film theory.

These disparate methodologies and disciplines are constantly being brought together in interesting and productive combinations by feminist scholars who seek new insights into the complex relationships between women and television.

Reclaiming television for feminism: the fat female comedy of Jo Brand

This case study consists of textual analysis of the television comedy of Jo Brand, who, along with performers like Roseanne, Dawn French and Victoria Wood, effects what Michel Foucault calls a 'reverse discourse',[14] by using the fat female body, which has traditionally been cast as the object of comedy, to reproduce herself as comic subject. There are, however, significant differences in the style, content, and political emphasis of these performers: Dawn French, for example, proposes that 'fat is beautiful', promoting inclusion of the fat female body, or an inversion whereby fat women become beautiful at the expense of thin women. Jo Brand operates very differently, and her work taps into the notions of carnival and the grotesque body as articulated by Mikhail Bakhtin.[15]

The medieval carnival with its emphasis on the carnal and excess is dominated, for Bakhtin, by the grotesque image, which is 'opposed to all that is finished and polished'.[16] But this is not incompleteness as partiality; the grotesque body is 'unfinished' because it constantly 'outgrows itself, transgresses its own limits',[17] embodying the loss of boundaries inherent in carnival, which 'does not know footlights' and 'does not acknowledge any distinction between actors and spectators'.[18] Like the laugh that bursts out, crossing from inside to out, grotesque realism initiates a (temporary) loss of boundaries.

The grotesque body is not an ugly body, but a non-conformist body, a body that exceeds its allotted space, breaking out to unite with the body of the people. It is body-without-end, and symbolises life-without-end; it destroys internal restraints, freeing laughter; and shatters social order in a creative, regenerative way. A comedy that uses grotesque realism, as Jo Brand's does, takes on that political potential to break down constructed social boundaries.

It can be argued, however, that the temporary inversions of carnival (the Lord of Misrule, mockery of the ruling classes, cross-dressing) were nothing more than a 'safety valve' allowing the release of social tensions and thereby supporting the *status quo*,[19] and comedy can be seen as operating in the same way. The medieval model of comedy was based not on laughter but on 'harmony and reconciliation',[20] and still today sociologists and psychologists, such as William Martineau, see humour as 'a "lubricant" and an "abrasive" in social interaction – especially in such common everyday interaction that constitutes the basis of the social order and makes the routine flow of social life possible'.[21] In this sense, comedy would seem to be essentially conservative.

The fat woman is the perfect figure to bypass this objection, for while her grotesque, fat, female body makes her part of the disruptive topsy-turvy carnival atmosphere of comedy, her fatness and femaleness also exceed the licensed space. Her body is real, not a silly costume or mask that can be removed when the time for comedy is over; it continues into the 'real world' and she cannot or will not return to her 'proper' place after the show. The fat female body can hold onto the political potential of comedy, allowing the subjective comedy of fat women to operate as feminist praxis.

Brand's grotesque identity was firmly established by her first television series.[22] The opening titles parody a cookery programme but re-establish a relation between food and appetite which is so often missing from that genre: this is not food for the eyes (pictures on plates) nor intellectualised food (marker of sophistication and specialist knowledge) but food for the mouth and the belly (Brand says 'Sod that' to the recipe when it threatens to delay her gratification).[23] Brand's excessiveness is embodied in the cake she creates with cream, more cream, ice-cream and custard; her off-centre inappropriateness is represented by the pork-pie garnish; and her refusal to submit to conventions that inscribe eating as a social event (and the message that excessive eating makes you a social outcast) is echoed in her advice to serve the cake with 'no friends'.[24] Yet the cutaway shot of the chair being wedged against the door emphasises that this is not a woman without friends, but one who values her own space and the time alone to indulge her own desires. The threat that such a set of images, such an identity, evokes can be witnessed in a press review: 'The opening sequence . . . illustrates her trademark food-lust, with a dangerously calorie-loaded cake, cream-covered, garnished with chocolate bars and topped with a sausage roll'.[25] The association of food with lust is interesting, as is the notion of calories (a scientific measure of energy) being dangerous, but most significant is the last remark, for it was a pork pie, not a sausage roll! The appetite, the 'food-lust' has been conflated with the 'danger' of eating to produce a devouring sexuality: a *vagina dentata*.

This introduction arouses rather than laughs away the fear of the fat female which is inextricably bound up with her location in comedy and the title and set take the process further. '*Through the Cakehole*' captures the moment of the breakdown of boundaries; it is an image of the point at which outside and inside meet and merge, the site at which food – that which is non-body – enters, is transformed, and becomes body or abject matter. This dangerous point of metamorphosis is represented by the gaping mouth, which dominates the studio set and looms over sketches, putting Brand firmly in the tradition of the grotesque, in which:

> a leading role is . . . played . . . by the gaping mouth. This is, of course, related to the lower stratum; it is the open gate leading downward into the bodily underworld. The gaping mouth is related to the image of swallowing, this most ancient symbol of death and destruction . . .[26]

But the fat female body can change the script, for swallowing is not death, just as food is not 'dangerous'; swallowing is the means of continuing, expanding life, an understanding embodied in the fat woman. When Jo Brand appropriates this symbolism from the Mystery-Plays,[27] the open mouth retains its connotations of devouring death, but is also re-presented as speech, the power of the word, and as the joyful, life-giving act of feeding.

Brand's comedy, which eschews Dawn French's inclusionism in favour of a focus on the threshold, risks alienating the audience. The body of the audience, which constructs itself as complete and enclosed, is loathe to consider the potential loss of boundaries which the mouth and belly of the fat woman imply. Brand ameliorates the threat by employing, in her opening stand-up set, a self-deprecatory humour. Casting her body as a failure in late twentieth-century terms, she reassures the audience by masking the fact that the body which her stage persona inhabits is not a twentieth-century body at all, but a reborn relic of the age of carnival. Brand encourages her audience to view her as a failure in the body market when she opens with, 'Now, you might be looking at me thinking, "You're a bit crap at seducing people." Are you? Cos I am, I'm crap at it.[28] However, she then turns the tables, asserting an aggressive, even violent, attitude towards men: 'On the very rare occasions that I do actually get a bloke in a room on his own, it just seems too good an opportunity to miss just to punch him in the bloody gob'.[29] This is the unruly woman,[30] expressing anger and valuing the expression of her anger over the social imperative to model her behaviour in ways attractive to men. As the laughter fades, Brand adds, 'Only joking, boys',[31] echoing the protestations of generations of traditional male comedians in the face of women who would not or could not laugh at misogynist jokes. This reflexivity, and awareness of the gender politics of comedy is part of what makes Brand's work understandable in terms of feminist praxis: the merging of theory and activism.

Another key factor is Brand's interest in women's history and the way she plays with it, transporting her persona intact to a different historical environment. The resulting mismatch offers a humour of incongruity, which masks a serious message about the position of women in the past or the present. The 'Amsterdam 1580' sketch, featuring Brand alongside Helena Bonham-Carter, demonstrates the differences between the body politics of Brand and Dawn French, suggesting a way in which comic inversion can be used not merely to redefine, but to destabilise hierarchies.[32] The scene is an artist's waiting room where two models discuss their careers and lives. This is the world French dreams of, where fat is beautiful and the slender Bonham-Carter is reduced to working for the 'Bruges Ugly Agency' doing 'character work' as plague victims. The reversal allows Brand to express comically, through the thin body, some of the pain and anger that in her own voice would become self-pity. Bonham-Carter's character can admit to envying the fat woman in a way that Brand could never admit to envy of supermodels; such an admission would be read as an acceptance that thin is 'better' and Brand's body would cease to symbolise transgression and excess, becoming instead a sign of failure.

By putting the words in Bonham-Carter's mouth, Brand raises a laugh (from within the audience's cultural moment, it is ridiculous for the thin woman to envy the fat) which sugar-coats the serious message. When Bonham-Carter says, 'I really envy you. You've got it all', the suggestion, reinforced by our reluctance to accept the thin woman's envy of fat, is that it is not the fat body *per se* which is desirable, but the status which a particular society has conferred on that body. Just as Freud's concept of penis envy[33] can be explained in terms of a female wish for the rights, opportunities and status which were available only to the bearer of a penis, so the modern woman's envy of, and desire for, a thin body can be explained in terms of the relative status of fat and thin female bodies in our society. The message of the sketch is that it is not female bodies which need to change (the 'Go and eat some pies' response of the Brand character is not given any validity) but rather it is the rigid value system that raises up one woman to the detriment of another which needs to change. When Brand said in an interview, 'I take a different approach to the "Fat is sexy" view . . . I'd be happy just to be not abused rather than hailed as a new sex goddess,'[34] she is apparently asking for a subtler shift than that advocated by Dawn French. In fact, Brand's aim is far more radical, demanding as it does not an extension of the definition of beauty and sexiness, nor an inversion that makes fat women sexy and thin ones ugly, but an end to judgment in terms of physical appearance. She does not say 'Fat is beautiful,' but 'Sod beautiful'. The 'Amsterdam 1580' sketch attempts to instigate such a change: by establishing a historic precedent for the inversion of body ideals, Brand makes explicit their contingency, and by representing the sixteenth-century 'ideal' as false and comical, she shows up the current 'ideal' as equally laughable, thus undermining the notion of an ideal female body and the structure of female oppression that such a standard supports.

The topsy-turvy of carnival is not rectified by Brand; she does not return us to the *status quo* but comically undermines our experience of the 'real world'. And this is the point of my argument: that the fat woman can draw on the shared history of grotesque bodies and comedy to upset the social order, and then use her very real, material body to deny the ephemeral nature of such a disruption. Because her excessive body exists in the real world, she is able to overflow the licensed bounds of 'comedy' and bring the instability she has created through her body into the everyday world.

Notes

1. Michèle Mattelart, *Women, Media and Crisis: Femininity and Disorder* (London: Comedia, 1986), pp. 5–18.
2. Gaye Tuchman, 'The Symbolic Annihilation of Women by the Mass Media', in Tuchman, Kaplan Daniels and Benet (eds), *Hearth and Home*, pp. 3–38.
3. Patricia Holland, 'When a Woman Reads the News' in Baehr and Dyer (eds), *Boxed-In*.
4. Ien Ang, 'Melodramatic Identifications: Television Fiction and Women's Fantasy', in Brunsdon, D'Acci and Spigel (eds), *Feminist Television Criticism*, p. 155 (originally published in Brown (ed.), *Television and Women's Culture*, pp. 75–88).
5. Judith Mayne, 'L.A. Law and Prime-Time Feminism' in Brunsdon, D'Acci and Spigel (eds), *Feminist Television Criticism*, p. 84 (originally published in *Discourse*, 10/2 (1988), pp. 30–47).
6. Alexander Doty, 'The Cabinet of Lucy Ricardo: Lucille Ball's Star Image', *Cinema Journal*, 29/4 (1990) pp. 3–22, and Patricia Mellencamp, 'Situation Comedy, Feminism, and Freud: Discourses of Gracie and Lucy' in Tania Modleski (ed.), *Studies in Entertainment: Critical Approaches to Mass Culture* (Bloomington: Indiana University Press 1986), pp. 80–95.
7. Gloria-Jean Masciarotte, 'C'mon Girl: Oprah Winfrey and the Discourse of Feminine Talk', *Genders* (Fall 1991) pp. 81–110.
8. Belinda Budge, 'Joan Collins and the Wilder Side of Women: Exploring Pleasure and Representation' in Lorraine Gamman and Margaret Marshment (eds), *The Female Gaze: Women as Viewers of Popular Culture* (London: The Women's Press, 1988), pp. 102–11.
9. Charlotte Brunsdon, 'Crossroads: Notes on Soap Opera', *Screen*, 22/4 (1981) pp. 32–7 and 'Feminism and Soap Opera' in Davies, Dickey and Stratford (eds), *Out of Focus*, and Christine Geraghty, *Women and Soap Opera: A Study of Prime Time Soaps* (Oxford: Polity Press, 1991).

10. Annette Kuhn, 'Women's Genres: Melodrama, Soap Opera, and Theory' in Brunsdon, D'Acci and Spigel (eds) *Feminist Television Criticism*, p. 146 (originally published in *Screen*, 25/1 (1984), pp. 18–28).

11. Patricia Mellencamp, 'Situation Comedy, Feminism, and Freud: Discourses of Gracie and Lucy' in Tania Modleski (ed.), *Studies in Entertainment: Critical Approaches to Mass Culture* (Bloomington: Indiana University Press, 1986), pp. 80–95.

12. Lynn Spigel, 'The Suburban Home Companion: Television and the Neighbourhood Ideal in Post-War America' in Beatriz Colomina (ed.), *Sexuality and Space* (Princeton: Princeton Architectural Press, 1992), pp. 185–217.

13. Ann Gray, 'Behind Closed Doors: Video Recorders in the Home' in Baehr and Dyer (eds), *Boxed-In*, pp. 38–54.

14. Michel Foucault, *The History of Sexuality* (London: Penguin, 1990), p. 101.

15. Mikhail Bakhtin, *Rabelais and His World* (Bloomington: Indiana University Press, 1984).

16. Ibid. p. 3.

17. Ibid. p. 26.

18. Ibid. p. 7.

19. Natalie Zemon Davis, 'The Reasons of Misrule', *Society and Culture in Early Modern France* (London: Duckworth, 1975), p. 97.

20. T. G. A. Nelson, *Comedy: The Theory of Comedy in Literature, Drama, and Cinema* (Oxford: Oxford University Press, 1990), p. 1.

21. William H. Martineau, 'A Model of the Social Functions of Humor', in Jeffrey H. Goldstein and Paul E. McGhee (eds), *The Psychology of Humor* (Academic Press: London, 1972), p. 103.

22. Jo Brand, *Jo Brand: Through the Cakehole* (Channel 4, 1994).

23. Jo Brand, *The Best of Through the Cakehole* (Polygram Video, 1995).

24. Jo Brand, *The Best of Through the Cakehole* (Polygram Video, 1995).

25. 'Scoffer Who Devours Men', *The Observer*, 10 April 1994, p. 23.

26. Mikhail Bakhtin, *Rabelais and His World* (Bloomington: Indiana University Press, 1984), p. 325.

27. Ibid. p. 348.

28. Jo Brand, *The Best of Through the Cakehole* (Polygram Video, 1995).

29. Jo Brand, *The Best of Through the Cakehole* (Polygram Video, 1995).
30. Kathleen Rowe, *The Unruly Woman: Gender and the Genres of Laughter* (Austin: University of Texas Press, 1995).
31. Jo Brand, *The Best of Through the Cakehole* (Polygram Video, 1995).
32. Jo Brand, *The Best of Through the Cakehole* (Polygram Video, 1995).
33. Sigmund Freud, 'Some Psychical Consequences of the Anatomical Distinction Between the Sexes', *On Sexuality* (London: Penguin, 1991), p. 186.
34. 'Scoffer Who Devours Men', *The Observer*, 10 April 1994, p. 23.

Bibliography

Baehr, Helen, and Gillian Dyer (eds), *Boxed-In: Women and Television* (London: Pandora, 1987).

Brown, M.E. (ed.), *Television and Women's Culture: The Politics of the Popular* (London: Sage, 1990).

Brunsdon, Charlotte, Julie D'Acci and Lynn Spigel (eds), *Feminist Television Criticism: A Reader* (Oxford: Clarendon Press, 1997).

Daniels, Thérèse, and Jane Gerson (eds), *The Colour Black: Black Images in British Television* (London: British Film Institute, 1989).

Davies, Kath, Julienne Dickey and Teresa Stratford (eds), *Out of Focus: Writings on Women and the Media* (London: Women's Press, 1987).

Hamer, Diane, and Belinda Budge (eds), *The Good, The Bad, and the Gorgeous: Popular Culture's Romance with Lesbianism* (London: Pandora, 1994).

Tuchman, Gaye, Arlene Kaplan Daniels and James Benet (eds), *Hearth and Home: Images of Women in the Mass Media* (New York: Oxford University Press, 1978).

Chapter 15

Advertising

Sarah Niblock

WHEN A WOMAN DISCOVERS she is expecting her first baby, she is more likely to see herself as a fecund mother-to-be than as the target for advertisers. Yet while 'Dinkies' and 'Yuppies' kept marketing account managers in business in the 1980s, now it is 'Fems' (first-time expectant mothers) who are being wooed as a highly profitable consumer group. Their nine-month magazine-fuelled shopping spree may end with a jolt almost as startling as the birth itself, with the revelation that they have spent their hard-earned cash on largely useless objects and products.

Motherhood aside, feminists have long feared the possible effects of advertising on women's life choices, employment prospects and overall self-image. From its origins, the feminist movement has analysed advertising from a range of perspectives and employing a variety of methodologies. The main questions asked include how do the words and images in advertisements influence our opinions of others, our world views, our social relations and behaviours and how, in turn, might those from other socio-cultural positions view us? This chapter will first provide an overview of the research and analyses which have proved most influential in feminist debates on advertising. Critiques of these feminist approaches and positions have inevitably followed, so I will briefly examine what flaws theorists have found in feminist strategies. Indeed, it is evident that women may now see a more positive reflection on screen or page as there has been an upsurge in advertising ostensibly portraying women who are active and hold down powerful jobs. However, by focusing on depictions of motherhood in advertising, I will examine whether the picture is really any brighter than it was when women first began questioning the 'feminine mystique'.[1]

It must be clear from reading this book that it is impossible to see the work of feminist theorists in isolation from their predecessors or contemporaries since so much of their individual research was produced in response to, or informed by, work in disciplines such as psychology. This is why it is impossible within the constraints of a chapter to identify everyone who has significantly contributed to feminist debates on advertising, and this chapter should therefore be read as a personal interpretation rather than a comprehensive account.

There is nothing new in selling to women. Alfred Harmsworth (later Lord Northcliffe) was the first in Britain to promote women to advertisers when, in the 1890s, he launched two weekly women's magazines. Then, in 1903, this early media baron introduced the *Daily Mirror* as a paper for 'gentlewomen'. Years later, the postwar consumer boom gave women's domestic role a new spin through advertising in the burgeoning media sphere. From her humble origins as an unpaid labourer and mother, the housewife saw herself reflected as a skilled expert with the latest technology at her fingertips. For instance, from the 1950s 'Katie' transformed the humble wartime Oxo cube into the basis of a beef stew and family harmony.

It was not until the mid-1970s that women's individuality began to gain recognition in commercials. Fragrance ads were enthusiastic in their lauding of women's uniqueness, such as 'Cachet: A fragrance as individual as you are', probably in response to the launch of assertive young women's periodicals like *Cosmopolitan* (nevertheless, many campaigns still adhered to traditional delineations). In the 1980s and 1990s, there was a feeling that feminist battles had been won and that women could have it all. Eventually, advertisers, who were slightly slower than magazines in picking up popular cultural trends, started to borrow the language of feminism and assimilate it into their copywriting. Recently, lesbian discourses, albeit of the 'lipstick' variety, have found their way into car commercials.

Defining sexual identity and gender is difficult at the best of times, especially nowadays when we live amid a cultural tapestry of advertising images telling us what being a man or woman should be about. Accordingly, feminists view what advertising says about gender as an important issue to understand, and it has formed the basic tenet of their investigations since the 1960s.

What has concerned feminists most is the construction and repetition of stereotypes. A stereotype is a standardised representation of a specific type of person or group of people which, while having little in common with real men or women, is so frequent and pervasive that it appears true. By making simple generalisations about a far more complex reality, stereotypes can allow us an insight into commonly-held beliefs and values. These concepts and images are frequently negative, yet are widely used in advertising, a medium devoted to creating worlds rich in ideals and myths. Moreover, an advertisement cannot create meaning on its own – it has to be seen by viewers or readers whose own attitudes may tally closely with those depicted in the text. This sets up a discourse about what it means to be a woman in society, and places women under pressure to look and act like these two-dimensional representations.

Feminists have catalogued innumerable stereotypes used to represent women in advertising at various points in history. By way of illustration, Myra Macdonald has defined three stereotypes of women used between the wars: the 'capable household manager', 'the guilt-ridden mother' and 'the self-indulgent flapper'.[2] She describes how these were not self-contained categories of actual women but manufactured versions of female responsibilities invented to effectively target products and services. The resultant hegemonic, or common consensus, position this ideology held was put in the spotlight by feminists in the 1960s and 1970s. One of their key inspirations was Betty Friedan's *The Feminine Mystique*, which was first published in 1963. Bearing the banner 'the personal is political', consciousness-raising groups of feminists sought to show women how far their own relationships and experiences were dictated by patriarchal social systems and discourses, including advertising.

A section of Friedan's book consists of a content analysis of popular magazine advertising. Content analysis is where researchers count the number of times a textual or visual element occurs in their sample. The idea behind it is that there may be a relationship between the repeated use of particular themes and representational devices and the intentions of producers and the responses of readers. There have been countless such studies, recording anything from occupations of women in adverts[3] to their poses in so-called 'sanpro' commercials.[4] From her own findings, Friedan concludes that the perpetuation of housewifery makes money: 'Somehow, somewhere, someone must have figured out that women will buy more things if they are kept in the under-used, nameless-yearning, energy-to-get-rid-of state of being housewives.'[5] For example, she gives an account of market research findings on how best to promote cake mix to women in 1945.[6] The findings showed that the most effective way was to appeal to a woman's underlying guilt – so that although the cake is in fact made from a mix, the woman still has to bake it, making it ostensibly homemade while allowing her to spend more time with her family. A further advertising tactic noted by Friedan is the attempt to upgrade mundane household chores through consumerism: be it a new all-purpose cleaner or a hi-tech washing machine, the aim is to make the purchaser feel less like an unskilled labourer and more like an expert.[7]

Another American feminist, Gaye Tuchman, observed later that much of the market research carried out just after World War Two explored men's, not women's, attitudes. Shifting her focus of study forward twenty-five years, Tuchman suggests that advertising still bore similar patriarchal overtones. For instance, she cites several quantitative studies which reveal a concentration of women represented as homemakers rather than as active members of the labour force. For example, in 1972 Dominick and Rauch counted that 75 per cent of a sample of advertisements featuring women were promoting products found in the kitchen or bathroom.[8] However, it is significant that an authoritative male voiceover accompanied the majority of television commercials in question, as if suggesting that only a man can really give a product sufficient credibility.

Erving Goffman's influential examination of visual imagery in his book *Gender Advertisements* was concerned with similar types of issues, although he instead asked another question: why do most advertisements not look odd to us? He suggests that male/female relationships are represented like parent/child relationships, and justifies his arguments with content and textual analyses to uncover what such portrayals say about the relative social status of men and women. For instance, he says women and children are pictured seated on floors and beds much more than men, and as these places are low down, and possibly dirty and exposed, women and children are perceived as having a lower status than men; the males depicted in Goffman's sample are generally upright and thus perceived as more alert, capable and powerful.[9] In all his illustrations, Goffman suggests that we try to imagine a reversal in the positions of the male and female models. Perhaps the reason the originals do not look strange to us, he surmises, is that advertisers highlight existing social relations and culturally specific gender codes: 'If anything, advertisers conventionalise our conventions, stylise what is already a stylisation, make frivolous use of what is already something cut off from contextual controls. Their hype is hyper-ritualisation'.[10]

Gillian Dyer's comprehensive and readable study of advertising as discourse highlights the significance of advertising images in particular, as opposed to text. Although we tend to think of photographs as realistic, images are subject to the same selection and editing as text. Importantly, she discusses how the act of 'seeing' is not essentially natural or passive but rather is culturally-inscribed. We will be attracted or repelled by images according to social conditioning, not just through the simple transfer of messages from the eye to the brain. Dyer expands on this by describing the array of non-verbal, image-based elements in advertisements which help create meaning, such as age, gender, race and size, as well as the actions and gestures of the humans represented: 'Superiority, inferiority, equality, intimacy and rank can be signified by people's position, size, activity and their relationship to the space around them, the furniture and to the viewer/consumer.'[11]

To exemplify this point, one can compare television commercials for men's and women's deodorants, all of which frequently depict men and women being active. But while Lynx advertisements portray a man keeping cool during a military coup, women in Sure commercials are shown keeping fit for leisure and, presumably, beauty. Such studies convey compelling evidence of the extent of gender inequality in advertisements but some theorists have dismissed such statistical dossiers for their lack of contextualisation. One argument is that empirical studies have no way of accounting for economic or political climates. Furthermore, studies might reveal the incidence of stereotyping but give no explanation as to why stereotyping is happening nor how an audience perceives it. This is why many feminists chose to adopt the structuralist approaches which gained popularity in Britain in the 1970s. Semiotics is a structuralist methodology which is defined as the study of signs, specifically their selection and combination. This approach, which is not without criticism, has been employed widely as an analytical tool to investigate how advertisements create and fix meaning. According to this methodology, all messages comprise a combination of signs or what Swiss linguist Ferdinand de Saussure called 'syntagmatic relations', meaning the way the signs are combined that creates the message. When applied to advertising, semiotics is an attempt to extricate explicit and implicit meaning from the interpretation of both verbal and visual signs. For example, semioticians can identify gendered representational differences in television advertisements aimed primarily at women. Carmen Luke describes how products targeted at females employ similar technical devices to soap operas such as extensive use of indoor and close-up shots, in direct contrast to male-targeted ads with their wide, outdoor shots, faster pacing and hard, metallic music.[12]

In *Decoding Advertisements*, Judith Williamson combined Roland Barthes' theory of myth production with a Marxist and psychoanalytical analysis to reveal the mechanisms by which advertising 'works' on the consumer.

> Advertising may appropriate not only real areas of time and space, and give them a false content, but real needs and desires in people, which are given a false fulfilment. We need a way of looking at ourselves, which ads give us falsely . . . we need to make sense of the world, which ads make us feel we are doing in making sense of them.[13]

In other words, advertisers have a knack of getting their market to consume a myth in order to buy a product. So, the potential appeal of, say, Milk Tray chocolates when compared with Dairy Box is to do with the connotations of sexual promise emanating both from the black-clad action man plus the purple and gold packaging. It has little to do with the contents of the box.

Marxist approaches have been accused of over-concentrating on production at the expense of consumption, and cultural studies might be accused of over-compensating on this in its focus on the latter. However, commodities have to be produced and sold before they are consumed, so advertising cannot strictly be separated from those processes. Fine and Leopold define a link between production and marketing which is manifested through advertisements: 'developments in production can themselves constitute the raw materials for advertising and for the cultural meaning of commodities more generally – the ideology of production.'[14]

Here we can see firm links with feminist investigations of myth production in advertisements. Advertising does not show how commodities are really manufactured: in the case of baby food, for example, what parent could bear to fill Tiny's tummy with gloop they have seen being stirred by a metal rod in huge metal vats? Instead, we are fed a diet of representations. First, science is used to show how the most sophisticated nutritional research has gone into that pot of Beef and Prune Treat. Secondly, the product is presented as wholesome via the use of 'mothers' recipe' ranges. From their labelling and marketing, consumers are given the impression that these foods are homemade and old-fashioned, enabling the full-time working mother to feel guilt free as she reproduces the wholesome dishes she imagines she was served by her own stay-at-home mother.

In a sense, myth can be seen as bridging the gap between the commodity as it really is and the commodity the consumer is encouraged to perceive, and feminists have shown that this perception is far from simply based on the consumer's individual desires. Formula baby milk, as opposed to breast milk, is a case in point. Breast milk substitutes based on cows' milk made an impact after World War Two to such an extent that breast feeding had declined dramatically by the end of the 1960s, aided by the efforts of manufacturers and pharmaceutical firms. More insidious is the fact that as midwives and health visitors managed to reverse this trend in the 1970s, formula manufacturers turned their attentions to a less-informed developing world, with the result that infant mortality went up, not down.

The way in which advertising has defended itself against feminist attack by incorporating contemporary women's issues into their promotions has not gone unnoticed. Content analysis would normally have to deem any apparent instance of a 'feminist' character as progressive, whereas qualitative approaches have blown their cover to reveal how the incorporation of feminist text or images might be divested of their original resonance. Williamson describes a television ad for the men's aftershave Censored, broadcast in the early 1970s, in which a woman is beating a man at chess. Before he loses, the man splashes himself with the scent, prompting his opponent to leap on him lustfully. Williamson argues that such ads are particularly sexist because of the male prowess they associate with seducing a strong woman as opposed to a submissive one.[15] To take another example, a television campaign for the Peugeot 306 car, broadcast in the summer of 1998, depicts a thirtysomething affluent couple, enjoying a trip without their children. It culminates in them making love on a beach. The female voice on the musical soundtrack and the visual objectification of the man suggest the audience is encouraged to identify more with the female on screen as protagonist. However, the fact that he is driving while she tempts him by smoothing down her short skirt shows that the ad is still defining masculinity in terms of action and femininity in terms of seduction. This technique, where advertising pretends to acknowledge a competing ideology but ignores its real challenge, is known as incorporation or co-option. So we are left asking whether much has really changed for the better since the 1950s. While earlier advertisements implicitly suggested women should keep out of the labour market and work a shift at home, now they are expected to do a double-shift of work and motherhood. With this is mind, I will now discuss contemporary representations of motherhood in advertising.

While the Millennium Fem has replaced the dewy-eyed depictions of expectant mothers in 1970s commercials, the advertisers' motivations are the same. The Fem 'is a much juicier target than she will ever be again. She holds the key to an average first year spend of £1,150 in a virtually recession-proof market.'[16] Sales of baby foods, drinks and milks alone regularly outstrip computer games markets. The Fem is probably richer than she will be ever again, for while she might be in full-time employment now, she might go part-time or stay at home after the birth.

A glance at contrasting portrayals of pregnancy and early motherhood in Mothercare catalogues in the 1970s and 1990s might, through content analysis, reveal a more progressive image for women. Illustrations from the 1970s depict an ironically virginal purity where props are mounted behind the models to resemble wings, while their eyes are turned in coy, sideways glances.

Supportive garments to conceal any postpartum bulge are marketed to enable the new mother to regain her sexual attractiveness immediately after the birth. In the 1990s, the emphasis is more on action rather than the static poses of their 1970s counterparts, but the look is still charged with patriarchal connotation.

Let us consider an advertisement for Mamas and Papas prams featured in *Practical Parenting* magazine in October 1996. First, although the product's purpose is to transport babies in safety and comfort, infants are absent from the image. Instead, the benefits of the product for the *mother* are being promoted, particularly style and ease. Central to the photograph is the pram itself, but the eye is drawn most to the woman pushing it, who is very young, with a fashionable hairstyle and tight, denim clothes. Real new mothers often look and feel exhausted and have no time for blow-drying hair or finding outfits which match the pram. Their bodies often take months to return to how they were before pregnancy. The female depicted may fuel the misapprehension in a first-time mother that it is possible to look and feel radiant and glamorous in those early months. Her appearance is symbolic of the multiplicity of potential roles this woman has. The jeans and jacket are dark, not faded, and when combined with the blue scarf and patent leather bag and shoes, are reminiscent of business attire. Overall, her look symbolises success, control and adaptability. Photographed full-length from the side, the model is looking ahead and moving forward while smiling – connoting social interaction – as opposed to the isolation many new mothers experience. It is significant that she has only one hand on the pram while the other clutches the strap of her rucksack, as if to signify that she is able to juggle her life to accommodate friends alongside baby. The draped backdrop is highly reminiscent of the Mothercare catalogues of the 1970s to which I referred earlier. White signifies purity and innocence often associated with babies but also with the young woman who has symbolically reverted to her purest, most perfect social role by becoming a mother.

White is also commonly used in the advertising of women's personal hygiene products as if to conceal natural bodily functions. Like obesity, dirt of any sort is abject in advertising. The housewife and mother is custodian *par excellence* of cleanliness and order.[17] It used to be that personal and household hygiene products were promoted for concealing dirt, hence the popularity of air fresheners in the 1970s and 1980s. Now advertisers prey on our fear of what we cannot see. Potty-training mothers are told to use cleaners that will make their toilet safe for vulnerable toddlers, yet an average two-year-old has developed an adequate immune system by the time they are crawling and will now be capable to washing their own hands. Nappies, once a familiar sight and smell in a bucket, are now manufactured and marketed to conceal their purpose. Many are even colourfully-decorated as a further distraction from what they might contain. In this way, products are advertised to women as if to make public an area of their lives that was once private and personal. In other words, it is no longer acceptable for a baby to smell or for a women to be sweaty – the intensive advertising of these commodities insists women have a social responsibility to ensure they and their children conform. In fact, this idea is seminal to 1950s and 1960s advertising. This is not surprising if we consider how in Western patriarchal ideology, women's reproductive ability has long inspired myths around sex, evil and dirt going back to Eve, the original seductress.

Most advertisers would scoff at this type of reading and would defend their production on the basis of what message they really intended to mediate. Even regulatory bodies such as the Advertising Standards Authority (ASA), the agency responsible for all print advertisements in Britain, do not always take action against agencies who promote women in an obviously pejorative way. For instance, *The Guardian* reported that Peugeot were allowed to continue a campaign, despite complaints, which depicted a woman's midriff tattooed with the image of a car along with the slogan 'Declare Your Independence' because 'it didn't convey a negative image of women or cause serious offence'.[18] Dyer points out how dangerous it is to base the analysis of a text solely on the intentions of the sender.[19] Yet critics of feminist text-based research argue that even their damning statistics and representational analyses do not provide sufficient evidence of injustice to women by the advertising industry.

Sut Jhally tries to unravel what lies behind the considerable power advertising seems to have over its audience but is suspicious about feminist explanations of active sexism. Justifying his scepticism, he maintains that advertisements are not read as representative of reality but rather they are abstractions from what they reflect. Therefore, the argument should not be about whether or not the representation of women is accurate, but rather that what we see in commercials is a ' "hyper-ritualisation" of gender relations and just one of the many sources from which we learn what gender means in our culture.'[20] He says that feminist attacks on representation also fail because they do not acknowledge the attraction adverts have. Thus, a critique of an advertisement becomes an attack on the reader, on people. Maybe, instead, we should not be attacking the images but rather the structures of power which are asking us to find pleasure from them and consume them and their products. I would agree that more work is needed on the reception of advertisements to avoid making unsupported generalisations. Additionally, an examination of recruitment and professional practice in the advertising industry might indicate whether certain ideologies are nurtured within the field. However, it would remain indisputable that stereotypical images of women have dominated, and continue to be perpetuated, in innumerable ads.

Through my examination of representations of motherhood, I have attempted to give an overview of the main currents of feminist thinking on advertising. It must be borne in mind that different people will interpret ads, and other media, in different ways, which means investigation into the actual conditions of reception and consumption is essential. This is particularly needed at a time of so-called 'post-feminism' when a further test of a woman's credentials (if more were needed) is whether she can see the 'joke' in advertisements such as 'Wanna Fila?' – metonymically depicting a pair of breasts barely concealed by a sports shirt – in magazines like *Loaded*. Furthermore, if it is not individual advertisements that come under feminist scrutiny but rather the message system, feminist text-based analyses have provided the materials for closer scrutiny of the institutional and ideological context within which advertisements are produced. It is ultimately here that a new slogan can be written which releases women from patriarchal obligations.

Perhaps we are seeing a true struggle for representation being fought in the unlikely arena of baby products. Where else are we witnessing such a hegemonic battle between portrayals of mothers-at-home and woman-who-work? Maybe advertising is closer to real life than we think.

Notes

1. Friedan, *The Feminine Mystique*.
2. Macdonald, *Representing Women*, p. 77.
3. Sullivan, 'Women's Role Portrayals'.
4. Havens, 'Imagery Associated with Menstruation'.
5. Friedan, *The Feminine Mystique*.
6. Ibid. pp. 212–13.
7. Ibid. p. 215.
8. Tuchman, 'The Symbolic Annihilation'.
9. Goffman, Gender Advertisements, p. viii.
10. Ibid. p. 84.
11. Dyer, *Advertising as Communication*, p. 101.
12. Luke, 'Reading Gender and Culture'.
13. Williamson, *Decoding Advertisements*, p. 169.
14. Fine and Leopold, *The World of Consumption*, p. 216.
15. Williamson, *Decoding Advertisements*, p. 170.
16. *The Guardian*, 2 February 1993, p. 12
17. Kristeva, *Powers of Horror*, p. 71.
18. *The Guardian*, 17 August 1988, G2.
19. Dyer, *Advertising as Communication*, p. 87.
20. Jhally, *The Codes of Advertising*, pp. 132–43.

Bibliography

Barthes, Roland, *Mythologies* (St Albans: Paladin, 1995).

Brierley, Sean, *The Advertising Handbook* (London: Routledge, 1996).

Davidson, Martin, *The Consumerist Manifesto: Advertising in Postmodern Times* (London: Routledge, 1996).

Dyer, G., *Advertising as Communication* (London: Routledge, 1996).

Fine, B. and E. Leopold, *The World of Consumption* (London: Routledge, 1993).

Friedan, Betty, *The Feminine Mystique* (Harmondsworth: Penguin, 1983).

Goffman, E., *Gender Advertisements* (London: Macmillan, 1979).

Havens, B., 'Imagery Associated With Menstruation in Advertising Targeted to Adolescent Women', *Adolescence*, 23, Spring 1988.

Jhally, S., *The Codes of Advertising: Fetishism and the Political Economy of Meaning in the Consumer Society* (London: Routledge, 1987).

Kristeva, J., *Powers of Horror* (New York: Columbia University Press, 1982).

Luke, C., 'Reading Gender and Culture in Media Discourses and Texts' in G. Bull and M. Anstey (eds), *The Literary Lexicon* (New York and Sydney: Prentice-Hall, 1996).

Macdonald, M., *Representing Women: Myths of Femininity in the Popular Media* (London: Routledge, 1997).

Ohmann, Richard, *Selling Culture: Magazines, Markets and Class at the Turn of the Century* (London: Verso, 1996).

Saussure, Ferdinand de, *Course in General Linguistics* (New York: McGraw-Hill, 1966).

Sullivan, G., 'Women's Role Portrayals in Magazine Advertising', *Sex Roles*, 18, 1988.

Tuchman, Gaye, 'Introduction; The Symbolic Annihilation of Women by the Mass Media' in Gaye Tuchman, Arlene Kaplan Daniels, and James Benet (eds), *Hearth and Home: Images of Women in the Mass Media* (New York: Oxford University Press, 1978).

Williamson, J., *Decoding Advertisements* (London: Marion Boyars, 1978).

Rebecca Arnold is a Senior Lecturer in the Cultural Studies department at Central Saint Martins College of Art and Design. Her book, *Fashion, Desire and Anxiety, Image and Morality in the 20th Century*, will be published by I. B. Taurus in January 2001.

Cheryl Buckley is Reader in design history at the University of Northumbria, Newcastle upon Tyne. Her research and writing deals with theories of design and gender, fashion and dress history, and the roles and work of women and ceramic designers.

Fiona Carson studied art history at the Courtauld Institute of Art, and sculpture at St Martins School of Art and Goldsmiths College. She has taught widely in art colleges and is now a Senior Lecturer in women's studies and art history at the University of East London. She has taught feminist art theory and practice since 1976, and is also a practising artist, currently making woven constructions.

Sarah Chaplin trained as an architect at Nottingham and Oxford Brookes universities, and has a Masters degree in architecture and critical theory. She is a Senior Lecturer in architectural and design theory at Middlesex University where she set up a Masters degree in digital architecture. She is also a director of the design consultancy Evolver. In addition to publishing articles on architectural criticism, design and digital cultural theory, she has co-authored *Visual Culture, an Introduction* with John A. Walker, and co-edited *Consuming Architecture* with Eric Holding.

Pauline de Souza is a freelance art historian. She has taught at Derby University, Cheltenham and Gloucester College of Higher Education. She is teaching at the University of East London and Birmingham University. She is currently working on *The Companion to Black British Culture* and *The New Dictionary of National Biography*. She also contributed an essay to *Women Artists and Modernism* (Manchester, 1998).

Jessica Evans is Lecturer in cultural and media studies in the sociology discipline at the Open University, and she researches in visual culture, and psychoanalysis and social relations. She is the author of many articles on photography, editor of *The Camerawork Essays*, and co-editor, with Stuart Hall, of *Visual Culture: The Reader*.

Anne Hole is currently completing a DPhil in women's studies at the University of Sussex, on the female body as a site of comedy. She has taught courses in the media studies programme at the Chichester Institute of Higher Education, and in feminism and culture and community at the University of Sussex.

Janis Jefferies is an artist academic. She is Reader in textiles and deputy head of visual arts at Goldsmiths College. She has published widely on contemporary textiles, and won a Betty Park critical writing award for textiles in the USA in 1996. Her solo exhibitions include 'Out of the Shadows: Towards (as) other Feminine' (Montreal, 1997), 'Locating Light' (Quebec City, 2000) and *selvedges* (Norwich School of Art Gallery and touring 2000/2001).

Julia Knight is Senior Lecturer in the department of media arts at the University of Luton, and she has published on various aspects of film and video culture. In the late 1980s she worked in the independent film and video sector in Britain and was a contributing editor to *Independent Media*. More recently she has edited *Diverse Practices: a Critical Reader on British Video Art*, and is now co-editor of *Convergence; A Journal of Research into New Media Technologies*.

Fran Lloyd is head of the school of art and design history at Kingston University and the MA Course Director for art and design. She is completing a PhD at Manchester University on new British sculpture of the 1980s. Her publications include *Deconstructing Madonna*, *From the Interior: Female Perspectives on Figuration*, and *Dialogues of the Present: Contemporary Arab Women's Art*. She is currently editing the symposium papers for *Displacement and Difference* (Centre of Near and Middle Eastern Studies at SOAS, University of London).

Sarah Niblock is Senior Lecturer in journalism at London College of Printing. She is also a freelance journalist, contributing to national newspapers, radio, and women's magazines. Her first book, *Inside Journalism* was published in 1996, and she is currently researching into The Artist Formerly Known as Prince.

Claire Pajaczkowska is Senior Lecturer in visual culture in the School of Art, Design and Performing Arts at Middlesex University. She has lectured widely in Britain, Europe, and the USA, and translated three books on visual culture and psychoanalysis from French. Her doctoral thesis was on psychoanalytic theories used in the analysis of culture, and her current research is on visual culture and the sublime.

Helen Potkin is Senior Lecturer in art history at Kingston University. Her academic interests are in contemporary issues and art practice and in public art. She is currently researching public sculpture and monuments as part of the national recording project.

Sally Stafford is Lecturer and Subject Leader for film studies at Middlesex University. She is currently working on a doctoral thesis on 1940s women's films and the themes of guilt and the confession. More generally, her research interests are in visual culture, gender, sexuality and representation.

Teal Triggs is Director of Postgraduate Studies and Research in the School of Graphic Design at the London College of Printing. She is co-founder of the Women's Design Research Unit (WD+RU) and has written and lectured extensively in the USA, Europe and the Far East on graphic design theory, women in design and digital technology. She also edited *Communicating Design: Essays on Visual Communication*.

Index

Note: page numbers *in italics* refer to illustrations. Works of art are listed under the names of their authors.